The Anglosphere

The Anglosphere

A GENEALOGY OF A RACIALIZED IDENTITY

IN INTERNATIONAL RELATIONS

Srdjan Vucetic

Stanford University Press

Stanford University Press
Stanford, California

Printed in the United States of America on acid-free, archival-quality paper

Library of Congress Cataloging-in-Publication Data

Vucetic, Srdjan
  The Anglosphere : a genealogy of a racialized identity in international relations / Srdjan Vucetic.
     p. cm.
  Includes bibliographical references and index.
  Summary: Focuses on Australia, Britain, Canada, New Zealand, and the United States.
  ISBN 978-0-8047-7224-2 (cloth : alk. paper)
  ISBN 978-0-8047-7225-9 (pbk. : alk. paper)
  1. English-speaking countries—Foreign relations. 2. Group identity—Political aspects—English-speaking countries. 3. Security, International—International cooperation—Case studies. 4. World politics—20th century. I. Title.
  D446.V83 2011
  327.0917'521—dc22   2010030488

Typeset by Thompson Type in 10/14 Minion

To the memory of Dedo

May his love for teaching be passed along.

ACKNOWLEDGMENTS

Writing is a way of interacting with many significant Others. Foremost among those who have guided me in this writing project are Ted Hopf, Jennifer Mitzen, and Alexander Wendt. No trio will have a greater influence on my professional and intellectual development. I was truly lucky to have them on my side for all these years: Without their unfailing encouragement, there would be no book. That it isn't better is entirely my doing. My luck continued when Peter Katzenstein expressed interest in my manuscript; I am very grateful for the extensive comments and criticism he offered.

I took my ideas to many conferences, workshops, and impromptu gatherings, where I met a number of wonderful scholars, who kindly helped me with this project. For written comments and correspondence, thanks are due to Tarak Barkawi, Emilie Bécault, Duncan Bell, Janice Bially Mattern, Zoltán Búzás, Bridget Coggins, Tom Dolan, Andrew Gamble, Eric Grynaviski, Yoram Haftel, Lene Hansen, Clarissa Rile Hayward, Richard Herrmann, Dane Imerman, Tahseen Kazi, Markus Kornprobst, Ronald Krebs, Autumn Lockwood Payton, Tim Lücke, Kim Richard Nossal, Dorothy Noyes, Inderjeet Parmar, Brian Pollins, John Oates, Marc O'Reilly, Thomas Risse, James Rosenau, Stéphane Roussel, Anna Stavrianakis, Robert Vitalis, Michael C. Williams, Byungwon Woo, Clément Wyplosz, Dvora Yanow, and Lorenzo Zambernardi. Special mention must be made of Brendon O'Connor, who facilitated my research in Australia in every conceivable way. As for David Dewitt and Arthur Rubinoff, I simply cannot adequately credit the importance of the advice I received from them over the years. In the broadest sense, I am also indebted to all the scholars appearing in my bibliography.

The financial burden for researching and writing this book has been shared by several institutions. First of all, I offer a grateful thanks to the fellows, staff, and friends of Pembroke College, Cambridge, for welcoming me to their wonderful and unique community, and to Mr. Randall Dillard, for having generously funded my research fellowship. At Ohio State, I received much-appreciated research and travel grants from the Graduate School, the Department of Political Science, the Office of International Affairs, and the Mershon Center for International Security. A research grant from the Social Sciences and Humanities Research Council of Canada was likewise extremely helpful. As for the editing and publishing burden, my heartfelt thanks go to Stacy Wagner, Jessica Walsh, Margaret Pinette, and the rest of the team at Stanford University Press.

My last acknowledgment concerns my most significant Others. My old and new families, the Vucetics, the Dunnes, and the Sahas, have been indispensable every step of the way in this long and laborious process. All of them, and especially my darling wife Anita, deserve my deepest gratitude.

CONTENTS

The Anglosphere

1 WHAT IS THE ANGLOSPHERE?

The Anglo-American relies upon personal interest to accomplish his ends, and gives free scope to the unguided strength and common sense of the people; the Russian centers all the authority of society in a single arm; the principal instrument of the former is freedom; of the latter, servitude . . . each of them seems marked out by the will of heaven to sway the destinies of half the globe.

—Tocqueville, *Democracy in America* (1835), Vol. 1, p. 434

If the population of the English-speaking Commonwealth be added to that of the United States with all that such co-operation implies in the air, on the sea, all over the globe and in science and in industry, and in moral force, there will be no quivering, precarious balance of power to offer its temptation to ambition or adventure. On the contrary, there will be an overwhelming assurance of security . . . If we are together, nothing is impossible.

—Winston Churchill, The "Iron Curtain" speech, 1946

Now Mr Churchill is starting his process of unleashing war (like Hitler) with a racial theory, declaring that only those people who speak English are full-bloodied nations, whose vocation it is to control the fate of the whole world . . . Mr Churchill and his friends in England and in America are presenting those nations who do not speak English with a kind of ultimatum—recognize our supremacy over you, voluntary, and all will be well— otherwise war is inevitable.

—Stalin, a *Pravda* interview concerning Churchill's "Iron Curtain' speech, 1946

THE ANGLO-AMERICAN "SPECIAL RELATIONSHIP" and the "Airstrip One." ANZUS and the "deputy sheriff." NORAD and the "51st state." These are some of the many representations, official designations, and popular caricatures of the special relationships between the United States on the one hand and Australia,

1

Britain, Canada, and New Zealand on the other. The relationship between the United States and Britain began with a revolutionary war in the eighteenth century, in which the former violently seceded from the latter. This germinal Anglo-American enmity is now all but forgotten, having been replaced with a remarkably durable alliance and a close friendship. Australia, Canada, and New Zealand established their special relationships with the United States more gradually, as they gained more and more sovereignty from Britain. Together, these special relationships are said to constitute a "core" of a distinct international, transnational, civilizational, and imperial entity within the global society, currently known as the "Anglosphere."[1]

Winston Churchill used to describe this entity as the "English-speaking peoples." As far back as the late seventeenth century, as he observed in his hefty *History of the English-Speaking Peoples*, the proverbial Anglos have been constantly winning wars, expanding trade, and promoting freedom, security, and welfare—all of this thanks to their liberal political culture and institutions.[2] As Churchill explained in his famous "Iron Curtain" speech delivered at a small college in Fulton, Missouri, on March 5, 1946:

> We must never cease to proclaim in fearless tones the great principles of freedom and the rights of man which are the joint inheritance of the English-speaking world and which through Magna Carta, the Bill of Rights, the Habeas Corpus, trial by jury, and the English common law find their most famous expression in the American Declaration of Independence.

For Churchill the "great man of history," this speech evoked a moment of victory for the English-speaking peoples against the Nazi-Fascist axis just as they were about to embark upon another war against Soviet communism. For Churchill the historian, however, this juncture was a mere chapter of modern history centered on the expansion of the Anglo experience. The English-speaking peoples were doubly special, to each other and to humankind, because the progress of liberal modernity depended on their unity and cooperation. The newly minted United Nations (UN), Churchill explained at Fulton, could provide collective goods only in one context:

> Would a special relationship between the United States and the British Commonwealth be inconsistent with our over-riding loyalties to the World Organization? I reply that, on the contrary, it is probably the only means by which that organisation will achieve its full stature and strength.

Churchill's theory of history continues to claim adherents, many of whom like to point out that Churchill was right. The processes of secession, dedominionization and decolonization destroyed the British empire but left behind a distinct yet loosely bounded community of peoples, who were fiercely committed to, among other items, freedom, democracy, the rule of (common) law, and the English language. This community's lack of formal institutional actorness merely disguises its exceptional longevity and power. Centered first on London and then on Washington, D.C., the Anglosphere has dominated international politics for the world for the past 200 years, perhaps longer. Its agents—companies, empires, states, nations—colonized and industrialized large swathes of the planet and moved millions of its inhabitants, often by force. They also acted as the market and lender of the last resort, the guardian of the reserve currency, and the bulwark against various revisionists and revolutionaries. As a result, the world has now gone *Ang*lobal. Though Australians, Americans, British, Canadians, and New Zealanders make up less than 7 percent of the world's population today, the standard triumphalist argument is that "their" language is the global language, "their" economies produce more than a third of the global gross domestic product (GDP), and "their" version of liberalism in society and economy defines most human aspirations.[3] If he were alive today, Churchill might well be pleased with the state of the Anglosphere. One can imagine him making a swift autocitation: "I told you so long ago: If we are together, nothing is impossible."

This book is one story of how the Anglosphere became possible. It focuses on Australia, Britain, Canada, New Zealand, and the United States—the five states that are said to constitute the "core" of the community—and considers how they came to exempt themselves from the rules that have shaped war, peace, alliances, coalitions, and other manifestations of international conflict and cooperation in world politics. The story begins with a contention that the origins of Anglosphere are racial. The turn-of-the-twentieth-century rapprochement between the expanding United States and declining Britain was caused by a discourse of identity that implied natural unity and moral superiority of the "Anglo-Saxon race." The loosely woven fabric of Anglo-Saxonism began to unravel in the middle decades of the twentieth century. In this period, the Anglosphere emerged as a broad-angled Western community made up of interdependent, institutionalized, and integrated special relationships centered on the United States. As the Cold War dragged on and then fizzled away, the Anglosphere positioned itself as the sovereign icon of liberal internationalism and the corollary human rights revolution. Across the decades, hitherto silent voices grew louder and louder, and antiracism went mainstream around the globe. These changes were sweeping and dramatic, yet they often occurred in such lopsided and contradictory ways that some of the old racialized privileges and hierarchies were left unscathed. At the beginning of the twentieth century, it was thus once again possible for the leaders of the old and new Anglo empires to jointly claim moral superiority in the international society. The main argument of this book is that cooperation among select English-speaking states became possible through a variety of racialized processes, which come together at home, abroad, and in-between. In short, the Anglosphere is a product of its racial past, a past that might not have receded.

A RENEGADE RESEARCH AGENDA

Despite having made an excellent early start on the subject, International Relations (IR) has little or nothing to say about the Anglosphere. E. H. Carr, the putative father of the discipline, long preceded Churchill in theorizing the "English-speaking peoples" as the "dominant group in the world." He was also much more critical. In his *Twenty Year's Crisis*, Carr provocatively argued that the Anglos were "consummate international hypocrites" bent on spreading their forms of politics under the guise of morality and neutrality.[4] Carr's book is still a classic, but these lines are often skipped over. IR hardly recognizes the dyadic Anglo-American "special relationship" (AASR) as an analytical category, much less the plural Anglosphere. On the surface, the absence has to do with the current hegemony of rationalist theories. These approaches have been extremely insightful about the ways alliances and economic blocs emerge out of strategic coordination among governments, businesses, logrolling coalitions, and other rational actors bent on solving collective action problems and generating joint goods such as security or trade. Yet, with respect to the seemingly more nebulous cultural groupings like the Anglosphere, rationalist accounts of world politics tend to obscure as much as they illuminate. A deeper reason lies in the traditional sway of a narrow materialist ontology focused on a system of sovereign, separate, and nominally equal states. Missing from this picture are racism, nationalism, colonialism, imperialism, and other macro-historical processes, which imply that sovereign states are also historical and cultural nations bound by all kinds of discourses, institutions, and practices.

The obvious ontological and theoretical home for the Anglosphere appears to lie in constructivism, particularly in its research agendas revolving around the concept of identity.[5] Much of social life, constructivist argue, can be explained in terms of the relations between the Self and Other. What social actors want and how they act is indeed determined by who they are, but the point is that the Self does not exist as a disconnected, unadulterated unit; instead, it always emerges in interaction with certain significant Others. To go back to Churchill's "Iron Curtain" speech, the "fraternal association of the English-speaking peoples" would have been meaningless without this interaction. In the speech, one first finds the temporal or historical Others, defined by a recent global war against the Nazi-Fascist enemies: "The awful ruin of Europe, with all its vanished glories, and of large parts of Asia glares us in the eyes." Then there are the territorially bounded Others: Soviet Russia, "Turkey and Persia," the "South American Republics," and, as a particularly menacing force within, "the Communist parties or fifth columns." Here, the Self–Other relations are in a transition, with Soviet Russia and Communist partisans changing their status from wartime allies to future foes. "Christian civilization" and the UN also appear in Churchill's speech, but mostly as the second-order extensions of the Anglo Self, rather than as significant Others.

Similar "us" versus "them" dynamics are present in countless international discourses, institutions, and practices across different social realms of world politics—from pop culture (for example, James Bond, Jason Bourne) to university scholarships and literary awards (such as Rhodes, Knox, Man Booker) to political economy (as in "Anglo-Saxon capitalism") to transgovernmental and intermestic relations (such as the Strategic Alliance Cyber Crime Working Group). The continuity and change in these ideas and actions has been subject to contingent and variable interactions among the "peoples" involved, but the main point is that the Anglosphere is meaningless without some other social group in time and space, whether one refers to a state/nation, international association or organization, transnational network, civilization, or some combination of these. Herein lies the usefulness of what constructivists call constitutive analysis—an analysis of intersubjective meanings that condition the social and political possibilities within a given community, site, or field. This type of analysis resembles "theories of reference" in philosophy or "theoretical identifications" in the natural sciences. On the latter, by showing how atoms constitute molecules or how average molecular kinetic energy constitutes temperature, constitutive analysis contributes to causal explanations of various chemical, biological, and physical processes. By analogy, an analysis of constitutive dimensions of the social kinds like the Anglosphere

can therefore contribute to causal explanations of international conflict/
cooperation.

It is precisely these types of explanations that motivate the constructivist
research program on "security communities" or groups of states in which a collective identity is said to lead to dependable expectations of nonviolent change.[6]
The same can be said about the constructivist work on transnational diasporas and "families of nations," which tends to treat preferential treatments in
diplomacy, foreign aid, trade, or tourism as a function of ethno(racial), (anti)
national, (neo)colonial, and (post)imperial identities.[7] That the Anglosphere is
absent in these literatures is surprising considering that it is both conceptually and substantively related to the "Atlantic community," "Black Atlantic,"
the Commonwealth, the *Francophonie*, and similar entities, which are more or
less acknowledged in constructivist IR.[8]

The absence of the Anglosphere agenda in IR is neither ontological nor
theoretical in nature, but sociological. The Anglosphere is unattractive as
an analytical category because it carries the burden of political and normative reappropriation. Most IR theorists would point out that the concept—in
fact, the conceit—of the Anglosphere must first be separated from the racist associations it carries from the era of Churchill and Stalin before it can
be used in the analysis of international relations. That this reappropriation is
inherently risky is evident in the fate of the conservative and neoconservative
discourse on the Anglosphere in the 2000s. Much like Churchill, who used
Anglosphere-talk to prop up anticommunism and empire, James C. Bennett,
Robert Conquest, and Keith Windschuttle, among others, have used it to legit-
imize or mobilize certain political projects—anything from Euroskepticism
to the U.S.–Indian nuclear alliance to assorted liberal orderings at a global
scale.[9] Unlike Churchill, this generation of thinkers never failed to underscore
the pluralist, postcolonial, anti-imperial and, indeed, antiracist nature of the
imagined community spanning sixty or so sovereign and "diverse" nations
from Antigua and Barbuda to Zimbabwe. What made these claims unper-
suasive to those on the political and cultural left was a certain consistency
in conceptualizing the Anglosphere as a hierarchy made up of the core and
mostly white Self on the one hand and on the other the peripheral and overwhelmingly nonwhite Other. Core/periphery—like the corollary metaphors of
concentric circles, nodal points, families of nations, clubs, or waiting rooms—
is a colonial-era concept that refers to the presence of historically or culturally backward Others. The new discourse on the English-speaking peoples

thus arrived with the old discourse in tow, in the sense that the talk of the linguistically bounded and hierarchically ordered "spheres" invoked the old images of empires and civilizations. Little surprise that liberals and Marxists rejected the idea of the Anglosphere, sometimes echoing Stalin's response to Churchill's Fulton speech, as not only insufferably outmoded and parochial, but also fundamentally racist.[10]

These connotations have rightly made IR wary of the Anglosphere. Recall how the discipline evolved mostly out of the English-language study of empire, colonial administration, and, in particular, race. In an effort to forget its racist past, IR turned race into a "taboo."[11] The practice is primarily sociological, not philosophical. In contrast to the so-called eliminativist constructivists in the philosophy of race, who eliminate race as the discourse of social construction, constructivists in IR tend to eliminate race because of the particular historical developments that continue to structure their discipline. This book takes a different approach. Following the philosophical teachings of antieliminativist constructivism, I will define race as *racialized identity*, a social kind that exists because people believe it exists. From this perspective, race is not real in the biological sense, but it is real in the sense that the social and political world is constituted by groups who have been, or were, treated as if they were races.[12] Originally introduced by the sociologist Robert Miles and later developed by Lawrence Blum, Linda Martín Alcoff, and others, racialization thus refers to a social and political process of inscribing group affinity and difference primarily onto the body (for example, "blood," phenotype, genes) as well as on other markers of lived experience (such as "character," eating, shopping).[13]

The concept of racialization is useful because it rejects inherent characteristics, differences, or hierarchies among groups and because it recognizes that race intersects with—without being substituted by—ethnicity, gender, class, and other identities that define groups. For example, as historically evolving and cross-culturally variable identities, "Anglo" or "white" are related, but not reducible, to ethnic, quasi-ethnic, religious, or class groups or their hybrids such as "English" or "WASPs" (White, Anglo-Saxon, Protestant).[14] Racialization is also useful because it acknowledges the continuing impact of racial histories and experiences on complex systems of separation, privilege, hierarchy, and inequality within, between, and among entities that Churchill so coyly called peoples in the contemporary world.

Much like race, the Anglosphere too has evolved over time and space as it defined patterns of inclusion/exclusion of billions of people around the world.

(Writing about the Anglosphere is related, but not equivalent, to writing about groups labeled by themselves and others as Anglos.) As an analytical category, the Anglosphere roughly approximates the idea of the "English-speaking peoples" as well as what students of history, historical sociology, comparative politics, and related academic fields and subfields have subsequently named "Lockean heartland," "Anglo-America," and "Anglo-world."[15] Each one of these alternative categories represents a different school of thought on what has made the world hang together—and apart—through large-scale historical change. While I cannot do them justice, I will document these arguments in the later chapters and consider how they might relate to my account. I also recognize that the questions of philosophy, ontology, theory, and sociology of knowledge cannot be separated from their normative implications. However, instead of separating positive from normative until the concluding paragraphs, as per the current practice of writing IR, I have decided to address the normative questions elsewhere.[16] In this book, the focus remains on the historical evolution of the racialized identities in the putative Anglosphere core and their influence on patterns of war and peace. To tell this story, I build on constructivist IR and its ideas on how "peoples" make friends, rivals, and enemies with each other in the world.

THEORIZING THE ANGLOSPHERE

One of the oldest typologies of IR theory is the so-called levels of analysis. Levels are defined by a spatial scale ranging from individual decision makers' heads to the entire planet. They are not theories but are broad ontological referents for the domain of the "causal" action. Using one scale as an example, the Anglosphere emerges (1) in Churchill's head (the "individual" level); (2) within and between various societies, states, nations, transnational corporations, and/or empires (the "unit" level); (3) within and between various groupings of states, nations, and/or empires (the "subsystem" level); and (4) within the global society as a whole (the "international system" level). Note the scare quotes around the word *causal*: As a matter of constructivist ontological principle, the collective identity of a global community of the English-speaking peoples cannot be sliced up into different levels. Instead, it is continuously constructed on, and across, all levels of analysis and therefore irreducible even to the sum of heretofore separately analyzed levels and/or structural and agential variables. Put differently, agents and structures such as elites and nations, societies and empires, states and the international system are *always* mutually constituted.[17]

For many constructivists and virtually all poststructuralists in IR, the ontological message is clear: Mutual constitution implies that social entities cannot be separated, "stabilized," or "bracketed" for the purposes of causal analysis. And yet no account of the social and political world can vary everything at the same time; language, after all, is successive, not simultaneous. Arguably, in any analysis—as opposed to the underlying ontology—one phenomenon (for example, state/nation) must always be stabilized or bracketed at the expense of some other phenomenon or phenomena (such as foreign policy, drive for recognition, security community). In recent years, the meanings of causation and causal analysis in IR have thankfully been broadened and deepened, partly due to the advent of critical realism.[18] Building on this growing pluralism, I propose that an analysis of Self–Other relations that constitute the Anglosphere is in fact compatible with an analysis of the various causal processes that produce the Anglosphere.

In making a causal claim, I first make an argument that identity at the level of the unit—which I call state/national identity—rendered some foreign policy choices more likely than others. State/national identity refers to the intersubjective meanings on the proverbial "who we are." The continuity and change in foreign policy, the argument proceeds, is a function of the debates on how reality fits the dominant discourses of identity and vice versa. This approach, I suggest, can help us theorize the multiplicity of identities at the unit level: All state/nations maintain multiple affiliations, but some of these affiliations tend to be more consequential in international politics than others. Identities that originate "inside" state–society relations are reproduced at the level of international, transnational, intermestic, and other levels "outside" the unit, where, in turn, they are consolidated, challenged, or diminished.[19] In evaluating this self-reinforcing dynamic against historical evidence I will indeed attempt to explain and understand why and how state/national identities in Australia, Britain, Canada, New Zealand and the United States gave rise to the Anglosphere as a racialized community in global society.

Various feedback loops across all levels indeed constitute an important part of this story. However, they are not its theoretical and analytical focus because it is impossible to theorize and analyze all dimensions of the Anglosphere simultaneously, at least not with the same depth. My framework is doubly state-centric in the sense that it treats the state as both the object and unit of analysis. In this story, the point at which Australia or America become international subjects comes only after we understand the political processes that constitute them in each historical period under investigation. Only after we understand these processes do we move to explain patterns of conflict or cooperation in the Anglosphere and beyond. Theory of interstate interaction is exogenous; here, I make a simple proposition about international conflict or cooperation should states or nations hold a particular understanding of each other. All being equal, a continued understanding of the Other as close and positive is likely to lead to more cooperation; conversely, a shift in the same belief is likely to lead to more conflict. And in the last caveat, my conflation of the state and nation is meant to be in line with a long-standing theoretical continuum on the relationship between the two: At one end, the state and nation are commensurate; at the other, they are separate.[20] Conflation is also useful because it allows for an openness to a wider range of meanings under the two rubrics, without sneaking in a prefab theory on the constitutive essence of either. The assumption is that state or national identities, while rich in content and contestation, can be empirically recovered in a given historical context.[21]

DISCOURSE, DEBATE, FRAMING, FIT, AND EVENTS

The first generation of constructivist scholarship in IR cast much of its focus on the concept of identity, mostly due to a desire to demonstrate how identities trump contrary seemingly obvious material pressures. Though it established constructivism as a mainstream paradigm, this focus actually diminished the power of identity-based explanations. In empirical studies, political actors were found to be subject to several identities, some of which mattered more than others in given policy situations.[22] In large part, the problem was theoretical. In conceptualizing and theorizing identity as intersubjective structures of meaning among social groups concerning their relationships to one another, constructivists paid much more attention to content, structure, and continuity than to contestation, process, and change. Second-generation constructivists have been better balanced, but the heaviest theoretical lifting still remains to be done. Seemingly basic questions such as under what conditions some identities trump others, how policy situations are legitimated in terms of identity, or how plausible alternatives are marginalized are still omitted from the theoretical agenda.

To attempt to answer these questions, let us begin by conceptualizing state or national identities as *discourses* or structured practices of communication over the proverbial "who we are." Rather than deductively specifying American or Australian identities by referencing certain self-evident institutions or political developments, this type of empirical analysis begins with a discourse analysis of what it means to be American or Australian at a specific historical point. A longer methodological discussion will take place later, but the goal of empirical analysis is to recover the basic counters of state or national discursive terrain: Some discourses can be expected to be dominant (hegemonic or governing), while others are challenging (counterhegemonic or subaltern). Allowing for the empirical character of multiplicity and dominance, foreign policy can be said to follow the dominant discourse of identity. This process is not automatic as even a single state or national identity can imply different policies. In this sense, foreign policy is made through arguing—a particular but socially pervasive form of communication aimed at winning an audience or audiences also known as argumentation, deliberation, rhetoric, spin, or, most simply, talk. IR theory has dealt extensively with the social-theoretic and social-scientific underpinnings of the independent role of arguing, so here we need only to derive a claim that the making of social facts such as foreign policy is always contested and never complete, in the sense that all political actors accept this construction of reality and knowledge (or accept it to the same degree).[23] By making arguments political actors make situations, that is, particular and partial readings of reality, rather than simply thinking and acting within situational constraints.

In this framework, what is fundamental to politics is the interaction between the structures of meanings on the one hand and the political actors who use them to articulate certain positions on the other. Here, arguing plays as important a theoretical role as discourse: While the dominant discourse shapes foreign policy by ruling out the proverbial "impossibles," it is arguing that makes some policy directions more likely than others. Arguing over the definition of an intersubjective reality goes to the core of the mobilization of public power in the sense that winning arguments are binding and have direct consequences for political outcomes. For our purposes, human agency is manifested through arguing among political elites, a category of people whose privileged institutional positions and reputations provide them with comparatively greater authority in social interactions. Arguing always takes place in front of the audience or the public; by default, it has more than two participants even when it occurs in secret or secretive cabinet-style deliberations. By talking to their interlocutors, speakers express or articulate reasons to justify ideas, positions, plans, actions, policies, and so on, but it is their audience who judges what is legitimate, that is, acceptable in terms of what is intersubjectively held as "true" and/or "valid" in a given context and, consequently, what can be done. Conversely, a legitimacy crisis occurs when the claims of what is true and/or valid cannot keep pace with shifts in the operation or location of political authority. Due to these intrinsic properties of arguing, political elites can therefore impact the environment within which they operate, sometimes radically so.[24]

One way to theorize the effect of arguing on foreign policy is to account for the role of foreign policy *debates*, which are part of the ongoing struggle for power and legitimacy among political elites.[25] Debates occur above the level of discourse and are relatively delimited, elastic, and variable, such that political elites need not say the same thing in all contexts, but they cannot say just anything—not without some risk of losing their privileged status in society. Within the realm of the discursively possible, however, elites wield the power to define or *frame* events, problems, and solutions in particular ways. The conceptual history of framing is long, and its uses in analyzing social interaction across the social sciences differ, but this outline selectively draws from the theories of social movements, rhetoric, and political communication as well as from their applications in IR.[26] The assumption is that elites maintain their positions of authority through framing and counterframing.[27] All frames are subject to construction and reconstruction in speaker–audience interactions as participants improvise and innovate, but they also repeat old truths. The simplest frames are known as topoi, keywords, markers, or slogans, and they are usually characterized by commonplace binarizations such as good/evil, advantage/uselessness, threat/opportunity, or facilitator/burden (for example, "evil empire" or "indispensable nation"). These can also be culturally and/or historically specific phrases and statements, such as the "celestial kingdom" or the "rainbow nation."

Useful in analyzing the framing process is the following typology of six mutually nonexclusive types of frames: diagnostic (such as problem representation, the "blame game"), prognostic (announcements of strategies and tactics), motivational ("call to arms"), abstractions (cause–effect syllogisms), comparisons (historical analogies, similes, and metaphors), and claims of appropriateness (rule following on the basis of identity). Framing moves typically involve several of these elements simultaneously, as in a statement that "we are the last, best hope for humankind." Here, the appropriateness of separating a collective identity (*we*) from a troubled social environment (*humankind*) leads to a metaphorical call to arms (*hope*). The link between *we* and *humankind* is abstract, but the implication is that the former is the sovereign vanguard of the latter.

In foreign policy debates, elites use frames and counterframes to identify threats and securitize, to mobilize their audiences for war and peace, and to make complex, novel, or controversial ideas appear tangible and simple, familiar and palatable. The debates are settled by endogenous and exogenous reasons because they involve multiple actors not necessarily covered by the analysis. But so long as the researcher can document the political gains and losses separately from the debate itself and control for other explanations between the debates and their external effects, it is possible to reconstruct the effectiveness of argumentation. In this explanatory approach, winning frames do not resonate with universal reason, ethicality, or correspondence to some objective reality, but with the deeper intersubjective structures of meanings. For our purposes, what decisively influences the competitiveness of frames in the foreign policy arena is their *fit*—also known as alignment, accessibility, click, consonance, congruence, or match—with the underlying discourses of state or national identity. As a greater fit emerges, the frames become more established, and so do practices, policies, and institutions supported by those frames. Conversely, consistent misfits intensify calls for change. For the purposes of our analysis, we can regard fit as a function of interaction between how the speaker defines the state or nation and what goes on in the wider world. The often-used phrases "reality constraints," "current state of the world," and "facts on the ground" point out that foreign policy is not a closed system. Any frame that invokes state or national identity logically generates a set of expectations about the future, which can be challenged by various new developments.

By embedding both discourses and arguing in a single framework, the theoretical ambition pursued in this book is to provide a dynamic account on how agents and structures are mutually constituted. Indeed, the very idea that reality might come to constitute a (mis)fit with identity and so shape political outcomes is a theoretical challenge to any constructivist approach in IR that—analytically speaking—treats structures and agents as discrete and reducible to one another. Anchoring one end of the theoretical continuum, here we indeed have discourse-based theories of foreign policy that accord no necessary and independent role to conscious human action and, on the other end, theories that regard arguing as a tool of strategic action, in which political actors are always fixing, rearranging, and redeploying discourses of identity in ways that maximize their power over other actors.[28] If the first school of thought suffers from a major structural bias, the other tends to ignore the fact that political actors may be severely constrained by discourses that go well beyond a specific policy situation.

To make an analytical shortcut into the dynamics of foreign policy debates, this framework foregrounds what historical sociologists call *events*, that is, shocks, new facts, reality gaps, ruptures, and other rare moments of significant disjuncture between reality on one hand and discourses, practices, and institutions on the other.[29] In a given political context, many occurrences can be seen as candidates for events: natural catastrophes, demographic shifts, knowledge breakthroughs, popular revolutions, declarations of war and peace, health or economic crises, and even unexpected outcomes in sports competitions. All of these are sometimes analyzed in terms of their material effects on fixed and coherent social units, but in this framework we treat them as political opportunities for shifting the meanings of state or national identity and, in turn, international conflict or cooperation. It is here that the analytical reach gains another ambitious goal: In addition to reconstructing the story of how collective identities are constituted over time, the task now becomes to analyze moments when the old structures of meanings are articulated anew, stretched, or constrained.

Events are doubly continent on agency, in the sense identities are made and remade in and through interactions with the significant Others whose agency influences the dominant interpretations of the Self. Even the most unexpected events never just happen to political actors so much as they are discursively "fitted," but the Self cannot control what the event means to the Other. A change in how a state or nation is defined either by itself or by its significant Others can significantly change their interaction on the international conflict–cooperation continuum. Faced with an event, elites may explain it using dominant discourse or provide a frame based on an alternative discourse. Ignoring it or calling it irrelevant is of course possible, but it is unlikely for the types of events described above because the authority of elites partly depends on their ability to provide continuous and consistent identity narratives in all circumstances. For this reason, as major events and acts emerge and reality constraints change, elites must reappraise state or national identity anew, in which case old narratives may prove unreliable, sometimes even compared to those authored by significant Others. Depending on the outcome of debates among elites, foreign policy orientations can be either strengthened or challenged. If the policy stakeholders deem the fit between frames and reality to be appropriate, the status quo in foreign policy is likely to be consolidated. Conversely, a demonstrable misfit may cause policy shifts.

It is by analyzing the making or breaking of the fit between identity and reality that we can show how foreign policy debates influence political authority to make decisions, sustain policies, or invest in institutions. If the representatives of the government succeed in demonstrating that their expression of state/national identity fits reality—for example, if they consistently interpret the actions of a significant Other state as harmful—the government is likely to reject the opposition calls for more cooperation with that Other. But if the opposition is able to convince the audience that the former rival has become friendly and helpful, then the government will be compelled to change the status quo. We cannot ascertain fit between identity and reality a priori, but we can analyze how it was made and with what consequences for the outcome under study. My analytical goals line up with the critical realist perspective on causation, which seeks to identify causal mechanisms within social processes and demonstrate how these mechanisms operate through the operation of human agents situated within social structures and institutions such as discourse, the state, international community, and so on. To support or invalidate the causal claim at the unit level, we can propose that two kinds of empirical findings would cast doubt on my argument: one, if a policy shifts to an alternative option in spite of a rhetorically demonstrated fit between who we are; and the facts on the ground; two, if a policy continues despite a comparable misfit. Conversely, if my argument is correct, we should expect that foreign policy should follow the outcome of debate on the identity–reality fit.

HISTORICIZING THE ANGLOSPHERE

Genealogy is a tool of interpretative inquiry, which defines itself against histories guided by a desire for the empirical and scientific status of historical knowledge.[30] It rejects objectivity and correspondence to the facts in favor of (inter)subjectivity and the multiplicity of interpretations. Central to genealogy is the notion of the so-called power–knowledge nexus, which posits that truth and validity are discursively produced and enmeshed with relations of power. Last, genealogy seeks to be "effective" in disrupting of what is regarded as natural, logical, or inevitable, rather than constructed, contingent, and haphazard. It is in this sense that genealogy is particularly promising as an antidote to Churchillian histories of the Anglosphere as *the* carrier of liberal modernity.

This particular genealogy is committed to the historical recovery of identity politics in four epochs of Anglosphere history: America and Britain in

1894–1903; Australia and New Zealand in 1950–1951; Australia and Canada in 1955–1956 and 1964–1965; and Britain and Canada in 2002–2003. At its most basic level, mine is a story about how competing articulations of Self–Other relations collided in the imagination of what it means to be a member of the Anglosphere core for over a century. But there is more: Embedded in this genealogy are four sets of pairwise comparative cases studies that I use to evaluate the theoretical argument. These are the Anglo-American "great rapprochement"; the Korean War and the Pacific Pact negotiations; the alliance politics of the Suez crisis and the Vietnam escalation; and the anti-Iraq "coalition of the willing."

A more ambitious genealogy would no doubt sacrifice theory to include more geography and more history. The idea of "origins" contradicts the philosophy behind genealogy, but there is no doubt that a broader vista would have been more revealing. After all, extant histories of the Anglosphere, whiggish or otherwise, typically begin in the seventeenth century, when the first Anglos in international life were the Dutch, and also geographically cover almost the entire planet.[31] But instead of enumerating the obvious omissions and various trade-offs between genealogical effectiveness and theory building, allow me to point out to what might be two distinct advantages of my Anglosphere story. First, the case studies in this book allow us to consider multiple and iterative causal flows among different units of analysis—the discourse of state or national identity, foreign policy, international cooperation, and community building. Where appropriate, I will reach back and forth in time to float the multiple points of entry into the research problem. Such broader empirical vista is necessary to demonstrate how some situations or decisions reproduce structures, while others overturn them, and what this means for the ways in which actors constitute themselves. It is indeed expected that this methodological framework will help us account for the continuity and change in the deep and slow-moving structures that are not readily visible in more limited historical forays.

Second and related, pairwise comparisons of the national discursive fields not only highlights the similarities and differences in the contestations over the state and empire, race and nation, and capitalism and democracy across the Anglosphere core, but they also help us understand how its identities are made on the "inside" and "outside" simultaneously. In this story, the Anglosphere Self indeed emerges in interactions with the "new immigrants," "Negros," the "Celtic fringe," indigenous peoples, Quebec, and Muslims at home, as well as with the "Latin races," Germany, "Asian communism," Saddam Hussein, and the Taliban.

The historical epochs, cross-national comparison, and policy situations selected for investigation are not put forward as certain critical junctures, which locked in the English-speaking peoples to certain path-dependent routes vis-à-vis their social environment. Yet they follow some standard methodological choices. The focus on the matters of war, military interventions, and alliances is deliberate because the domain of national security is said to constitute the least likely case for international cooperation and community building and thus offers the strongest sort of evidence possible for the existence of Anglosphere identity in world politics. Further "hard" case selections are nested within this domain. Instead of retelling the story of how the Anglosphere core cohered in World War II or the Gulf War, we consider cases where at least one core pursued a policy that contradicted the idea and practice of the English-speaking alliance. The American and British empires twice clashed over Venezuela at the fin de siècle, while the Pacific Pact, Suez, Vietnam, and Iraq each stand as bywords for energetic disagreements and disputes within the Anglosphere, as well as for unexpected exclusions and defections from the alleged common cause. In this sense, pairwise comparisons of Australia and Canada in Suez and Vietnam as well as of Britain and Canada in Iraq are "structured-focused," in the sense that they differ as little as possible from each other except on the dimensions to be explained.[32] The last rationale behind case selection was substantive. As I will show in the subsequent chapters, each case study is also motivated by a question that may be regarded as puzzling for at least some IR theories.

In this book, genealogy and comparative case studies are designed to work symbiotically with each other, and to that end both research tools are grounded in discourse analysis (DA), a qualitative and interpretative recovery of meanings from texts.[33] In each case study, the task of DA is to contextualize identities, that is, to interpret and code identities, as they are present in an individual text; and then intertextualize them, that is, to interpret and code identities across an archive. The objective is to find which identities in a given context are present and which predominate, across different sources, and in terms of both their salience and frequency. In much of social theory, identity is usually binarized in terms of similarity or difference with significant Others. The friend-rival-enemy distinction, the staple of IR theory, follows this continuum. This DA breaks this continuum into two axes of meaning:

distance, or the placement of the Other as close or distant; and value, or the assessment of the Other as positive or negative. This produces a typology of Self–Other relations that covers the standard racialized distinctions between settler and nonsettler colonies, partners and junior partners, trusteeships and failed states, or barbarians and savages.

The archive refers to a sample of texts sufficiently wide and diverse to pass as representative within the national discursive field (the Appendix contains a detailed list of sources and sampling criteria). Because we are considering not only what is understood but also who said what to whom, when, and where, the archive is divided into three sets, provisionally labeled society, foreign policy debate, and decision. To minimize the risk of tautology, these sets are isolated in advance of accessing data, and the DA proceeds from society to decision, not vice versa. Once again, there is a difference between ontology and analysis. On the one hand, these sets of texts are inseparable, mutually constitutive, and dialectical, as is discourse and fact, language and society, identity and foreign policy. On the other hand, separation, stabilization, and bracketing are inevitable from an analytical standpoint.

The very first methodological objective is to recover the broad discursive topography in society for the purposes of identifying the dominant discourse of identity. Society is treated as historically variable: how state or national identity has varied across, and has been mediated by, the identities of race, gender, ethnicity, region, profession, class, education, travel, and so on is an empirical question that directly informs the way in which DA assembles the context and intertext. For example, in the late nineteenth century, laying an authoritative and exclusive claim on American identity was infinitely easier for a societal minority consisting of educated, employed white males of the Anglo-Protestant descent who formed the backbone of the government, business, and the media. By the early twenty-first century, this process was opened up, if ever so slightly, to other members of the American society.

Next, in subjecting foreign policy debates to DA, we focus on the texts authored by people whose job or role is to explain how the world hangs together to an audience—in principle to the general public, but also to more exclusive audiences such as the legislators or academics. Some texts analyzed in this category will seek to justify the state's place in the world, while others will criticize it, but what is important analytically is that they attribute meaning to the state or national Self relative to external Others. It is in this analytical step that we trace the ways in which key international problems and solutions were framed by different texts in this period by elites. The majority of frames will probably follow the dominant discourse of identity, but also probable are the differences within it such that we can identify the main discursive "positions" or "schools of thought." These may or may not correspond to party identification, generation, gender, region, or class but are always influenced by the asymmetries emanating from the unequal capacities, authorizations, ranks, and credentials of speakers and their audiences. The influence of these asymmetries in foreign policy debates is an empirical matter.[34]

As for the recovery of events, these are sequences of contention in foreign policy debates produced by historical actors (for example, the media) and then used by a researcher for purposes of observation and comparison. The analysis makes no claims that an event X gained more headlines in a period than an event Y; rather, its goal is capture the patterns of discursive contestation in contemporary texts. The processes of linking of new events to extant frames is expected to follow patterns of contestation among elites speaking from different discursive perspectives. Because some arguments will be more persuasive than others, the dominant interpretation of the fit will influence the likelihood of one policy option being taken over others.

The third and last analytical step concerns foreign policy decisions. If my argument is correct, we should expect that foreign policy choices follow the outcome of foreign policy debate on the fit between the discourse of identity and reality. All else equal, the greater the fit, the more likely it is that a policy will continue; conversely, the greater the misfit, the more likely it is that a policy shift will take place. Two kinds of findings would cast doubt on my argument here: If a policy shifts to an alternative option despite the presence of the rhetorically demonstrable fit between the dominant understanding of state or national identity and new events, or if a policy continues despite the rhetorically demonstrable misfit. Where there are *no* plausible alternatives, the likelihood of a policy shift will be minimal.

In evaluating this theoretical framework against alternative explanations, special attention will be paid to rationalist perspectives on world politics, such as realism and liberalism. While both realist and liberals tend to argue that what actors say and do is ultimately a function of the distribution of material capabilities at home and abroad—anything from guns and butter to information about guns and butter—they, too, put evidentiary premium on intersubjective meanings in their historical case studies. The purpose of "process tracing" is to assess the congruence between the actors' evaluation of the policy situation on the one hand and the actual policy choices on the other: the more congruent this link, the greater potential for causal imputation about the actors' influence on the decision.[35] This type of analytical assessment provides realists and liberals with an opportunity to examine whether their theoretical logics and mechanisms operate as advertised. For example, a finding that a majority of actors "think and act" like ideal-typical realists (as do security-seeking nationalists) and not like ideal-typical liberals (such as community-building liberal democrats) is counted in favor of realism. The methodological choices made in this book mean that outside the scope of inquiry lie numerous aspects of the Anglosphere, such as, for example, patterns of conflict or cooperation in the domain of international political economy or various explanations of these patterns. At appropriate points in the chapters that follow, I will therefore address selected interpretations of my subject that go beyond the realist-liberal-constructivist triad in IR.

The archive of primary source texts used in this book consists of nearly 3,000 discrete and closely analyzed units—books, newspaper and news-magazine articles, speeches, and other historical documents. The secondary literature was consulted to guide, substantiate, corroborate, and correct the analysis, depending on the analytical stage. As general rule, my analysis relied on cultural, gender, imperial, intellectual, political, and social history in the first analytical step and on diplomatic history on the second and third. The secondary source cross-check also enabled a comparison of my recovery of the ideal-typical structures of meaning to the interpretations of seasoned historians.[36] As ever, to detect and analyze continuities and changes in the patterns of separation, exclusion, hierarchy, and inequality in international life, multiple readings of history are required. Once again, chapters to come weave but one story of the Anglosphere. Chapters 2 through 5 present four sets of case studies, along the lines discussed above. The composition and use of primary sources in these chapters is explained in the Appendix. Chapter 2 looks at the Anglo-American relationship in the period between two Venezuela crises, the boundary crisis of 1894–1895 and the blockade crisis of 1902–1903. What constitutes a puzzle for IR theory is the way in which the Anglo-American war became "unthinkable" while peace and cooperation became dependable. An explanation can be found in the rise of Anglo-Saxonism, a racialized identity that established American and British empires as vanguards of civilization. Chapter 3 turns to the making of the Pacific Pact in 1950–1951 and considers how the pact came to be reduced to ANZUS, thus excluding Britain as well as the so-called island states. By examining the role of Australian and New Zealander identities in diplomatic negotiations, the chapter shows how the pact came to be based primarily on racial, rather than strategic or anticommunist considerations. It also argued that the existence of a collective identity rendered the exclusion of Britain and, later, New Zealand, nominal.

Chapter 4 conducts a pairwise comparison of Australia and Canada and asks why foreign policies of these two seemingly similar core Anglosphere members diverged in the Suez crisis (1956) and the Vietnam escalation (1964–1965). In the first case study, which covers the most important Anglo-American conflict of the twentieth century, the dominant discourses of Britishness equally compelled Canberra and Ottawa to side with Britain. By going against the motherland, the Canadian governments overrode the Canadian identity, but not without a series of canny framing moves. In the second case study, the argument is that the status of the American Other in the debates on Australian and Canadian identities profoundly shaped Australian and Canadian policies in Vietnam. While the Australian government discovered exceptionally pro-American leanings of its audiences, the Canadian government attempted to define Canada as a unique nation with a necessarily ambiguous foreign policy. Chapter 5 relates to the run-up to the Iraq War from the perspectives of Britain and Canada. The analysis finds that British participation in the U.S.-led "coalition of the willing" followed a powerful pro-American undercurrent of the British identity, but not after considerable framing wars in which the government managed to build its own discursive coalition at home. In Canada, a similarly powerful but anti-American identity compelled the government to sit out the war, which it did. Chapter 6 draws the main conclusions, engages mainstream IR in theoretical and substantive terms, directs for future research, considers some questions of policy relevance, and ends with a reflection on the path dependence and future of the Anglosphere as an actor in international relations.

2 EMPIRE, VENEZUELA, AND THE "GREAT RAPPROCHEMENT"

Evidently, the Anglo-Saxon is doing for the modern world what the ancient Greek did for the ancient.
—Josiah Strong, 1893

America for Americans, and to hell with Britain and her Tories.
—Senator "Pitchfork Ben" Tillman (D-AL), 1896

We are a part, and a great part, of the Greater Britain which seems plainly destined to dominate this planet.
—The New York Times, June 24, 1897

What is our next duty?
It is to establish and to maintain bonds of permanent amity with our kinsmen across the Atlantic.
There is a powerful and a generous nation. They speak our language. They are bred of our race.
Their laws, their literature, their standpoint upon every question are the same as ours.
—Joseph Chamberlain,
Colonial Secretary, Birmingham, May 13, 1899

AS I SUGGESTED IN THE INTRODUCTION, the Anglosphere developed gradually, across oceans and over centuries. Yet all genealogies must begin somewhere in the recorded history. This story begins in the 1890s, a time when Britain and the United States were, in Stephen Rock's memorable words, "almost destined to be enemies."[1] Instead of the inevitable enmity, what occurred was the "great rapprochement."[2] What is puzzling here is not the rapprochement itself: A cursory look at the contemporary alliances, pacts, condominiums and spheres of influence suggests that many imperial projects were simultaneously competitive and cooperative, varying by the period, region, and issue area. Rather, it is the depth, consistency, and quality of the Anglo-American cooperation. Consider a brief transhemispheric comparison of the politics among empires. As a leading protagonist of "scrambles" and "carve-ups" in the eastern hemisphere, Britain pursued a conspicuously inactive policy in the Americas. Conversely, the United States never moved to annex—either through force or purchase—a single part of British territory in Canada, Newfoundland, or the British West Indies, in contrast to large parts of territories owned by Denmark, France, Spain, or Russia.[3] Why, then, did London acquiesce to U.S. expansion in the Americas but elsewhere vigorously fight off bids for expansion from other empires? Conversely, why did Washington tiptoe around British possessions in what it usually saw as the home hemisphere?

According to Kenneth Bourne, British foreign policy makers in this period "consistently" identified Americans as friends, using "criteria which lay outside their professional terms of reference."[4] Historical evidence shows not only that friendly attitudes were reciprocated by the American officials but also that a steadily growing number of elite figures on both sides of the Atlantic—government and opposition leaders, clergymen, businessmen, soldiers, artists—felt compelled to publicly express a conviction that the Anglo-American war was "unthinkable." Declarations of the unthinkability of war are logically evidence of its thinkability, but what is indicative is the absence of such declarations and attitudes toward other states and empires.[5] Along the same lines, "Greater Britain" had no peers in the marketplace of bold ideas. It was Charles Dilke in 1868 who pointed out that "if two small islands are by courtesy called "Great," America, Australia, India must form a Greater Britain."[6] Later in the century, the term came to identify arguments for closer integration of the English-speaking peoples into the "imperial federation" or the "Anglo-American union." As Duncan Bell recently showed, there was an entire transnational advocacy network behind the idea of Greater Britain, whose supporters, much like Churchill at Fulton, argued that assorted advances in industry, science, and technology combined with "moral force" and certain other intangible qualities to make greater integration in the English-speaking world possible.[7] From the perspectives of the American and British elites, analogous arguments in favor of integration with some third polity, nation, or society were virtually unimaginable at the time.[8]

To go back to Bourne, why was the idea of the Anglo-American war so consistently delegitimized by the individuals who were both empowered and responsible to keep the possibility of such outcome real? Put differently, how did the two empires destined to fight each other come to view each other as partners to the point that outright political integration became a legitimate topic of discussion among their elites? The argument of this chapter is that the "great rapprochement" was caused by Anglo-Saxonism, a discourse of racialized identity that obliged the British and American elites to think of themselves as the twin vanguards of modernity. Simply put, London and Washington claimed the obligation to resolve intramural disputes peacefully to claim the right to lead civilization forward, by example as well as by military might. Anglo-Saxonism and the rapprochement fed off each other. The more Americans and British believed that they together constituted a special edition of humankind, the more dependable the Anglo-American peace became. By the early years of the twentieth century it appeared that "two branches of the Anglo-Saxon race," to use a contemporary metaphor, were destined to rule the world for one hundred years. Indeed, it was the cooperation based on race and racism that paved the way for the Anglo-American "special relationship" as well as other special relationships that crisscross the Anglosphere core.

The empirical focus of the chapter falls on two crises: "Venezuela I" (winter 1895–1896) is a U.S. intervention in a boundary dispute between Venezuela and the British Empire and "Venezuela II" (winter 1902–1903) is a U.S. intervention over the Anglo-German naval blockade of Venezuela. Less focused, but equally structured is my approach to two further cases: the Spanish-American War (1898) and the South African War (1899–1902). In the previous chapter, I suggested that international security constitutes a hard case for making the link between identity and cooperation. The challenge of this case study is compounded by the fact that the United States emerged as an actor in its revolutionary war against Britain at the end of the eighteenth century. If identity were to play any causal role here, it should spell conflict as well as cooperation. Further, the Anglo-American conflict is also predicted by theories that emphasize the violent nature of power transitions: Why peace "broke out" between the rising United States and the declining Britain is an old puzzle for these and other theories in IR.[9] Last, Venezuela I is paradigmatic to the first-wave debate on the democratic peace thesis in the 1990s.[10] Liberals argued that the Anglo-American war over Venezuela was averted thanks to the pacifying effect of democratic norms and democratic political structures. Realists underscored the role of appeasement or the British decision to back off. Rather than a poster child for the democratic peace, they argued, Venezuela I was a "near miss." As neither side could explain an overdetermined outcome, the debate ended in a draw, apart from the fact that liberals agreed to add a subclause to their thesis: Democracies never *or almost never* fight each other.

This realist-liberal debate is a useful repository of alternative explanations because in it both sides accepted that political actors interpret, rather than simply reflect, their strategic position. As I suggested in the introductory chapter, notwithstanding the significant difference in the ontological and theoretical status between cognitive misperceptions on the one hand and discourse and debate on the other, it is still possible to read their accounts against mine.[11] If realists and liberals are right, relevant political actors should make sense of the world mostly in terms of geographic proximity, relative capabilities/ threats, and regime type. If my account is right, actors should follow the discourses and debates over identity, wherever these might take them. The positive influence of Anglo-Saxonism on the fin-de-siècle U.S.–British relations has long been known among historians, but in IR liberals and realists have minimized or dismissed its significance.[12] I will therefore attempt to correct the interpretations advanced by IR scholars while adding novel theoretical narrative to explanations offered by historians.

ANGLO-SAXONS AND OTHERS

In an ideal-typical reading of the American and British discourses of identity in the 1890s, there are several similarities. The elites in both societies strongly identified with Protestantism, modernity, and civilization. Protestantism invoked obedience, help, and family. Modernity was mainly understood through liberal education, industry and science, and technology. And civilization combined with modernity to imply competition and progress in a world divided in nations, states, and empires. The last three terms were used interchangeably with races, human collectives coded by geography and/or physiognomy. Implicitly or explicitly, most texts from this period assumed a world composed of different human races at different stages of civilization.

Because all national elites at the time cultivated myths of superiority and declared positive human attributes to be distinctively national or, indeed, racial, it is not surprising to discover that the contemporary Anglo-American elites believed that "their" race constituted the most mature stage of human civilization. What is surprising, however, is that the professed superiority was neither American nor English/British, but *Anglo-Saxon*. In this discourse, the ancestors of people who ruled the American and British empires were the Saxon tribes who moved to England in the fifth and sixth centuries. What made these continental immigrants special was their love for self-rule as well as their resilience against the authoritarian Latin races, initially Roman, then

Norman, followed by Spaniards and French. When and how the Anglo-Saxon legend became racialized is outside the scope of the book, but it should be noted that it was foundational to both polities under study. First it helped glue together an English–Scottish union (1707) under a German monarch (1714) that found itself isolated among the warring states of Europe. Then it helped the thirteen revolutionary colonies secede from the empire (1776). Texts left behind by Thomas Jefferson, John Adams, Benjamin Franklin, and other founders are peppered with claims to the Anglo-Saxon past, in which the Americans emerge as "better" and "truer" Anglo-Saxons, especially when compared to the despotic and dissolute King George.[13]

In a backward reading of history, it can be said that the discourses of Anglo-Saxon identity had been used to make and break states and empires for centuries, but it was only in the nineteenth century that they went global. One factor was the spread of the English language, while another was a spectacular decrease in communication and transportation costs, which led to a significant rise in the transnational flows of people, goods, services, and information. But what drove this globalization of Anglo-Saxonism was also racial thought. Consider the example of the transatlantic marriage, that famous upper-class fad of the late nineteenth century.[14] What made this practice possible was not a fortuitous mix of money, status, language, and the steamship with a multiple expansion engine but primarily a belief that the bride and the groom shared Anglo-Saxon racial heritage. No American lady and no British gentleman could even imagine marrying into the richest and most English-speaking of native families in Havana, Honolulu, or Hyderabad. Wealthy Anglo-American bourgeois doubtless regarded Europe's aristocratic families as attractive, but these tendencies were racialized, too. Consider the meaning of Germany. Among "red men," Asiatics, Slavs, and other frequently enlisted significant others in the Anglo-American meditations on "who we are," it was the Germans who most frequently and least ambiguously stood out as close and positive. Most historians, at least before mid-1890s, subscribed to the "Teutonic origins" or "germ" theory, according to which the rule of law, constitutional liberties, and other political and legal institutions that made the American and British so pleased with themselves originated in the Witan, a mythical assembly of Saxon patriarchs from the other side of the Roman limes. For some elites, Teutonism in history implied Teutonism in politics: an alliance of the United States, Britain, and Germany as the main branches of the grand Germanic race.[15]

As always, class, gender, region, religion, and other identities all played important parts in defining what it means to be American and British at the time, but in both contexts it was race that stood as the hub, the icon as well as the main anchor of state/national identity.[16] What helped race dominate the intersubjective meanings was its discursive coalition with science. In the 1890s, recently developed theories of physical and social evolution had long been grafted onto theories of social inequality, which held that race caused one's place in society. No agreement existed on whether race was primarily in "blood" (nature or biology) and/or in "spirit" (nurture or history), but nearly everyone believed in the existence of social hierarchies composed of discrete racial units—anywhere from two to sixty-three, but usually three to five. For example, between 1865 and 1895, anthropologists surveyed 25,000,000 Europeans to demonstrate that a single white race was really three different races, Teutonic, Alpine, and Mediterranean.[17]

While the meaning of race wildly varied across texts, there was one common denominator: Even those authors who argued that race was biological did not necessarily believe in the permanence of extant hierarchies. This had to do with the popularity of evolutionary science ideas such as the "survival of the fittest," "natural selection," "struggle for existence" and "fitness," which tended to imply that if the circumstances that led to a racial hierarchy changed, an inferior race could easily catch up and "overtake." From the American and British perspectives, the Anglo-Saxons were indeed superior on a scale of racial development and worth, but the scale was in flux. The Australian Aborigines and Native Americans were "dying"; China and the "Latin nations" of Spain, Italy, and France were "slipping"; while Japan, Germany, and Russia, at least in the Far East, were resolutely moving upwards.[18] In this discourse, the "danger" of racial overtaking was simultaneously internal and external. The last decade of the nineteenth century saw a major spike in immigration of "dark whites" from the Austro-Hungarian, German, and Russian empires and, indeed, Ireland. The fact that many of these "new immigrants" were non-Protestant or even non-Christian was understood to have adverse consequences for both economy and culture of the receiving Anglo-Saxon societies.[19]

The social and political processes related to globalization, evolutionary science, and immigration all helped catapult Anglo-Saxonism to the top of the American and British discursive fields at the time.[20] Yet the pervasiveness and power of this discourse had little to do with its consistency and coherence.

Some critics, possibly echoing Darwin, pointed out that in an evolutionary vista of thousands of years the idea of distinct human races made little sense, while others, echoing Herder, said that races were not coterminous with nations.[21] Discursively, at least three foreign policy baseline orientations were therefore possible. Anglo-Saxonists posited that the Americans and British were cousins, Teutonists agreed but added that all Germanic races were related, while skeptics denied the relevance of race-based disaporic identities in international politics. As we shall see next, the debates over which of these ideas best approximated the real world had dramatic effects on world history.

ANGLO-SAXONISM AND EMPIRE

In Britain, Anglo-Saxonism was hegemonic at all levels of discourse, including foreign policy. Indicative is the "Irish Question," also known under the rubric of "Home Rule." Rather than being attributed to parliamentary or constitutional politics, Gladstone's resignation in 1893 over this question was interpreted as a result of a failure of government to solve the problem of national unity, namely how to bring "order" to the "Celtic Fringe." The parallel problem was imperial unity. The imperial Self typically extended to the "self-governing" colonies in Australasia, Canada, and the Cape but not to the vast areas defined by military rule or "enlightened despotism." It was in the periphery that London faced the seemingly unending litany of upper-case Questions the empire faced in 1894–1895—Eastern, Egyptian, Far Eastern, Indian, South African, and so on. Because of the dual threats from within and without, the empire was in the state of "decline" ("deterioration," "decay," and "weariness"). Lord Seeley's wildly popular *Expansion of England* (1883) had put it in the starkest of terms: Britain must either strengthen the empire or become a "second rate" power.

British foreign policy debate had two main discursive positions—"traditionalist" and "constructive imperialist."[22] Traditionalists came from the political mainstream and included most old Conservatives like Salisbury and Hicks Beach as well as some senior Gladstonian Liberals like Kimberley. They and their supporters relied on the old tropes of "splendid isolation" and "masterly inactivity" and called for staying the basic imperial course, though some called for expansion ("wider still and wider"). Constructive imperialists called for the reform of empire. Here we had not only the ubiquitous Cecil Rhodes but also Conservative and Liberal Unionists leaders Chamberlain, Lansdowne, and Balfour; old Liberals Rosebery, Campbell-Bannerman, Asquith, Dilke, Playfair, Morley, Harcourt, Grey, and Haldane; navalists Beresford and Selborne; writers Kipling, J. A. Henty, Buchan and H. G. Wells; influential editors and commentators Curtis, Milner, Amery, Garvin, W. T. Stead and Stratchey; and scientists and eminent academics Pearson, Egerton, W. A. S. Hewins, Pollock, Mackinder, Milner, Curzon, Stubbs, and Acton. Imperial consolidation, they argued, could be achieved through a combination of "tariff reform," "devolution," "moral unity," "coherence," and "efficiency."[23]

Imperial consolidation implied imperial defense: The pound always depended on the Royal Navy and vice versa.[24] This expanded the debate over decline to include the question of regional peacetime alliances. Judging by private and public documents, London considered four imperial capitals as possible allies at the time: Berlin, Paris, Tokyo, and Washington.[25] From an objective-interest perspective, each alliance would have significantly reduced at least some of Britain's spectacular commitments around the globe. But from the perspective of state/national identity defined by Anglo-Saxonism, the most probable was the American alliance or, as Balfour and Chamberlain sometimes called it, the "race alliance."[26] Both constructive imperialists and traditionalists endorsed it: Dilke and Chamberlain advocated a formal alliance publicly, while in private Lansdowne and Salisbury spoke of an unspoken "understanding" with Washington. The grip of Anglo-Saxonism was so powerful that British "race patriotism" (again Balfour and Chamberlain, but also Alfred Milner and Andrew Carnegie) implied not only a "race alliance" with America but also a "federation of race" (Balfour). Thus the boldest proposals for reversing Britain's decline called for a political integration with the "cousins" and "brothers" in the United States—a project usually known under the rubric of "reunion" but also implied in the ideas of "Greater Britain" and the "United States of Empire."[27] Unification with the former colony had its vocal critics (Dilke and James Bryce come to mind), but much of the critique was in fact internal—namely, whether the new entity would be a federal or confederal or which Anglo-Saxon "branch" would lead. Equivalent proposals were not possible with respect to Germany or France, much less Japan. That the British elites set their foreign policy in reference not only to their empire but to the entire Anglo-Saxon race had a direct bearing on the way London approached Washington over the matters of international security well beyond the period under this case study.

Much like their counterparts in Britain, the American elites also worried about racial unity at the time, but their foreign policy debate centered on the problem of imperial expansion, not decline. From the metropolitan Eastern seaboard, where most texts in the archive generated for this chapter were authored, it appeared that the nation—"empire" was never employed to describe the North American homeland between the Rio Grande and the forty-ninth parallel—was under racial consolidation. In the West, the old problems with the "Indian" and "Mexican" Others were slowly coming under control, as did that with the Mormons of Utah, whose ideas anyway challenged only the dominant discourses of modernity and Protestantism, not race. America's two main political parties, the Democrats and the Republicans, both welcomed what they regarded as the North–South unification of the country, which was based on the Northern endorsement of the Southern desire to oppress the once enslaved "Negro" Other with segregation, disenfranchisement, and "lynch laws." The last racial problem at home was "new immigration"—the arrival of the Alpine, Mediterranean, Slavic, and Jewish Others in the big cities like Chicago and New York. As parallel histories of Irishness demonstrate so clearly, American whiteness had hitherto been more unsettled and elastic than the British counterpart, but the influx of European "dark whites" redefined the United States in 1894–1895 as the province of very white, propertied, Protestant adult men of British extraction.

The American foreign policy debates in the period under study can be stylized in terms of three slogans: "Manifest Destiny," the "Monroe Doctrine," and the "frontier." Each served to simultaneously imply America's distinction from the Old World and its expansive mission in the New. The Manifest Destiny refers to a widespread contemporary belief in the inevitability of American territorial expansion, while the Monroe Doctrine relates to Washington's long-standing program for eliminating European colonization of the Western Hemisphere. The importance of the frontier was famously captured by Frederick Jackson Turner who confronted the Teutonist theory of history with an argument in favor of a distinct American identity.[28] Because the 1890 national census map lost the frontier line for the very first time, Turner continued, the Americans needed to rethink who they are. These three slogans were subject to two framings and counterframings coming from two discursive positions— "exceptionalism" and "expansionism."[29] Consider the Hawaii debate in 1894. At that time, the islands were occupied but not annexed because it was legally unclear whether and how the constitution "follows the flag" and, politically, whether and how Manifest Destiny applies to the Pacific, a vast geographic space over which the Monroe Doctrine did not apply and where white settlement ended but colonial administration began. In the exceptionalist reading, which was preferred by Democrats, Populists, and a few Republicans (Senator Hoar), the main argument held that America's republican mission was legitimate only when applied pushed against its "virgin" frontier. Turner's thesis was that the entire American history can be reduced to the "colonization" of the "Great West," a space bounded by the Rio Grande, the Pacific, and an undefined point in the north. Beyond this space, claimed exceptionalists, America's mission mandated leadership by example, rather than conquest.[30] This position was institutionally bolstered in the Anglophobic agrarian movement as well as in the Anti-Imperialist League, whose leaders argued that the mission to conquer and socialize the biologically "inferior" or "lower" races was self-defeating.[31]

The fate of American exceptionalism is a thrice-told tale. The question whether territories could be administered without being settled was answered affirmatively in the aftermath of the Spanish-American War, specifically in the form of the Teller resolutions and the annexation of Puerto Rico, which legislated and legitimated colonial administration as a form of the American mission overseas. In 1894, exceptionalism faltered because of the misfit of its frames with the dominant discourse on race. Senators Beveridge, Davis, Lodge, La Follette, and Platt all wrote in favor in racial conquest, as did such distinguished academics as Henry Baxter Adams, Franklin Giddins, Alfred Mahan, George Wharton Pepper, Harry Powers, and Francis Amasa Walker. This camp won the debate thanks to two arguments in particular. The first was that the denial of America's Anglo-Saxon identity was naïve and even dangerous in the face of mass influx of uncivilized Europeans. If full assimilation of new immigrations was an imperative for the preservation of national character, so was the recognition of the fundamentally Anglo-Saxon content of that character.[32] Note that anti-immigrant Anglo-Saxonism far outweighed the potential effects of the so-called ethnic Anglophobia. Amounting to 8 percent of the American population at the time, the Irish-Catholics were the largest of all new immigrant groups, but the sheer size of this community translated into political power in the cities, not in Congress.[33]

The second argument was that the Manifest Destiny defined the frontier, not the other way around. For expansionists, racial theories implied that the "Great West" was what the Americans made of it: If one conceded to evolutionist theories on why the "red man" was "pushed out," then it was unclear why the national mission should ever stop at the "water's edge." As for the racial supremacist argument against empire, expansionists defeated it by emphasizing the evolutionary and historical nature of racial inequality. In this view, imperialism served not only to develop the unfit Cubans but also to prevent the fit Japanese from "overtaking" in the Pacific. Despite the presence of dubious tautologies (Anglo-Saxon supremacy legitimized colonialization, which then proved Anglo-Saxon supremacy), double visions ("Slavic Russia" was both inferior and threatening) and teleologies (one world ruled by the fittest race), the expansionist arguments based on race resonated with the American elites as much as similar arguments resonated with constructive imperialists in Britain. Let us now examine how these two elite worldviews interacted in select international crises between 1895 and 1903.

OLD RIVALS, NEW FRIENDS

It was in June 1895 that the U.S. government decided to intervene in a long-standing British–Venezuelan border dispute over what appeared to be a gold-rich piece of land. In a communiqué sent to London, Secretary of State Olney invoked the Monroe Doctrine and demanded submission of the dispute to U.S. arbitration because, he explained, the United States was "practically sovereign" in the hemisphere. An initial British dismissal was followed by another invocation of the Doctrine, in December of the same year, this time by President Cleveland before Congress, and so Venezuela became a crisis.[34] Once Senator Lodge, former president Harrison and many others called for a show of resolve, the issue gained bombastic headlines in the U.S. press ("War if Necessary," ran one title page), and war talk caused a temporary collapse of stock exchanges both on Wall Street and in Chapel Court.[35] That winter saw a great deal of public and private diplomacy across the Atlantic. Petitions like the "Anglo-American Memorial" were signed by thousands.[36] The pressure worked on both sides: By January, the entire American press called for peace, and London accepted arbitration in February.[37] Causing a transatlantic sigh of relief, the British government accepted arbitration in February. Later that year, London signed an arbitration agreement, which was favorable to its colony in Guyana. The Monroe Doctrine, the British press concluded, served the interest of both branches of the Anglo-Saxon race.[38]

Historians have long interpreted the Anglo-American crisis over Venezuela as "synthetic."[39] From a theoretical perspective that links discourse and debate to foreign policy, crises tend to be synthetic in the sense that they are spoken in and out of existence. Indeed, there was no objective and strategic reason for the Cleveland administration to intervene in the border dispute between

British Guyana and Venezuela while ignoring the contemporaneous border dispute between French Guyana and Brazil or an earlier British occupation of Nicaragua.[40] What needs to be explained, however, is the process by which the American and British elites came to see Venezuela as synthetic and not worth a colonial war. To that end, let us begin with an observation that in Britain not a single text advocated an American war. Considering that imperial jingoism and rowdyism in objectively similar crises was the order of the day until the 1956 Suez crisis, the silence might be regarded as odd. In these terms, the interpretation of the Kruger telegram, a congratulatory note Germany's Kaiser Wilhelm sent to the president of the Transvaal in January 1896 for defeating a British paramilitary invasion is also odd. In objective terms, the events in Venezuela and South Africa were virtually identical, as each involved a foreign government's public protest over an act of British aggression. So why was there such sharp contrast between the anti-German jingoism on the one hand and meek and conciliatory position toward the United States on the other? Lest one writes this puzzle over with a realist explanation involving a changing threat environment, note that Britain was equally conciliatory toward the United States before the news of the Kruger telegram reached London.[41]

From a point of view centered on identity formation in world politics, Venezuela I was a crisis over equal recognition. Ernest May argues that before 1895 the British understood America as a "metaphysical conception"—a former colony with curious imperial claims to an entire hemisphere; accordingly, saber rattling coming from the United States was simply not as credible as that coming from by France or Germany.[42] Archival records suggest that Prime Minister Lord Salisbury initially planned to "repudiate" the United States but backed off in the course of events. Opposition to government policy came from every direction, including Salisbury's own cabinet, but especially the parliamentarians, who apparently discovered America once again.[43] The antiwar rhetoric was shot through with Anglo-Saxonism: "We expect the French to hate us and are quite prepared to reciprocate the compliment if necessary; but the Americans, no!"[44] Balfour and Chamberlain, with the authority of cabinet members, took turns in declaring the Anglo-American war "unnatural," "fratricidal," "absurd," a "horror," and a "crime against the laws of God and man."[45] Rosebery and Harcourt, from the Liberal opposition, agreed that "war with America must be avoided at all costs and irrespective of all Party considerations" and that the future of both Christendom and human civilization depended on peace between the "mighty nations of the Anglo-Saxon race."[46]

From the theoretical perspective developed in this paper, Salisbury's tough line collapsed because it did not fit the dominant Anglo-Saxonist discourse that regarded the American people as family and the American government as an ally and even a (con)federal partner. On the American side, there was a similar misfit within the rising expansionist discourse that, in abstract, called for both the Monroe Doctrine over Venezuela and the Anglo-Saxon brotherhood with Britain. Former State Secretary Bayard captured this misfit by asking why "two Trustees of Civilization" should fight over "the mongrel state of Venezuela."[47] Business leaders agreed, and even Pulitzer and Reid, whose media often empires thrived on jingoism, called for peace.[48] Not unlike Salisbury, Cleveland gave up conflict because he could not meaningfully explain it to the public. This reading significantly complicates the democratic peace thesis. The Anglo-American elites indeed understood each other as fellow democrats, but their antecedent ontology was always race, not regime type.[49] In the flurry of public petitions sent to London and Washington, many cases for peace were made, but the idea that democracies should be able to resolve conflict peacefully was not one of them. Rather, the typical framing motivated peace with family metaphors, as in the case of a large British petition that stated: "All English-speaking peoples united by race, language and religion, should regard war as the only absolutely intolerable mode of settling the domestic differences of the Anglo-American family."[50] To the extent that democracy was related to peace, this argument was always made in the context of a racial theory of history in which democracy was in short supply everywhere but in Anglo-Saxondom. As a supplement to the liberal explanation of the crisis, it can therefore be said that what caused peace over Venezuela was *Anglo-Saxon* democracy, not Anglo-Saxon *democracy*.

That the idea of democracy was deeply racialized in the contemporary discourse can be surmised from the so-called arbitration movement. Founded on the idea that war among civilized nations should be outlawed, the movement gained in popularity among the Anglo-American elites in the 1870s, when the last of disputes concerning British policies toward the Confederacy in the American Civil War was settled. To Lord Playfair, one of the supporters of the movement, democracies are most likely to resolve their disputes peacefully when they share racial ties: "We are both the common inheritors of the traditions and glories of the Anglo-Saxon race from which we have obtained the spirit of conciliation, a spirit that has so aided the national development of both countries."[51] An Anglo-American "permanent" arbitration treaty was indeed signed in 1897, but never ratified, yet this very process is a significant embodiment of the ways in which the outcome of Venezuela I came to shape transatlantic ideas and institutions, from the rough blueprint for the "Anglo-Saxon Olympic Games" to the influential lobbies such as the Anglo-American Committee and the Anglo-American League. Among these was *The Anglo-Saxon Review*, a magazine founded by Lady Randolph, Winston Churchill's mother.

In the imaginary of the Anglo-American elites, the Venezuelan Other was recognized not only as distant and negative but also as partially equal. In this sense, the Venezuelan crisis significantly differs from the major crises that followed it. In the Spanish-American War, Britain turned out to be America's sole supporter among empires. From London, the rational for the war and its outcome fit perfectly with the discourses of race and racial evolutionism: the United States, that ever-stronger branch of the Anglo-Saxon race, took on and overpowered an ancient and miserable enemy. The support was virtually unanimous: Star and Stripes went on display everywhere, hundreds of British subjects attempted to enlist in the U.S. Navy, and dozens of resolutions, declarations, and poems encouraged America to teach Spain a lesson in proper imperialism. And, typically, this support was articulated in racialist terms in which the American victory was a victory for the entire Anglo-Saxondom. By going to an imperial war, argued one commentator, "the American Republic has now reverted to the hereditary policy of the Anglo-Saxon race."[52] In *The Spectator's* symposium on "Are Americans Anglo-Saxons?" published on the eve of the war, five British contributors said yes, while one (token Irishman) said no.[53]

In the United States, the news from Britain both surprising and reassuring. Rumors of tacit cooperation between the U.S. Navy and the Royal Navy against the Spanish squadrons sounded eminently believable, while even the most Anglophobic among the American elites warmed up to the idea of a curious Anglo-Saxon bond between the two English-speaking empires. This group included Olney, Lodge, and Roosevelt, all of whom were ready to go to war over Venezuela.[54] In 1898, Roosevelt wrote to his British friend Arthur Lee: "I feel very strongly that the English-speaking peoples are now closer together than for a century and a quarter . . . for their interests are really fundamentally the same, and they are far more closely akin, not merely in blood, but in feeling and principle, than either is akin to any other people in the world."[55] (In 1902, he said to Lee: "The attitude of England in 1898 worked a complete revolution in my feelings and the attitude of the consentient at the time opened my eyes of the other side of the question."[56]). Much like *The Spectator* in 1898, *The*

New York Times asked in 1900 if Americans were Anglo-Saxons and, as Belich notes, "concluded with relief that they were."[57]

Britain's "benevolent neutrality" in the war appeared consistent with the implications of Anglo-Saxonism. In the United States, the easy victory solidified the expansionist position and in particular the frame that held that the Anglo-Saxon master race was destined to lead the human civilization to modernity. In 1900, the year of the formal acquisition of formerly Spanish colonies, one academic proposed that "it may well be our destiny to carry on the work of subjecting the world to the sway of Anglo-Saxon civilization," while another observed:

> The entry of our country upon what appears to be a new policy of foreign conquest and colonization must evidently impart a doubled impetus to that active extension of Anglo-Saxon civilization for which the mother country alone has been in modern times so conspicuous.[58]

From the perspective of Anglo-Saxonism, America's destiny was not geographical, but historical, but to the extent that it was geographical, then the Far East was really America's "Far West."[59] Roosevelt made this point quite clearly in the 1900 edition of his multivolume *The Winning of the West*. America's "campaigns," the future president argued, were basically the same "in the old West against the Shawnees and the Miamis, in the new West against the Sioux and the Apaches, or [in] Luzon against the Tagals."[60] Support for American expansionism indeed peaked during the Spanish-American war. In July 1898, *Literary Digest* noted that even traditionally anti-imperialist editors supported expansion, and a *Public Opinion* survey of 65 newspapers found that only 24.6 percent opposed the American "retention" of the Philippines. In December of the same year, a *Herald* survey of almost 500 newspapers discovered a majority (61.3 percent) to be in favor of expansion, with clear margins everywhere except in the South.[61] As I said earlier, it was in the aftermath of the confrontation with the Spanish Empire that colonial administration overseas became consistent with the promise of the American republic. Exceptionalism resoundingly lost the foreign policy debate in the 1890s, but it never lost track of American imperial development overall. In the decades that followed, exceptionalism rose several times to shape the development of numerous America's imperial, transnational, and international ideas—from collective security and the League of Nations in 1917 to, as we shall see in Chapter 5, the anti-Iraq "coalition of the willing" in 2003.

The symbiosis of Anglo-Saxonism and expansionism in American foreign policy debates in the last decade of the nineteenth century had immediate and direct consequences for further institutionalization of the Anglo-American rapprochement. It facilitated the creation of a joint commission for the resolution of extant disputes in the Western Hemisphere in 1898, the Hay-Pauncefote Treaty in 1901, which renegotiated the terms of the building of the isthmian canal, as well as to the 1903 Alaska Panhandle Treaty, which finally settled the U.S.–Canada Pacific boundary. In realist interpretation of history, these events mean one thing only: What enabled North American power transition to occur without violent struggle in the Western Hemisphere had little to do with Anglo-Saxonism but with Britain's time-honored policy "apaisement." In this reading, London backed down not only in Venezuela but also in every single subsequent dispute with Washington, all the way to the Suez crisis in 1956.[62] With respect to the appeasement thesis, my analysis accords with Stephen Rock's, in which he concluded that London's conciliatory stance had little to do with the fear of the mighty United States and more to do with collective identity. "Had push come to shove," noted Rock, "Americans might well have taken a more conciliatory stance."[63] The counterfactual is in fact quite historical. In a discourse that understood British concessions to the United States as a net gain for the Anglo-Saxons, appeasement was not a meaningful category. Britain backed off in the Venezuela crisis not because of a cold reassessment of its overall threat environment but because its elites could not come to legitimately explain to their publics why they should fight white Anglo-Saxon Protestant men like themselves. For similar reasons, Washington not only reversed its policy but also made sure that its arbitration in the boundary dispute eventually came to benefit British Guyana, not Venezuela. In this reading, the expansion of the American empire in Alaska and the Caribbean was not a function of appeasement so much as of willing cooperation based on the idea of global interracial competition in which Americans and British were one and the same. I will return to this point in the conclusion.

The limits of the realist interpretation of the "great rapprochement" are also in evidence in the texts left behind by Alfred Mahan, America's preeminent strategic thinker from the period. In his widely cited *Influence of Sea Power upon History* (1890), Mahan famously argued that the United States needed a powerful navy to counterbalance the influence its rivals in the Western Hemisphere and in Asia-Pacific. Yet he identified Germany and Japan as strategic rivals but not Britain, the obvious candidate from the objective-interest perspective that realism foregrounds. Behind this curious absence lies Mahan's own Anglo-Saxonism.[64] Much like British strategists such as Seeley and Dilke, Mahan consistently treated international relations as interracial relations too. The same can be said of the texts left behind by Theodore Roosevelt later. Here was one American leader who lived and breathed European-style *geopolitik* and who, like a good realist, obsessed about foreign threats to American interest. Yet, unlike a good realist, Roosevelt also called for the global hegemony of "men who spoke English."[65]

The Spanish-American War also helped produce Anglo-American collective identity through outside recognition. From the point of view of Madrid and most other European capitals, there was little doubt as to the collusion between the American and British forces in the Manila Bay and even less doubt over the fact that racial bonds were at play.[66] This time, too, the politics among nations was at once the politics among races. So while realists and liberals are right to point out that Britain and the United States competed over territory, borders and markets in what they saw to be their spheres of influence in the Americas and Asia, it is also important to note that their significant Others came to regard this competition as something of a sham in the 1890s. According to Alan Pitt, for the contemporary Parisian elites

> The collective term "Anglo-Saxon" came to dislodge the place previously occupied by England alone in French thought . . . [and] the tensions of imperialism provoked a tendency to conceive the United States and England as part of a unified political/cultural bloc that threatened to swamp the francophone world.[67]

Subsequent international events, as we shall see next, only reinforced the continental discourse of a single "Anglo-Saxony" in international politics.

From the perspective of the construction of the Anglo-Saxon identity, the "Latin races" of Spain and France were perhaps the most obvious oppositional Others, considering the presence of a centuries-old Protestant–Catholic divide in Europe and its offshoots. The same point can be made with respect to Russia, Japan, and numerous lesser powers and peoples, whose distant and negative alterity was not questioned in the dominant discourses on the American and British Selves. For this reason, it is an imperative to extend the analysis to the construction of Anglo-Saxondom to more ambiguous collective identity terrain that would involve international confrontations with the fellow Germanic races.

THE LIMITS OF TEUTONISM

If the Spanish-American War represents a triumph for Anglo-Saxonism, then the South African War stands for its downfall. The latter refers to a culmination of a long-standing confrontation between the British Empire and the Boers, then known as settler people of broadly Germanic racial extraction who stubbornly refused imperial authority. Around the world, the war became framed as a story of David and Goliath, two minuscule Boer republics willingly taking on the world's mightiest power. American elites were split. Support for the Boers was expressed by scores of important public figures—not only from the usual suspects among the populists and Democrats (William Jennings Bryan, Senator Bacon, Pulitzer), but also from proven Anglophiles such as the business tycoon Andrew Carnegie, the writer Henry Adams, and former Republican President Benjamin Harrison. Support was also expressed through numerous public declarations, petitions, and resolutions of sympathy as well as in the form of 300 American volunteers who joined the Boer war effort. To many of them 1899 was the new 1776: Here too was a group of independence-seeking rebels standing up to London's unreasonable dictates.[68]

The pro-British camp was reduced to the governing Republican Party, most big business leaders and, importantly, Hearst's media. This support was enough, however, to enable a continuous support of the British war effort with a stream of much-needed supplies, from food and medicines to ammunition and transport animals to cash loans. In private, the government's neutrality was framed as "repayment" (or "gratitude") for British support during the Spanish-American War and as an act of solidarity between two empires carrying the burden of civilizing the world. Already, at the beginning of the war, the Secretary of State John Hay wrote in 1900: "The fight of England is the fight of civilization and progress and all our interests are bound up in her success."[69] Roosevelt's reasoning was similar and even more telling. Despite his "Dutch blood," as he explained to his friends and relatives, he maintained that "it would be for the advantage of mankind to have English spoken south of the Zambesi just as in New York."[70] What helped the official position was a rereading of the Boers against the Southern slaveholding landowners from before the American Civil War. In this frame, the Boers were socioeconomically backward, and therefore their republics deserved to be placed under the authority of the modern British state, following the fate of the Confederacy in 1865.[71] Also helpful to the government was the contemporaneous colonial war in the Philippines in which Washington was playing a role quite similar to that of London in South Africa, hence disabling easy moral superiority claims.[72]

As the war progressed, American identification with the Boers loosened, and the policy of the McKinley and Roosevelt administrations came in line with reality. The outcome is indeed remarkable: Seemingly for the first time in history, the American government sided with an empire, the British Empire at that, against white rebels.[73] The South African war threw sand in the wheels of the budding Anglo-American cooperation, but it failed to change its overall course. The relative weakness of the racial dimension in the American interpretations of the South African War was boon for the proponents of the official policy. Rather than pursuing a difficult framing of the Boers as a negative racial Other to the Anglo-Saxons, the U.S. government defined them as half civilized and therefore inferior to the British. Also effective was the Othering of the Boers on the basis of faith, namely, their "religious fanaticism"[74]

As useful as these frames were for carrying the "great rapprochement" through difficult new realities, none of them were applicable to the coming confrontation between the two Anglo-Saxon empires on the one hand and imperial Germany on the other. Unlike the backward Boers, here was a racially close Other who was also an equal in terms of fitness, efficiency, and other contemporary measures of modernity and civilization. The more the Germans excelled in industry, commerce, science, and education, the more American and British elites fell under the spells of racial Teutonism or "Anglo-Teutonism." The very presence of this discourse suggests that, at some point in the late nineteenth century, claims for racialized identity in international politics could have been conceivably lodged in the name of Anglo-German, American-German, or Anglo-American-German combinations. The Rhodes Scholarships, as Cecil Rhodes conceived them in 1901, were meant to solidify Anglo-American unity as well as to promote peace with Germany.[75] While it was of course not illegitimate for the American and British elites to believe in the Teutonic origins of liberty and to be anti-German, Germany enmity in world politics was comparatively unlikely precisely because it was understood as the source, extension, and continuation of pan-Teutonic racial development. For this reason, it is an imperative to closely examine the less studied of the two fin-de-siècle Venezuela crises. Before Venezuela II, Germany hovered between the position of a potential friend and that of an actual rival for the budding Anglosphere; thereafter, it turned into a chronic threat—a role it played consistently at least until the middle years of the twentieth century.

It was in December 1902 that Britain and Germany, as tactical allies (later joined by Italy), deployed their gunboats in the Venezuelan waters with the objective of forcibly collecting debts. At that time, naval blockades were standard policy, even within the domain of Monroe's hemispheric claim, whose proponents, including President Roosevelt, agreed that the unruly countries to the south of the United States needed "spanking" from time to time.[76] After all, it was known that the United States, too, had long had parallel claims against Venezuela, together with Mexico and several other European states. Yet also standard was the reaction to such blockades of the American press, which would normally express irritation to European attempts to forcibly collect "American" debts. After some heavy-handed bombardment of Venezuelan ports, the American press exploded in condemning the action and once again induced the American government to react. Now it was Roosevelt who explained to his audiences at home and abroad that moderate gunboat action to collect debts was entirely appropriate but that the possibility of a long-term territorial occupation of Venezuelan territory, including its customs houses, was not.[77] Like in Venezuela I, the secretary of state then demanded arbitration, and the president backed him up; this time the United States possessed naval capability and so dispatched a battleship squadron under Admiral Dewey to the crisis area. Less than two weeks into the blockade, European allies agreed to arbitration "in principle." But when German warships destroyed another Venezuelan fort in January 1903, the agreement collapsed, and the crisis gained wind. Washington then confronted Berlin with an "ultimatum," which led to the signing of the new arbitration agreement and to the "ultimate" withdrawal of the European empires from the New World. Indeed, America's enforcement of the vast hemispheric claim that is the Monroe Doctrine has not come under a European test since, save perhaps for the Cuban Missile Crisis in 1962.[78]

In terms of the Anglo-American interaction, Venezuela I and Venezuela II are similar in the sense in each case the idea of a "fratricidal war" was framed as a disaster for the entire humanity, and both sides worked hard to resolve the dispute. But this time, the Anglo-American peace and cooperation rose against a hitherto unknown entity: the "Hun Germany." The label belongs to Rudyard Kipling, who as the "Voice of Empire in English Literature" published the poem "Rowers" in which he chastised his government for its tactics over Venezuela: "With a cheated crew, to league anew/With the Goth and the shameless Hun!" According to the *Oxford English Dictionary*, this poem is among the first English uses of the word *Hun* to describe a German, meaning one of "brutal conduct or character."[79] From the perspective of collective identity formation in interimperial politics, this poem supplemented Kipling's much more famous "White Man's Burden," written three years earlier, in which the author urged the Americans to extend their empire to the Philippines for the latter's benefit.[80] Kipling's verse aptly delineated the boundaries between Anglo-Saxon and Teutonic communities and, in particular, set the tone for the dominant framing of the crisis on both sides of the Atlantic, in which Anglo-Saxons predilection for "compromise" and "arbitration" was juxtaposed against German preference for brutal confrontation.[81]

From the British perspective alone, Venezuela I and Venezuela II were similar. Here, too, the press gave the government the benefit of doubt at first, but once it learned the news of the U.S. reaction, it turned sour.[82] There was an utter absence of anti-American jingoism and not a single report in the British press attempted to contemplate a possible colonial war with the United States.[83] And constructive imperialists, mostly in the opposition, also attacked traditionalists, mostly in the government, for testing Anglo-American specialness. Parts of the cabinet's "White Paper on Venezuela," which showed how London colluded with Berlin, found their way to the newspapers on December 15, 1902, and immediately caused such parliamentary and public uproar that the Salisbury government was almost toppled.[84] The problem, as British editorials as well as opposition leaders noted, was that Britain was on the "wrong side."[85] In the British debate, the development of what looked like a naval face-off with the United States in the Caribbean proved to be a major misfit for the dominant discourse of identity. One way of minimizing this misfit was to blame Germany for creating the crisis and London for foolishly tagging along with it. Thus, in consideration of *both* British and American public opinion and its precarious position, the government first admitted it got "roped" by Berlin and then moved to abandon its German ally.[86] The policy shift was comprehensive: Balfour was so eager to make it up to their national and transnational audiences that by mid-February he went on record in claiming British co-ownership of the Monroe Doctrine.[87]

The American press read the crisis almost identically: Germany was the ringleader of the European "conspiracy" or "concert" against the Monroe Doctrine. German actions were attributed to the militarism and aggressiveness of the German *people*; British actions, in contrasts, were explained away as a product of German manipulation, that is, a matter of misjudgment and foolishness in their *government*.[88] For example, already in December, the U.S.

press commented how the German navy sought to sink Venezuelan gunboats, while the British aimed for capture. But in January, when German cruisers flattened the fort of San Carlos in response to small weapons fire coming from Venezuelan coast, the difference between two European allies acquired a much sharper meaning. Germany's "neo-Teutonic principles" of revenge and destruction were so "impulsive," "disproportionate," and "uncivilized" that they "disgusted" the entire "English-speaking civilization."[89] The point lost in the coverage was that, in January, a British warship had joined a German cruiser in an almost identical destruction of the fort of Puerto Cabello. The British ambassador duly noted this double vision and wrote home: "The outburst in this country against the Germans has been truly remarkable, and suspicion of the German Emperor's designs in the Caribbean Sea is shared by the Administration, the press and the public alike."[90]

Arguably, the Anglo-Saxon Atlantic had little space for Teutons long before Venezuela II such that the negative representations of Germany were both a cause and an effect of Teutonism's lack of discursive footing in British and American societies. Earlier we compared the Kruger telegram to the Cleveland communiqué to suggest the presence and power of Germanophobia in Britain. A similar comparison can be made with respect to the differing reception of two speeches on the subject of racial alliances given by Chamberlain. In the first, given a month into the Spanish-American War, the colonial secretary described the United States as a "powerful and generous nation, speaking our language, bred of our race" and concluded that "their feeling, their interest in the cause of humanity and peaceful development of the world are identical with ours . . . Stars and Stripes and the Union Jack should wave together over an Anglo-Saxon alliance." In the second speech, in November 1899, Chamberlain called for "New Triple Alliance between the Teutonic race and the two great branches of the Anglo-Saxon race." That the first speech was a major success with its audiences, while the second was a major flop, shows both the power of Anglo-Saxonism and the limits of Teutonism at the time.[91] On the U.S. side, ideas about Teutonism, both pro and con, were similar but more muted. The large German-American community was disunited by faith and politics, and there were no known figures in foreign policy debates who argued for a race-based understanding with imperial Germany. In the years before Venezuela II, the U.S. press was sympathetic to Germany but critical of German imperialism, at least in comparative terms. To use but one example, the German occupation of China's Jiaozhou in November 1897 was regarded as more threatening to the United States than similar and reoccurring British actions in the same region and at around the same time.[92]

These discrepancies may be puzzling for realists and liberals in IR, but they can be explained from a framework based on the idea of discourses of identity. In both Britain and the United States, Anglo-Saxonism was more dominant than Teutonism and was growing ever more dominant thanks to the outcome of framing wars during Venezuela I, the Spanish-American War, and the South African War. Rather than dislodging realist ideas about the centrality of balancing against threats in international politics, my perspective can help explain some old puzzles in this school of thought. For one, the grip of Anglo-Saxonism on the American official mind, to use Paul Kennedy's language, explains why the United States felt more threatened by the objectively "hypothetical" threat posed by Germany than by the objectively "tangible" threat posed by Britain.[93] Similarly, my perspective complicates but does not dispute the validity of the democratic peace thesis advanced by liberals. In British eyes, to use Kennedy's words some more, Germany appeared to be a *racial* outsider because of its low scores on some unspecified indices of "democracy" and "liberty." In other words, Germany's excessive "pride" and "aggressive nationalism" had to do with the failure of democratic institutions, but the institutional failure, in turn, had to do with that nation's relative lag in the process of racial evolution. Objectively, American and German democracies were comparable for the British, but intersubjectively they significantly differed so much Germany was distrusted over Belgium while the United States was trusted over Canada.[94] This was so because racial thinking preceded liberal-democratic thinking, logically, historically, and, indeed, ontologically.[95]

It is worth to pause over the historical "Canadian Question." From a crude realist perspective, as a foundationally anti-American yet militarily vulnerable entity, Canada should have not survived the end of the nineteenth century.[96] The realist logic was indeed at play in American foreign policy debates at the time—recall that both expansionist and exceptionalists regarded the Great West and the Great North as a single space subject to the Manifest Destiny. Historians also found evidence that both Hay and Roosevelt welcomed the South African War as an opportunity to extract concessions from the British over the outstanding disputes in Alaska and the proposed isthmian canal.[97] In a realist world, the British empire was stretched so thin at that point that Washington could have mounted a more aggressive territorial challenge in Canada's west coast, which had long separated Alaska from America's mainland. In a liberal world, the United States never mounted such a challenge because liberal democracies do not annex other liberal democracies. Canada, both as a part of the British Empire and as Britain's most advanced self-governing colony, was a liberal democracy.

From the perspective of collective identity, however, Canada survived thanks to the transnational presence and power of Anglo-Saxonism. In this hypothesis, American expansionists decided to forgo annexation plans because they believed Canadians would voluntarily apply for membership in the union, much as other white settler colonies in North America had done earlier.[98] As for Canadians, they too played the racial game such that their elites declared themselves as Anglo-Saxons in front of American audiences, thus reinforcing the discourse of collective identity. Speaking in Chicago during the South African War, Wilfrid Laurier, Canada's first French prime minister, used vintage Anglo-Saxonist frames with strong religious overtones to call for an Anglo-American unity in the "defence of some holy cause, in the defence of holy justice, for the defence of the oppressed, for the enfranchisement of the downtrodden, and for the advancement of liberty, progress and civilization."[99] I will revisit the role of self–other relations in this broader Anglo-Saxon Atlantic in Chapters 4 and 5.

Conversations among constructivist, realist, and liberal interpretations of the history of Anglo-American relations will indeed continue in subsequent chapters, but we have covered enough ground to revisit an old critique of materialism. Rather than speaking for themselves, whether to rational assessments or misperceptions, material features such as military capabilities or regime types are subject to interpretation. From the perspective of a constructivist perspective taken by this book, the meanings of these features emanate from identity relations—similar and positive Others are friendly, distant and negative Others are threatening. The findings in this chapter indeed strongly support constructivists who have argued against a transhistorical assignment of realist and liberal subjectivities and interactions. Numerous studies inspired by constructivist assumptions have shown, first, that states balance, bandwagon, and hide on the basis of their identities,[100] and, second, that because democracy is but one of these identities, democratic states are not inherently peaceful with each other.[101] I will return to these points later; for now, let us also conclude that the first battery of cases studies, though examined to varying degrees of depth, are generally supportive of the theoretical argument developed in this book. Looking at Britain and the United States and across four discrete international security situations, we can observe that Anglo-Saxonism shaped every single foreign policy choice under study. The more this discourse explained the new events, the greater its grip on foreign policy debates became. The sole confounding case for theory arises the dual reading of the South African War on the American side. Here, the Republican government pursued benevolent neutrality, while the Democratic opposition and the rest of foreign policy elites supported the Boer cause. Anglo-Saxonist frames were effectively muted in favor of those based on religion and civilizations, but a far more grained analysis is needed to explain how exactly the White House managed to avoid a rhetorical defeat and, in turn, crisis of legitimacy during this long war.

In terms of the American and British foreign policy debates prior to Venezuela I, the colonial wars against Spain and the Boers were cumulative, rather than revolutionary. The British victory in South Africa came at a huge loss of imperial political capital at home and abroad. Though the empire succeeded in annexing the Boer republics, there was a widespread sense that the war precipitated the steady imperial decline. In contrast, America's quick victory against Spain proved to the domestic and international audiences that the U.S. empire was rising, perhaps too much and too fast. In the context of Anglo-American relations, these two wars also followed the cooperative trends set in Venezuela I. The same argument can be made with respect to Venezuela II: When Britain and the United States found themselves on the opposite sides of an international conflict, the incongruence between discourse and reality was interpreted as an anomaly—nothing more than a folly on the part of incompetent politicians in London.

Venezuela II also created at least one new trend in interimperial politics. It was in the winter of 1902–1903 that imperial Germany crossed the boundaries drawn on an Anglo-American racial map of the world such that it shifted its role as a potential cousin to a likely enemy. As the crisis progressed, this transition appeared more and more certain such that Teutonism eventually lost all discursive ground in the American and British societies, never to recover. In Britain, the idea of an Anglo-German alliance had its supporters among constructive imperialists until December 1902, but the subsequent events buried it for good. Anti-German hysteria never enveloped the United States as it did Britain during the Kruger telegram incident, but the events over Venezuela helped the Americans organize pieces of Germany's earlier transgressions into a coherent whole. Kaiser Wilhelm's quirky musings about *Weltpolitik* became mortal threats, while the annoying German diplomatic talk of the "United States of *North* America" turned into major insults.[102] Had Germany lowered its aspirations to build an overseas empire, especially in the areas claimed by Washington and London, a wider Teutonic rapprochement in world politics would have remained a possibility. But because Berlin continued to antagonize them, imperial Germany became cast in a role similar to that of Spain, France, and other rivals and enemies against which Anglo-Saxondom came into existence. Previously understood by many as both a modern, industrious state run by a fellow Germanic race, Germany became rewritten as a wild empire of Huns, those Asiatic hordes who once upon a time smashed the Roman civilization and forced the Saxons to move to England. With this shift in some of the main historical and political ontologies in American and British foreign policy debates, Anglo-Saxonism became the only transnational game in town. For British foreign policy makers, this was a bonanza:

> Germany is now taking Great Britain's place in the American mind as the "natural foe" and the more general this feeling becomes, the more will the American people be instinctively drawn toward the pole of Great Britain with whom they have so much in common.[103]

The dynamics of imperial and racial identity politics that developed in Venezuela II produced the Anglo-American unity at least twice, first through another discovery of a uniquely Anglo-Saxon predilection for comprise and then through the construction of common German enemy. In Britain, the idea of a German alliance could no longer be sold after the winter of 1902–1903. The idea of a German war, however, became so likely that the portfolio of British formal and informal alliances soon grew to include agreements with France (1904) and Russia (1907). Similar ideas rose in the United States. When Admiral Dewey stated in 1898 that America's "next war" would be with Germany, few in the foreign policy establishment agreed with him, but in 1903 his statement rang true. In the end, Britain and the United States together fought and won not one but two wars against Germany. World War I dispelled illusions of racial identity among Germanic nations. Here, the enemy was the Hunnic empire, whose barbaric practices in Belgium and other territories it occupied shocked the English-speaking world but also appeared consistent with the German record in Venezuela a decade ago. Like democracy or appeasement, moral superiority was severely racialized as well.

By the time World War II broke out, the barbaric Huns had long turned into degenerate, totalitarian Nazis, under whom the German empire reached a new civilizational low. This war began to shatter ideas on race as a legitimate principle for politics precisely because these ideas were appropriated by these new German barbarians. Indeed, only a handful of people in the English-speaking world could relate to Hitler when he spoke about shared racial identity between the ruling classes of the Third Reich and Britain. Indeed, in the guise of a liberal and democratic Weimar republic, Germany attempted to position itself as equal member of the Western civilization in the 1920s, but this attempt failed. Cooperation between America and Britain on the one hand and Germany on the other became possible only in the late 1940s, once it became possible to imagine a single Western civilization. In a sense, the key effect of the "great rapprochement" was not the rise of the Anglo-American peace and cooperation but the lasting alienation of Germany from the family of civilized nations.[104]

Before moving to a concluding section, let us briefly compare the argument in this chapter to the social and economic histories of the same period, starting with James Belich's masterful study of the "rise of the Anglo-world."[105] Here, the argument is that the Anglo-world—Belich's term for the Anglosphere—rose to dominance not simply because of its comparatively superior agriculture, industry, or military but also because of the peculiar nineteenth-century culture of settlerism, which saw the need for the reproduction of own society at distance—in the "new world," "overseas," and on the "frontier." The effects of this culture were remarkable: "When Anglos went, they tended to stay, in contrast to most other peoples." According to Belich, the "settler revolution" predated the Industrial Revolution and the new technologies of communication and mass transfer, but it was the latter that facilitated the process of "re-colonization," which he defines as the economic and cultural integration of the "oldlands" centered on New York and London on the one hand and the North American, Australasian, and southern African "newlands" on the other. In this interpretation, "the proto-ethnic regional differences of Old America were structurally similar to those of Old Britain," meaning that British and American state/national identities curiously mirrored each other in racialized hybridities and hierarchies. Partly for this reason, when the oldlands exchanged money and migrants in return for virtual "protein bridges" to the newlands, they paid no attention to political boundaries. "Between the 1870s and the 1890s, the American West fed London, as well as New York," while London had more American banks and more American stocks listed on its stock market than New York. In short:

> Greater Britain was a relatively short-live entity, with a life-span of less than a century, say 1880s–1960s. But it was big and powerful in its day, a virtual United States, which historians of the period can no longer ignore, nor dismiss as a failed idea.[106]

From parts of Belich's story, it might appear that the Anglo-American rapprochement in security and defense merely followed the integration of Anglo-American capital, as Marxist approaches to IR have long argued. In the writings by Kees van der Pijl, to name but one well-known contemporary theorist of this tradition, the Anglo-Saxon Atlantic appears as what he calls the "Lockean heartland."[107] In this theory of history, the capitalist bourgeois rule developed in late seventeenth-century England and then spread to across the world through a series of confrontations with assorted "Hobbesian" contenders, from Bourbon and Napoleonic Frances to Wilhelmine and Nazi Germanys to Soviet Russia to, indeed, present-day China. It was during the fin-de-siècle that the Lockean heartland became a proper transnational space. In the aftermath of World War I, the United States gained the Lockean throne in both credit and industry.

That special relationships in international security build on the zigzag flows of capital, goods, and labor is obvious in Belich's and van der Pijl's interpretation alike. Yet it is important to note that both authors balance their socioeconomic explanations with the accounts of culture and identity. Belich maintains, for example, that great financial powerhouses of the nineteenth century like George Peabody, J. P. Morgan, or the Barings succeeded partly because they "operated as both Britons and Americans" or that Greater Britain, that "Anglo-worldwide imagined community" of the last two decades of nineteenth century, was enabled by the "rhetoric" of Anglo-Saxonism.[108] For van der Pijl, the expansion of capitalism beyond England was greatly facilitated by certain precapitalist ideologies unique to seventeenth-century English society, namely, the rule of common law (which fostered the idea and practice of self-regulation), individualism (private property), and Protestantism (missionary empire).[109] With the Industrial Revolution, these ideologies matured and then spread around the globe, propelled by ever newer technologies of communication, transportation and, indeed, war-fighting. To the extent that we could rewrite rhetoric and ideology as discourse and debate, the arguments made in this chapter can be situated in the primarily materialist as well historically and sociologically more ambitious interpretations of the Anglosphere. From my point of view, neither the magnitude nor the intensity of social and economic interactions in late nineteenth century Anglo world/Lockean heartland can be understood without reference to the ideas and practices that constituted an imagined community of Anglo-Saxons at a global scale.

WHEN DID THE FIRST SPECIAL RELATIONSHIP BEGIN?

This genealogy of the Anglosphere has begun in the 1890s, a time when international relations were profoundly racialized. This chapter has attempted to demonstrate how Britain and the United States came to be constituted as Anglo-Saxon empires—the brotherly polities divided by history and geography, yet united by a transnational and sometimes antinational collective identity based on race, as well on gender, class, and religion. The dominance of Anglo-Saxonism in American and British societies implied Anglo-American cooperation, but this cooperation became possible also because the discourse received continuously positive reinforcement in a variety of contexts in what must be regarded as the "international/interracial" system of states.

Against the backdrop of an earlier realist-liberal debate on Venezuela I, this chapter has suggested that the Anglo-American decision makers responded to the crisis neither on the basis of appeasement alone, which is the realist argument, nor mainly on the basis of interdemocratic friendliness, which is what liberals believe. Rather, peace broke out in large part because of the ways in which Anglo-Saxonism was mobilized to delegitimize conflict between Britain and the United States. So articulated, this analysis can be said to supplement the realist-liberal debate: The explanatory power of appeasement and the democratic peace would be significantly increased if one historicizes the meanings of threat and democracy, respectively. If the Spanish-American War followed the politics of Anglo-Saxon identity set in Venezuela I, then the South African War unsettled this identity but not its main foreign policy and international outcome: the practice of benevolent neutrality. Venezuela II followed these trends but also reinforced them by completing the racial boundaries of Anglo-Saxondom. In this crisis, Germany, hitherto racially close and occasionally positive in the American and British discourses of identity, became reracialized as an empire of Hunnic miscreants. Britain and the United States never signed a formal alliance against imperial Germany, Spain, or any other empire, but there developed a pattern of self–other relations that paved the way for what became known as the AASR.

The first public invocation of this term can be found in Churchill's 1946 "Iron Curtain," which we briefly considered in the introductory chapter. The wartime alliance against the Nazi–Fascist axis had brought the two English-speaking empires together as never before, in the sense that it created a legitimate security community. The authority the United States gained over Britain during World War II—specifically during the Washington conference in 1941–1942—is still felt today, as is the overall cooperation pattern in the domain of international security. This analysis joins those who argue that the AASR existed long before World War II.[110] The bonds forged in the era of Anglo-Saxonism implied a much stronger alliance than that regarded as a mere counterweight, even a liberal democratic counterweight, to either Nazi Germany or Soviet Russia. From this perspective, the "Iron Curtain" speech was never simply a transparent attempt to enlist the United States in the defense of the declining British empire or even in the British-led war on communism in Europe. Rather, it was a fairly uncontroversial reflection on the existence of the English-speaking fact in international life.[111] The fin-de-siècle ideas of Anglo-American unity never led to a customs union, much less a single polity, yet they nevertheless reflected, as well as produced, a significant economic, social, and cultural reality, which was still very much in existence in the postwar period. This reality also obtained in international security such that we must ask, following Daniel Deudney, whether the "most important and successful inter-state alliance of the twentieth century [is] actually a type of a non-state national unification."[112]

The question is provocative because it makes us reflect both on the historically brittle nature of nationhood in global society. As Marilyn Lake and Henry Reynolds have shown, W.E.B. DuBois's 1903 declaration that the problem of the twentieth century was the "problem of the color-line" referred to the global problem and to the global line—at least judging by the way the imagined communities of "very white men" in the English-speaking world expressed racial solidarity and shared ideas about national sovereignty and the concomitant monopolies on human movement.[113] Close transnational consultations continued through the 1930s, when Anglo-American political diplomatic relations again came under much strain, while the 1940s saw another flowering of calls for the Anglo-American federation. Deudney mentions those authored by Clarence Streit, a *New York Times* journalist. Streit never tired from advocating transatlantic federations. His manifesto for an American-style union of Anglosphere and European democracies, which was initially rejected by several publishers, became an instant bestseller when it came out in 1939, as did his 1941 book, in which he suggested that Britain and the United States should upgrade their wartime alliance into a political federation. He completed his trilogy in 1961, this time arguing that the member states of the North Atlantic Treaty Organization (NATO) should form a federal state of "Atlantica," freedom's last frontier.[114]

Deudney's question is provocative from the perspective of theories of alliance formation as well. If military alliances form and endure on the basis of transnational and, indeed, transstate collective identity, then the most functional and durable alliance in modern history is not the much-vaunted NATO but the far less formal AASR or, more broadly, the "English-speaking alliance."[115] In 1947, London, Washington, and Ottawa acted on the earlier recommendations of U.S. General Dwight Eisenhower and British Field Marshall Bernard Montgomery to harmonize their military forces.[116] The result was the ABC program—the "plan to effect standardization" among the American, British, and Canadian armies. In a continual quest for greater "interoperability," ABC has been updated and deepened ever since. Across the decades, it has expanded membership only twice. Australia joined the program in 1963, turning ABC into ABCA, while New Zealand gained associate status in 1964 and then, in 2006, full membership.[117] No multinational treaty ever supported this alliance, and it never gained a headquarters and a permanent staff, yet ABCA has been no lesser fact of international life than NATO. Though ABCA overlaps with NATO, it operates outside and, at times, against the Atlantic alliance.[118]

A parallel development was the institutionalization of Anglo-American intelligence sharing, which was made possible by a collective understanding—still occasionally broken—to discontinue all intramural spying. On this front, the UKUSA agreement of 1946 eventually became a five-state institution known, to various degrees of accuracy, as "Echelon," "Five Eyes," the Quinquepartite Partnership, AUSCANZUKUS, and ABCANZ.[119] In all likelihood, Echelon is the premier signals intelligence network in history. By any reasonable measure, Echelon bested its Eastern bloc competitors in the Cold War, while today it serves as the model—and possibly as a competitor—to the equivalent networks in the EU. There will be more on ABCA and Echelon in the concluding chapter; meanwhile, note that most of Churchill's Fulton visions materialized. As

America's postwar polices shifted in reaction to what came to be regarded as aggressive Soviet expansion, the Anglosphere became reality. In early 1947, the United States. bombastically "took over" from Britain in protecting Greece and Turkey from communism—a policy choice that became known as the Truman Doctrine. In the following year, the United States endorsed a Canadian proposal for a North Atlantic defense treaty and, together with Britain and France, moved to airlift supplies to the besieged West Berlin, and so the civilized world drew its boundaries once again against the new batch of barbarians from Europe. How the Anglosphere drew similar boundaries in Asia in this historical period will tell us more about its racialized nature.

3 ANZUS, BRITAIN, AND THE "PACIFIC PACT"

I did not like the ANZUS Pact at all.
—Winston Churchill, House of Commons, 1953

New Zealanders belong to a branch of New World civilization, the main centres of which are Sydney, San Francisco, and Auckland—the Pacific Triangle.
—Keith Sinclair, *A History of New Zealand* (1959)

ANZUS works on the tactical level because it feels right.
**—Peter Leahy, Australian brigadier general,
testimony to the Australian parliament, 1997**

We are a European, Western civilisation with strong links with North America, but here we are in Asia.
—John Howard, Australian prime minister, interview 1999

The United States and Australia are separated by geography— and a lot of it—but we're united by common values.
—George W. Bush, American president, 2007

ANZUS (AUSTRALIA–NEW ZEALAND–UNITED STATES), a military pact with claims to collective defense created in 1951, is one of the main institutional expressions of the Anglosphere in the area of international security. The pact is racial in its origins in the sense that its drafters deliberately kept the so-called island states out of what they saw to be an exclusive Anglo-Saxon club in the Asia-Pacific. This pact has not quite passed: In contrast to NATO, its European counterpart that in the 1990s and 2000s welcomed a dozen of its Cold War–era enemies, ANZUS never evolved into a larger and more plural "Pacific Pact," that ephemeral entity unsuccessfully pursued by U.S. diplomats in 1950–1951. In this genealogy, the significance of the pact also lies in its two intramural exclusions: Britain at the creation and New Zealand in 1985–1986. The first development is especially puzzling from the perspective of collective identity.

Given that most Australians and New Zealanders regarded themselves as British at the time, how was it possible for their governments to sell the tripartite treaty to their audiences? Canberra and Wellington made an alliance without London in 1944, but this arrangement did not exclude the motherland in favor of another country.

In the historiography of Australian and NZ foreign relations, the ANZUS case is associated with the so-called Anzac dilemma, a term that superbly captures the dynamics behind the putative shift of New Zealand and Australian alliance portfolios from Britain to the United States.[1] Traditionally, explanations have followed a basic bargaining model in which the pact emerged as a compromise between America's desire to enlist support in containing communism and Australia's craving for a superpower's long-term guarantee against future invasion from Asia.[2] As for a larger regional pact—that ephemeral entity known to contemporaries as the "Pacific Pact" and to IR theorists as the "NATO in Asia" counterfactual—racialized identities played a role even during the "pactomania" of the 1950s. In 1953, Australia, Britain, New Zealand, and the United States joined in a strategic planning forum named the Five Power Staff Agency, and then, a year later, in a more famous South-East Asian Treaty Organization (SEATO), a pact that formally linked the said five powers to Pakistan, the Philippines, and Thailand.[3]

British exclusion from ANZUS, too, loses its mystique when situated within a broader history of collective security institution building in post-war Asia-Pacific. Indeed, ANZUSUK almost materialized in April 1946, when American, Australian, British, and New Zealand diplomats discussed the idea of an "American-Commonwealth Pacific Pact." As David McIntyre notes, even if a four-member English-speaking alliance had come into existence, it would have probably served as "something of an interim measure along the road to a more comprehensive regional security arrangement."[4] The puzzle of British exclusion is further reduced by the contemporary discourses and practices in ANZUS. ANZUS never became "ANZUSUK," but it always had the full blessing of the British Foreign Office. Rather than weakening either the AASR or imperial/Commonwealth ties, the pact probably strengthened each, by adding yet another institutional link to the broader English-speaking alliance.[5] In practice, Australian and NZ diplomats treated ANZUS as if it was ANZUSUK. As Canberra and Wellington duly dispatched copies of every document related to the pact to London, "nothing could be done in ANZUS which the United Kingdom did not know about."[6]

Once we take advantage of hindsight and archival records, the questions raised by the limited institutional membership of ANZUS are not particularly puzzling. Britain was only nominally excluded, and in any case the pact was designed as one institutional step toward a broader and more inclusive Pacific pact. At the same time, these explanations would make no sense to Australian and New Zealand decision makers, who had to sell the new pact to their audiences in 1950. It is worth recalling, as per the first epigraph, that Churchill did not like ANZUS at all. Under the Attlee government, London was generally quiet about the pact. Not so under Churchill. When the British bid for ANZUS membership was politely turned down by the Americans in September 1952, Churchill's protests struck a chord across the British and "old Commonwealth" press and, in turn, caused anxiety and even regret among the members of the Australian government.[7] A similar sense of unease was palpable in 1951, yet the signing of the tripartite pact went ahead. My contention in this chapter is that the Korean War destabilized Australia's heretofore dominant "Britishness" enough that Canberra and Wellington were able to make a successful argument for ANZUS as a way to "bolt the back door." In this abstract yet motivational frame, any security gain achieved by Australia and New Zealand could never be anything other than a net gain for Britain as well. In a world in which a globe-spanning English-speaking alliance led the free world in containing communism, the ANZAC dilemma was therefore moot.

RACE AND THE UNMAKING OF THE PACIFIC PACT

"The histories of Australia, New Zealand, and Canada as independent nations share a curious characteristic: nobody knows when they began."[8] In the year 1950, Australia and New Zealand were more British than independent. The two countries emerged as sovereign and independent from World War II, yet their elites still regarded themselves as the "outposts," "bastions," and "custodians" of the British Empire in the Asia-Pacific. In this discourse, Britain "seeded" Australasia and then devolved its powers to its colonies, which then did their best to mimic and perhaps surpass the motherland. This status was not necessarily inferior. To use memorable phrases coined by J. G. A. Pocock and Belich, the Antipodes saw themselves as "neo-Britains" and even "better Britains."[9]

That dedominionization and independence had little effect on the discourses of Britishness is evident from the unwillingness to let go of the word *empire*. The new terms "British Commonwealth" and the "Commonwealth of

Nations" were regarded as diplomatic and even "proper,"[10] but few Australians and New Zealanders at the time passed on the opportunity to observe the existence of two Commonwealths. The "new" Commonwealth referred to Ceylon, India, and Pakistan—former colonies of Britain who had recently and, many added, quite optimistically chosen independence. On their part, Australia and New Zealand belonged to the "old" Commonwealth. Also specified by the adjectives "real," "original," and "white," this community also included Canada and South Africa, but its racialized logic pushed its boundaries further to include all Anglo-Saxons.[11]

The continuity of this discourse of identity to those analyzed in the previous chapter is evident in the way newspapers reported on the British Empire Games (February), the plans for the 1952 royal visit (September), or British immigration seamlessly shifted "we" and "they" back and forth, as per the fin-de-siècle ideas of British race patriotism and Greater Britain. Yet state/national identity in the postwar Antipodes was more pluralistic, in the sense that there was a greater tendency to incorporate the cultural heterogeneity of the British Isles and other parts of Europe and Christendom. That old discursive brew of race, gender, language, and religion that once gave rise to Anglo-Saxonism was now complicated by ethnicity, which rendered the inside/outside dynamic slightly more open. In each national discursive field, there was some toleration of any slight to the white, Anglo-Saxon, Protestant (Anglican, Methodist or Presbyterian) ideal. Australia's "Anglo-Celtic" identity did not exist in New Zealand, while unique to New Zealand was "Aryanism"—a belief that the British and the Maori were the vanguard races of Europe and South Pacific, respectively. The latter discourse did not make the Pakeha accept the Maori as their equals; yet, in ways that might be absurd in the present, it helped New Zealand accept its indigeneity significantly better than its cross-Tasman neighbor.[12]

The discourses and practices of Britishness shaped Australian and New Zealand foreign policy in profound ways. Wellington kept wartime rationing policies for years after the war ended to help feed the motherland, while Canberra let the British conduct atomic tests on the Australian soil as a matter of course.[13] And, most tellingly, more than a few ANZAC representatives to Japan and the United States would ask to be introduced as "representatives of Britain."[14] The status quo position in foreign policy debates was a simple dictum: "where Britain goes we go."[15] Both prime ministers, Australia's Robert Menzies and New Zealand's Sidney Holland, repeatedly subscribed to this view, as did most other elites.

Texts in the Australian archive were notably more critical of the motherland than those in New Zealand, however. The word *Singapore* invoked Britain's failure to defend its main naval base in the Pacific against Japan in February 1942 and so carried collective memories of the metropolitan insolence in the times of war. Calls for greater independence in Australian foreign policy built on this discursive platform in particular. At a minimum, independence meant a more equitable footing in the British family of nations, but more typically it implied a desire for "new roles." This was clear in the ideas shared by the external affairs ministers Percy Spender and Richard Casey, the opposition leader Herbert Evatt, and the prolific academic expert Peter Russo. Australia, they argued, was not only a Commonwealth nation, but also a "middle power" in the U.N. system (Evatt) as well as a "metropolitan power" and a "good neighbor" (Spender, Casey). The "middle power" idea emerged at the San Francisco conference in 1945, first with the Canadian diplomatic team and then also with the Australian team led by Evatt, who himself also liked the term *security power*.[16] Because of its military and its geographic location, Evatt argued, Australia deserved a special status in international institutions relative to other states, save only for the permanent members in the U.N. Security Council. The "metropolitan power" and the "good neighbor" both related to the old racialist idea of a British outpost, which implied that Australia had special rights and responsibilities in the region.

All of these new roles departed from the status quo, but the one that sparked the most intense foreign policy debate in the period under study was the role of the U.S. ally.[17] The status of the United States in the discourses of Britishness was liminal, after all. Assorted folk theories of history followed family metaphors to suggest that Australia and New Zealand were Britain's daughters, while America was their somewhat estranged sister or a distant cousin. That the Anglosphere was assumed, not explained, is evidenced in a historical snapshot of the opening of the trans-Australian railway in 1912:

> As a part of the ceremony three rockets were fired—one releasing an Australian flag, one a Union Jack, and one of the Stars and Stripes. Thus in an atmosphere of international amity which in the light of subsequent events was almost prophetic.[18]

Similarly, Australian newspapers never explained why Australian literature should be situated between English and American; why Miss Australia was modeled after Miss America; and why the Australian government should raise funds for the Australian American Memorial in Canberra.[19] Australians and New Zealanders required no answers to these questions because the United States was the extension of their Self, at least in some contexts.

The "American alliance," or, as Spender used to call it, the "American guarantee," was meaningless outside the contexts of the ANZAC relationship to communism and Asia. The communist Other was simultaneously external and internal. The first dimension referred to the Cold War, which was regarded as a growing and global confrontation between the Soviet empire and the Western, Christian civilization.[20] On the internal dimension, a revolutionary form of democracy advocated by homegrown communists had nothing to do with democratic pluralism and everything to do with Moscow. Thanks to espionage and communist internationalism, labor relations became a matter of national security.[21] Unlike communists, not all "Asiatics" were necessarily threatening. Closest to the Self, were the poverty-stricken, but generally friendly, populations of "new Commonwealth" South Asia. Then came the "youthful and still uneasy" people of Burma, Indonesia, and Thailand in Southeast Asia as well as the Philippines, "unique as the only Christian democracy in the Far East."[22] Anchoring the far side of the Self–Other continuum was the old Japanese enemy, followed by the newly established People's Republic of China. With Moscow and Beijing now acting as a "team," more of Asia was poised to turn red. If Malaya turned communist, argued Menzies in the parliament, Indonesia would, too, and with dreadful consequences for Australia.[23]

A cold geopolitical calculus would dictate the creation of an anticommunist coalition in the region, yet Australian and New Zealand audiences would have none of it. Consider the Australian reactions to proposals for an Asia-Pacific defense pact and economic and technical assistance to Southeast Asia, made at the Commonwealth Foreign Ministers' conference in Colombo in January 1950. Australian's new foreign minister Spender claimed authorship of the proposals.[24] On the premises that Australia was a "good neighbor" and that "peace is indivisible," Spender posited that the best way to combat communism in Asia was to offer economic and technical aid to the newly established Asian governments. At home, his argument fell flat. The press bought neither the idea of peace indivisibility nor that of a good neighborhood. A *Bulletin* editorial suggested that

Asia has been unstable ever since Australia has existed as a country . . . so long as the dominating air power and sea power remain in the hands of the English-speaking peoples and their Western European allies, as they do today, the centre of gravity of the world must lie in their centres of production and not with the seething masses of Asia, which are, at the present and will be for years, incapable of overseas aggression far beyond their borders.[25]

Even the *Sydney Morning Herald*, which had earlier shown enthusiasm for Colombo (as well as Spender), felt the need to remind the government that "our religious faith, our national philosophy, and our whole way of life, are alien to Asia."[26] The debate over the Colombo conference shows how the idea of race connected the discourses of communism and "Asian expansionism" in Australian thinking. In a racialized world, the rising tide of communism in Asia appeared historically continuous with the Japanese aggression in World War II.[27] The survival of Australia "as a country" was a matter of containing the "seething masses of Asia." In this view, even the Philippines, that one Christian and democratic nation in the region, could be nothing but alien to the Australian "way of life." The media never used the word *race*, but most Australians could easily decipher the message, which held that the alterity of Asia was not simply political, philosophical, or socioeconomic. In this framing, the policy of helping the Asian Other was imprudent. Rather than buttressing Asian democracies against communism, what the audience wanted was Canberra to join the Anglo-led West in containing all of Asia.

It was precisely these discourses of racialized identity that put an end to Washington's blueprint for a broader Pacific Pact. In December 1950, John Foster Dulles, President Truman's main troubleshooter in the region, submitted to Australian and New Zealand diplomats a proposal for a "Pacific Ocean Pact." The American plan was to use the ANZACs to prop up the "island states" of Japan, the Philippines, and "possibly" Indonesia against communist encroachment. In public, Dulles and his team argued that the Pacific Pact, like all of America's alliances, would be made up of states, not nations. The argument made for a strong antiracist and postcolonial message. Private diplomatic notes reveal a more complex story. The United States refused British membership in the pact not because of Britain's colonial commitments to the Asian mainland (for example, Malaya), but mainly because it did not want to create "a closed club for Anglo-Saxons," wrote Dulles to the British ambassador in March 1951. Here, membership shaped alliances, not the other way

around. The inclusion of the Philippines, as Dulles pointed out often, constituted a limited propaganda gain considering that this island state was widely
perceived as America's "ward," "little friend," "stooge," and "stepchild." Indonesia, he argued, was "more truly representative of Asia"[28]

Despite its legitimate and well-formulated desire to use alliance membership as a political weapon in the Cold War, Washington still ended up with
an all-white pact. The first draft of the ANZUS pact, produced in February
1951, was a compromise between the American and ANZAC diplomats over
the question of membership. For Dulles, the first step for a "big pact" was
a "soft" or "liberal" peace with Japan. Without "peace with reconciliation,"
argued Dulles and his diplomatic team, there could not be a long-term "Pacific settlement." A similar plan was said to have worked in Europe, where
West Germany was turned into a valuable Cold War ally. To Australian and
New Zealand diplomats, this analogy made no sense: Japan was Asia, West
Germany was Western. One of them wrote: "Our acceptance of this, which
would turn Japan from an enemy into a firm ally overnight, would give rise to
political complications in Australia."[29] Another pointed out that an alliance
with the Philippines or Indonesia but not Britain would be "unthinkable" in
New Zealand.[30] Archival documents suggest that Canberra and Wellington
rebuffed Philippine demands for inclusion on the grounds of the shortage of
time and money, but internal memos indicate deep doubts in the "stability,"
"seriousness," and "importance" of Asian governments.[31] Once the pact was
drafted, Spender was able to explain to British diplomats that they should use
racial language in their correspondence:

"A white man's pact," is, in our opinion, both unjustified and dangerous. It
is unjustified because the original Dulles proposals contemplated Japan, the
Philippines, and possibly Indonesia as parties, so that the pact could scarcely
be described as a "white man's pact." Secondly, a "catch phrase" of this kind, if
it comes to the ears of any Asiatic country (as it well may) or finds its way into
the press, gives a flavour to the proposed security arrangements in the Pacific
which could arouse susceptibilities and passions as between East and West.[32]

There were, indeed, many ideas in the ANZAC diplomatic correspondence
that "could not be said publicly," including a belief that Chinese communism
in 1950 and Japanese militarism in 1941 were both types of "Asian expansionism."[33] Australian and New Zealand foreign policy elites avoided nineteenth-
century language of racial conflict to describe the world, yet decision making

was informed in precisely those terms. It was the ongoing racialization of the Asian Other that compelled most Australians and New Zealanders to believe that Japan and Indonesia would turn against the West if the Cold War turned hot.[34] Indeed, when Menzies expressed his worries about the enemy arc forming to the north of Australia, he worried primarily about Asian dominance, not communism. It was this racialized ontology of security that carried the day of the Pacific Pact negotiations. Despite a presidential demand to lend the pact an "air of colour respectability," Dulles gave up on Asian members, including the Philippines.[35] Thus, the idea of a big anticommunist community with rhetorically defensible claims to postcolonial and multicultural identity gave way to an Anglo-Saxons–only club. To British loyalists in Canberra and Wellington, the tripartite pact was clearly the second choice, yet "by far the best solution" under the circumstances of the overall American policy in the Asia-Pacific.[36]

The swiftness by which the boundaries of ANZUS were closed against its potential Asian members might suggest a continuing life of the idea of Greater Britain. Indeed, the ANZAC campaign for a "limited pact" had direct consequences for the finale of the Pacific settlement saga in San Francisco in August–September 1951. Here, too, the ANZAC and British campaigns worked hand-in-hand.[37] Officially, London insisted that the closeness of the U.S.–Philippine relationship made any formalization of that relationship redundant, but internal memos show worries about losing prestige if an institutionalized arrangement came to pass between ANZUS and Manila, before that between ANZUS and London. And so Washington ended up signing three separate treaties in 1951, nearly simultaneously: the U.S.–Philippines mutual defense pact, the Japanese peace treaty, and ANZUS, a pact David Lowe aptly described as being "'about Asia' but not 'of Asia.'"[38] Dulles's Pacific Ocean Pact died with ANZUS, but the general idea of a larger pact "of Asia" was partly revived with creation of SEATO during the Eisenhower administration. But here, too, Japan found itself on the outside, much in line with the foreign policy thinking of Australians and New Zealanders.

The discovery of the confluence of communism and Asian expansionism in the minds of Australian and New Zealand policy makers correctly predicts the exclusion of Japan as well as the creation of a limited Pacific pact in the form of ANZUS. What it cannot explain is the resolution of the aforementioned ANZAC dilemma. In the past, Canberra and Wellington were able to explain away disagreements with London in terms of different definitions of what it meant to be British in a particular context. In January 1950, for example, Britain attempted to take advantage of the Colombo conference to have the entire Commonwealth recognize the communist government in Beijing, hoping that recognition would enable the survival of old trading links. The ANZACs took the credit for thwarting the plan because it was possible to criticize the Foreign Office in London as un-British in choosing commerce over democracy. As one diplomat wrote, "New Zealand alone had saved the Commonwealth from complete disgrace."[39] In this policy situation, the agreement with the United States and the rest of the Commonwealth (save for India) was helpful, but not decisive. ANZUS was different in the sense that it was Canberra and Wellington, not London, who broke the Commonwealth ranks. Here, the ANZAC dilemma looked real, at least for a time. In the rest of the chapter I will consider how the Malayan emergency and the Korean War helped resolve this dilemma. In debating what action to take in these new events, the Australian and New Zealand policy makers learned that the most effective ways of pursuing an independent foreign policy was to demonstrate that an alliance with the United States and loyalty to Britain were two sides of the same coin.

NEW EVENTS, OLD PERILS

In 1950, the main problem of Australian and New Zealand security was the Malayan emergency, a communist-led guerilla uprising against the British colonial rule. Sending troops to Malaya was an obvious response, in line with secret defense agreements as well as with good Britishness, but this time the motherland asked for much more. In addition to its requests for help with the ongoing Cold War contingencies in Europe (the Berlin blockade) and emergencies in Asia (Malaya), London was asking for a "permanent" military commitment to the oil fields and the lines of communication in the Middle East. In a gallant display of loyalty to Britain, the government of New Zealand called a referendum on conscription and thus affirmed its Middle East contribution in April 1950.[40] Prime Minister Holland said: "New Zealand very proudly, and after the greatest consideration, has assured Great Britain that where Britain goes we go, that where she stands we stand, and that we shall support her to the hilt in every way."[41] Privately, one of its diplomats wrote:

> My mind still finds it difficult to reconcile the arrangements we are making—An agreement for the Pacific, but commitment in reality in an area of the M[iddle] E[east] where we have no representation and no intelligence of our

Own . . . I have the feeling that we [are] getting into a curious colonial status. But I'm sure it must make sense somewhere in W[ellington].[42]

Wellington's decision may be puzzling from the perspective of realist or liberal IR theory, but it is entirely consistent with the constructivist ideas about identity. Recall that New Zealanders had no less intense memories of Singapore than did Australians. Like his trans-Tasman counterpart, Prime Minister Menzies epitomized loyalty and argued for "dual commitment." Against this position, Foreign Minister Spender called for a policy shift, away from the British "interests" in the Middle East and toward American "containment" in Asia. The policy was debated between April and June, but the final decision was made in December. Indeed, it was the height of the war in Korea, and in parallel to the conflict in Malaya, that the Australian cabinet decided to commit its best troops to the Middle East.[43] In Canberra, much like in Wellington, reality confirmed identity. From the objective-interest perspective typically emphasized in realist theories, the ANZACs went to the wrong region. They also stayed in the Middle East until 1955, when the British concluded that it was prudent to concentrate their own troops in Europe, while concentrating the Australians and New Zealanders right against the communist insurgents in Malaya. The next chapter will consider the Suez crisis as one important consequence of these decisions.

If asked, in early 1950 to choose between a joint imperial defense scheme of questionable strategic benefit to Australasia and an American-led commitment to the Asian mainland, most Australians and New Zealand foreign policy would have chosen the former, acting on their sense of Britishness and loyalty to the motherland. By the summer, this understanding of the world shifted. It was in June that communist North Korea, seemingly unprovoked, invaded pro-Western South Korea. The subsequent events—namely the escalation and Americanization of the war—created the conditions of possibility for ANZUS to go ahead.[44] The Australian and New Zealand naval commitment to the theater of operation was swift and nearly simultaneous with that made by Britain, but the decision to commit ground troops was not. London ruled out a ground war and, for a day or two, it looked as if the ANZACs would follow the motherland's lead.

Then came an American call to arms, aimed at Canberra and Wellington individually. Never before had a new role presented itself so clearly. With the wind in his sails, Spender asked the government to "scrape the bucket" and

send troops to Korea right away.[45] Ten days into the war, London changed its
official mind and decided to send army regiments to Korea after all. From
the Antipodean perspective, this reckless flip-flopping discredited the motherland and brought back the memories of Singapore, when London's poor decision making left the dominions to fend for themselves. The talk of a more
independent foreign policy was put into practice. In a race to publicly an-
nounce their significant military contributions to Korea before London, Wellington beat Canberra by a few hours. As ever, the ANZACs made a valiant
effort in defending the Western civilization against its enemies. In terms of
the military contribution per capita to the U.S.–led U.N. force in Korea, New
Zealand and Australia came third and fourth, trailing only South Korea and
the United States.[46]

The North Korean invasion fit with everything Australians and New Zealanders knew about Asia and communism—that it was powerful, militaristic,
and aggressive. On June 7, *The Bulletin* explained that the war was necessary
to "hold back a wave of barbarism such as the world has never seen since the
invading hordes of Asia put out the lights of Rome and set the world's civilisation back a thousand years."[47] At the same time, the event also demonstrated
that Australia and New Zealand could pursue new roles in the U.S.–led system
of collective security independently from Britain without in any way jeopardizing colonial ties. Contrary to some historical narratives, a comprehensive
"switch" from loyalty to the empire to the American guarantee was impossible
from the perspective of the Australian and New Zealand identities in 1950.
But thanks in small part to the events surrounding the conflict in Korea, it
became possible for the ANZAC elites to argue in favor of an independent
foreign policy within a broader framework of the English-speaking alliance
set in a total war against Asian communism. As the allied troops were pour-
ing across the North Korean border in pursuit of its enemies, Menzies sent an
official message to his citizens:

> The danger to us goes deeper than when the Japanese almost reached Austra-
> lia. If Japan had succeeded then, Britain or America might have rescued us.
> But from a world of tyranny there could be no rescue.[48]

In short, the Korean War rendered all ANZAC dilemmas false, from those
emerging from the Pacific Pact negotiations to those in the Middle East–Malaya
deployment debates.

Consider a speech Menzies gave in Adelaide in June 1950, hours after the news of the North Korean invasion. The United States, he said, was an "amazing country . . . the centre of gravity of democracy," but Australia's cries for the American guarantee were "pessimistic, distorted, and, therefore, unreal." A wider alliance between America and the Commonwealth was much more sensible because the "British peoples of the world need the Americans [and t] he Americans need us. . . . we are the same kind of people, with the same ideas, with the same ideals, with the same high faith, with the same basic belief that governments exist for the people, that they are the servants and not the masters." It was these two nations, British and American, who were responsible for the "freedom of man."[49] This framing echoed the Anglo-American discourse on Anglo-Saxonism and, as Chapter 5 will show, also foreshadowed the British discourse on Atlanticism.

The same move was made to frame to defend the ANZUS treaty when it was made public in July 1951. The opposition Australian Labor Party (ALP) described the product as "un-British," while their counterparts across the Tasman, the New Zealand Labour Party, called the proposed pact "disloyal."[50] Both governments countered with a claim that the traditional Commonwealth defense and the new American alliance were now two parts of a single and indivisible project. In New Zealand, the government issued a set of public statements arguing, variously, that ANZUS was "not incompatible with devotion to the mother country," that it was a "backup to Commonwealth defence, not a new association," and, ultimately, that it was not a case of "selling out to the Americans."[51] The fact of the war in Korea greatly disarmed the opposition critics. Once Britain committed ground troops to the peninsula, the basic identity between the Commonwealth and the United States firmly held such that potential ANZAC dilemmas were resolved. As the U.S.–led coalition forces in Korea assembled under the U.N. flag, the other dilemma of contemporary foreign policy debates was resolved, too. The ALP leader Evatt used to argue that the U.N. system offered a new role for Australia, yet the war questioned the novelty of this role. Thanks to the Soviet boycott of the institution, the U.N. Security Council indeed authorized the U.S.–led war, which made it easier for the government to rhetorically demonstrate to its audiences that it was leading Australia along the right path of history.

As the U.S.–led military intervention in Korea grew in the allied flags and its firepower, so did the idea of the American guarantee in Australian and New Zealand hearts and minds. Like in the two world wars, the Anglosphere became a fact on the Korean battleground, too, prompting the use of family metaphors and terms such as the "English-speaking cause" or the "Anglo-Saxon unity." The ANZAC elites came to agree that the American guarantee in the Asia-Pacific was indeed a long-standing foreign policy goal for their nations, as evidenced in the fact that their governments had already asked the United States to extend the Monroe Doctrine to the Pacific Ocean, in cooperation with Britain.[52] Moreover, a positive recognition of these ideas came from the Americans themselves, especially from Dulles and General Douglas MacArthur, the U.S. commander in Korea intimately familiar to the Australians and New Zealanders from the days of World War II.[53] For the historian Keith Sinclair, this particular narrative was so resonant and influential in New Zealand that it was possible to talk about "double nationalism"—the notion that New Zealanders identified with Britain as well as the United States.[54] Sinclair's interpretation is hardly far fetched. As I said above, most ANZAC newspapers invoked familiarity with America without interrogating it. The only counterargument left for the critics of ANZUS was to frame the American guarantee as already present on the basis of identity, which would render the formal institutionalization of the alliance moot.[55]

From this Antipodean perspective, the creation of a limited Pacific Pact was a small part of a larger effort to contain the communist enemy on a global scale. ANZUS, as the ANZAC leaders recognized, was meant to be a part of a "regional defence system extending from the Pacific through South East Asia and South Asia to the Middle East."[56] In the discourses of political geography, Australia and New Zealand were identified by themselves and others as Western and as Northern. The prima facie absurdity of this logic was never lost to even moderately critical observers, which normally paid homage to the prime minister, who in April 1939 observed that Britain's Far East is Australia's "Near North." Texts dealing with the ANZAC role in the Commonwealth defense routinely engaged with the variable meanings of the obviously nonlocal signifiers Near, Middle, and Far East. Yet these engagements typically served to sustain, not undermine, the Western and Northern essence of the Antipodes. Menzies's observation was an illustration of his wit, not a thoughtful postcolonial critique of Europe as the geographic center of the world. Only in a frivolous world, therefore, was it possible for the Australian Self to be in the East.

In a world where a racialized destiny determined geography, British exclusion from ANZUS was not necessarily a mistake. The preamble of the ANZUS treaty in any case acknowledged that Australia and New Zealand had certain

Commonwealth obligations, in addition to their obligations to each other as well as to the United States. It was this Anglobalization of the Cold War that enabled Canberra and Wellington to frame British exclusion as moot in a larger scheme. The text of the treaty itself recognized that the archipelago of anticommunist pacts movable, such that the division of labor among allies was shifting and overlapping. This particular framing was a winner. During the tripartite Canberra talks of February 1951, Spender argued that the purpose of the pact was "bolting the back door," such that more generous ANZAC contributions to the Commonwealth security could be made elsewhere.[57] The metaphor made sense only because the Australians thought of themselves as Western, in which the front door opened toward Europe and the Atlantic. Spender's counterpart in New Zealand, Doidge, used the same language. Building NATO but not following up with a similar arrangement in the Pacific, he argued, was "like locking the front door and leaving the backdoor open."[58] More than any other, it was this particular framing of ANZUS that diluted the resonance of the ANZAC dilemma in front of audiences at home.

The outcome of Australian and NZ debate on ANZUS had remarkable consequences for alliance politics in the Cold War. Looking at the "old" Commonwealth in the post-1945 period, Francine McKenzie observed that "paradoxically, one consequence of American-dominion rapprochement was to enhance the value of the British connection to the dominions."[59] This paradox can be explained in terms of collective identity. In an Anglobalized view of international security cooperation, the American alliance could not possibly "trump" the Britishness of Australia and New Zealand—any national security gain was simultaneously a net gain for the Anglosphere as a whole. The "back door" that ANZUS "bolted" in 1951 belonged not to the ANZAC house but to the Anglosphere. This seemingly simple frame resolved not just the ANZAC dilemma but also similar dilemmas faced by other dominions at different times.

RATIONAL AND RACIALIZED DESIGNS

ANZUS proceeded without British participation because the Australian and New Zealand governments succeeded in convincing their audiences about the basic unity of purpose of the English-speaking peoples in the Cold War. As David Capie (2003) demonstrated, realist teachings cannot quite explain patterns of alliance formation in postwar Asia-Pacific. Capie's arguments are strongly supported by the analysis in this chapter. The archival documents on the ill-fated Pacific Pact indicate that American, ANZAC, and British policy makers paid no shortage of attention to the questions of military capabilities and containment strategies. But the balance of power was never as important to them as the balance of race. The main issue in negotiations was not the extent to which each party would give up its autonomy to aggregate the collective capability but rather how to simultaneously satisfy the ANZAC demands for racial exclusiveness on the one hand and the American desire to form a racially pluralist club on the other. The first vision prevailed: For Canberra and Wellington, no military and strategic benefits could ever outweigh the political costs of including Asians in collective defense.

Liberal arguments on alliance formation, too, are of limited purchase considering evidence that shows that nations like India, Japan, or the Philippines were primarily evaluated in terms of racialized identity, not on the basis of their democratic credentials. Indeed, just as national and transnational advocacy networks reached milestones in antiracist struggle in the form of the U.N. Charter, the Universal Declaration of Human Rights, and the first UNESCO statement of race, foreign policy decision makers in the democratic world were dividing the global society into racialized clubs. The foundational moments of both NATO and ANZUS were indeed each shot through with the discourses of Anglo-Saxonism, to say nothing of the fact that neither was intended to be open to participation of predominantly nonwhite democracies in their respective regions.

From the perspective of this chapter, liberalism is much more helpful with respect to its ideas on the rational design of international institutions.[60] Most liberals would indeed agree with the classical interpretation of ANZUS as a purposive quid pro quo between Australian and U.S. diplomats bent on advancing individual interests of their constituencies. In comparison to realists, who tend to focus on security, liberals would add that the bargaining parties traded individual autonomy for other joint goods as well, such as efficiency and legitimacy. In the end, the pact was determined by the relative bargaining power of the participations, in which the ANZACs gained less than they wanted in terms of the institutional depth. The final draft came to specify that the Americans provided due consultation, not automatic protection. Spender's much-vaunted American guarantee was therefore not an actual guarantee. Articles 4 and 7 of the pact obliged any two members to consider the attack on the third as "dangerous," not to come to its aid. In contrast, Article 5 of NATO integrated the North Atlantic region into a tripwire system of collective defense, such that an attack on any member was an attack on all. The comparison is historical despite the fact that NATO was only beginning to acquire its elaborate institutional features, such as a permanent secretariat, dedicated forces, or integrated defense structures. Arguably, it is NATO that Menzies had probably in mind when he described ANZUS as an alliance with the "foundation of jelly."[61] From a sociological perspective, however, the foundations of the tripartite pact were in fact laid through the many Cold War–era debates among ANZAC and American officials, who would work together for months reflecting on the conditions and nature of collective defense as stipulated in the treaty and on the precise meanings of the words *attack*, *danger*, and *aid*.

The rational design perspective correctly predicts that U.S. preferences would carry the day in negotiations on the institutional features of ANZUS. The negotiations that led to the pact were subject to power asymmetries, with the United States as the dominant side. But what remains puzzling is the question of membership. As I said earlier, Dulles and his team were instructed to bring back a comprehensive Pacific Settlement, which would include a peace treaty with Japan as well as a big and culturally diverse collective security pact. In contrast, the diplomats from Canberra and Wellington sought no alliances with Asian nations, especially with Japan. On the issue of membership, power asymmetry did not help the Americans. The ANZACs managed to convince the Americans not only that Japan should be treated as a separate issue but also that any British exclusion must be contingent on Asian exclusion. The fact that Washington deliberated with its junior allies during the negotiations and lost, instead of simply overruling them, reveals the operation of collective identity in practice. As constructivist research on security communities shows, it is a sense of shared identity ("we feeling") that compels friends to accommodate each other, regardless of extant hierarchies and asymmetries. America's willingness to offer separate security to Australia and New Zealand against its own initial preferences shows just how racialized identities shaped rationality in this context.

The standard constructivist alternative hypothesis that liberals must grapple with in their research for rational design is whether international institutions are parasitic on collective identities, rather than bargaining outcomes among utility-maximizing state actors. This constructivist alternative is often overdrawn. Liberals are not wrong to analyze actor choices and strategic interactions over assorted distribution problems and membership issues. These involve multiple equilibria, which is an important research question considering that the variations in the size of alliances, coalitions, or other international institutional forms are puzzling to constructivists and liberals alike. But constructivism can help liberals to more adequately theorize the intersubjective nature of institutions, which is ultimately what shapes the ideas about both "who gets what, when, and under what conditions" as well as the ideas on "who's who."[62] But while liberals could do well to acknowledge that bargaining strategies depend on identity politics, constructivist should also recognize the self-reinforcing dynamics at play: Political actors who define themselves as X, but not Y, can and do frame their identities in terms of *practices* of such interstate bargaining on alliance membership. I will return to this point in later chapters.

FRIENDS, BUT NOT ALLIES?

In the history of racism and the making of international institutions, the success of ANZAC diplomacy in the Pacific Pact negotiations stands next to that famous moment at the Paris peace conference in 1919, when the Australian prime minister Billy Hughes almost single-handedly sabotaged the "racial equality" initiative proposed by its Japanese ally.[63] Most of this history is yet to be written, but the historical analogies are instructive for the story told in this book. This chapter has shown that the national, transnational, and international processes that created the Anglosphere in the middle years of the twentieth century were no less racialized than those in the previous century. ANZUS never came to approximating NATO in its depth, but it was a Monroe Doctrine of sorts, with Asian expansionists in the postwar Pacific playing a role similar to European imperialists in the nineteenth-century Atlantic.

As we shall see more clearly in the next chapters, racial thinking disappeared from the discourses of the Anglosphere identity over time. But the sense of belonging this thinking created remains with us to this day. In closing, let us then suggest that the ANZUS identity still survives ANZUS as an institution. The pact indeed unraveled in 1985 when New Zealand's Labour government failed to reach an agreement with the United States over keeping the South Pacific nuclear free, and it now continues to be in force between the United States and Australia as well as between Australia and New Zealand, but not between New Zealand and the United States. But let us consider the events from 1985 once more. In New Zealand, the year was marked with two roughly comparable events. In February, the so-called port access dispute saw the Labour government deny access to USS *Buchanan*, a nuclear-armed ship of its U.S. ally. A year later, Washington suspended its ANZUS obligations to the South Pacific nation. Public opinion polls from that time showed another form of double nationalism in New Zealand. The majority of respondents at once supported the United States and the American alliance and their government's antinuclear stance.[64]

Now compare this policy situation with that playing out in July, when French secret service agents blew up *Rainbow Warrior*, British-registered Greenpeace ship in Auckland harbor, killing one of its crew members, a Portuguese photographer. France had been conducting nuclear atmospheric testing in the South Pacific since the 1960s, much to the displeasure of most New Zealanders. The nuclear tests in the French possessions of Mururoa and Fangataufa in the 1970s had in fact led international court action against Paris, as well as other protests, the Greenpeace harassment of French operations being one. The destruction of *Rainbow Warrior* was interpreted as an act of state-sponsored terrorism, even an act of war. The ensuing Francophobia reached such sky-high proportions that French fries were renamed "Kiwi sticks"—long before that more famous case in 2003, when the cafeteria of Congress renamed the same dish "freedom fries" in protest against French decision to sit out the U.S.–led intervention in Iraq. In this sense, the New Zealander reaction to the attack on *Rainbow Warrior* cannot be understood outside the historical relationship accorded to the French Other in the constitution of the English-speaking peoples. At no stage in the Pacific Pact negotiations did the U.S. and Anzac diplomats find a reason to reach out to France as a possible partner in regional collective defense. In theory, given its bona fide white, European, and democratic identities, as well as its significant political and military presence in postwar Southeast Asia, France was a potential ally for the ANZACs. Yet in discourse and in practice, an alliance with France was akin to that with Catholic Philippines: curious, but not serious.

Much like British exclusion in 1951, New Zealand's defection in 1985 does not disprove the existence of the ANZUS and Anglosphere identities in world politics. For one, the United States never punished New Zealand, but the superpower did express its dissatisfaction symbolically. For two decades, the U.S. diplomats would refer to the South Pacific nation as a "friend, not an ally," as if friendship alone was insufficient for the maintenance of the New Zealand–U.S. special relationship or, specifically, for the New Zealand army to maintain its interoperability with U.S. forces through the ABCA program.[65]

Be that as it may, on July 25, 2008, Secretary of State Condoleezza Rice spoke at the War Memorial Museum in Auckland and described the host nation as "a friend and an ally." The next day, *New Zealand Herald* interpreted the event as the proverbial "thaw" in the bilateral relationship. This was an overstatement. Experts trace the diplomatic thaw back to early 1990s,[66] while I would propose that special relationships that glue the Anglosphere together could be cold at times, but never ice-cold; hence they cannot thaw. The next and subsequent chapters will assess this proposition in detail.

4 SUEZ, VIETNAM, AND THE "GREAT AND POWERFUL FRIENDS"

> *Britain is not always right and the United States is not always wrong.*
>
> **—Canberra Times, 18 March 1955**

> *I do not believe that Canada is a variant of the United States.*
>
> **—John Conway, "What Is Canada?" (1964)**

IN THE GLOBAL SOCIETY, Australia and Canada have long been regarded as mirror images of each other.[1] What explains their similarities is their common Anglosphere history. At the turn of the nineteenth to the twentieth century, Australian and Canadian elites defined themselves as members of a world-leading Anglo-Saxon race. Yet unlike their American counterparts at this time, they additionally defined themselves as specifically British peoples. By the middle of twentieth century, Australians and Canadians were still British in many contexts, but few among them self-identified as the instruments of racial supremacy. In lieu of Anglo-Saxonism, Greater Britonism, and its corollaries, the dominant discourses of identity now revolved around capitalism, liberal democracy, and anticommunism. Indeed, at the forefront stood the Cold War, in which Australia, Canada, and their "great and powerful friends" fought against the Eastern bloc.[2]

In the attempt to shed light on the constitution of the Anglosphere in the Cold War era, this genealogy will now examine Australian and Canadian choices in the Suez and Vietnam conflicts. Each war led to a split in the English-speaking alliance, in which Australia and Canada played different parts despite their many similarities. In the Suez crisis, Canberra went with London; Ottawa, with Washington. Here, the discourses of state/national identity in both Australia and Canada suggested that Britain and its allies were right to invade Egypt, even during the contemporaneous Soviet invasion of Hungary. Canberra "blindly" supported the British-led war, but the "liberal internationalist" government in Ottawa called for a U.N. cease-fire, together with the Americans and the Soviets. Tellingly, Canadians framed their policy as a reasonable disagreement between two friendly Commonwealth governments, rather than a dispute of one independent state with another. This pattern reversed itself in Vietnam. When the American president Lyndon Johnson moved to escalate and Americanize the conflict in 1964–1965, Australia jumped at the opportunity to help by contributing combat troops.

Canadian assistance in Vietnam was bloodless, ambiguous, and disappointing. As the U.S. campaign progressed, the Johnson administration came to accept that various circumstances prevented many of its allies from sending troops, but it nevertheless continued to press for political support. Canada stuck to its peacekeeping role in Indochina, which also included a daily provision of field intelligence to its American allies. At the same time, not only did the Canadian government refuse to cheer the war on, but its prime minister made a diffident speech questioning American wisdom in the war. The following chapter explains how Australian and Canadian policies in these conflicts were consistent with certain national discourses and debates, as well as with certain international roles that give rise to the Anglosphere in world politics.

MIDDLE POWERS AND THEIR FRIENDS

Anticommunism was an identity that united the Australian and Canadian societies across both of the periods under discourse analysis, 1955–1956 and 1964–1965. The capitalist, liberal Self related to its communist Other in nearly every quotidian domain. Athletes trained specifically to beat the Russians at the Olympics (especially those in Melbourne in 1956); new universities were built in response to Sputnik; and unions and political parties constantly revamped their programs and images to appear more anticommunist. The defections of Soviet embassy officials, Petrov in Canberra and Gouzhenko in Ottawa, inspired endless spy sagas.[3] The Australian and Canadian geographies of anticommunism were distinctive, however. Apart from the fifth column elements at home, Canada's Communist Other was predominantly in Europe. "The German problem," as explained by Canada's external minister to his peers in 1964, "is the centre of the European problem and . . . the relations of the west with communist countries."[4] In contrast, Australia's communist enemies were mostly Asians. By 1955, Japan had become an "important trading partner" and "Cold War ally," and the new locus of Australia's fear of Asia was China. In Indochina, communists were Chinese equipped and Chinese led; in Malaya, they were *really* Chinese—hence the term "Chinese Communists terrorists."

Britishness was similarly shared, in the sense that most Australians and Canadians tended to define themselves as British in 1955–1956, but post-British or at least less British in 1964–1965. Much of what was concluded about the British identities of Australia and New Zealand in the previous chapter applies to Canada in 1955. To use the term coined by a Canadian historian this time, here was yet "another Britain," similar to the rest of the Old Commonwealth in everything except its significant "French fact."[5] For example, Victoria Day, quipped *The Globe and Mail* on May 23, should be about history, not about long weekend leisure: "It is not good for a nation so to slight the truth of its historical beginnings." And when India's Nehru came on a state visit on December 18, the same newspaper concluded: "We do not wish to be a British colony today; but we count ourselves fortunate to have been one yesterday." Their independence from Britain did not stop Canadians from supporting what was left of the British Empire. Those who convincingly argued, like the *Globe and Mail* editors, that India deserved its independence, could be no less convincing in arguing that Cyprus or the Gilbert Islands required further tutelage. In the discourse of British identity, the idea of the Commonwealth was valued in part because this new arrangement allowed for gradual, variable, and multispeed processes of decolonization.[6]

ANZUS and the Korean War did not make the Australian elites any less British. As in 1950, Prime Minister Menzies again argued in favor of closer cooperation with London-based partnerships. As one pundit explained, the American alliance was complementary, but not central to the Australian defense:

> Despite occasional allegation to the contrary, post-war emphasis upon geography has not involved neglect of historic association with the United Kingdom and other members of the Commonwealth. Post-war governments in Canberra have also tried to make good use, with some variety of emphasis, of opportunities to strengthen Australia's more recent associations in contemporary history with the United States.[7]

The dominance of Britishness was reflected in Australia's international practices: Canberra followed London in anything from U.N. voting to nuclear weapons policy. Much as in the first half of 1950, the most-talked-about foreign policy issue in 1955 was the Malayan Emergency. This time, however, it appeared that the motherland finally got it right. Britain's creation of a defense pact with Iraq, Iran, Pakistan, and Turkey seemingly freed up Australian troops in the Middle East, which were then redeployed to the Commonwealth's "strategic reserve" in Malaya.[8]

Another major event during this year was the "offshore crisis"—a clash over the Chinese Nationalist island possessions of Quemoy and Matsu, which later became dubbed as the First Taiwan Straits Crisis. Here, Australia agreed with Britain that Formosa was "not worth a great war."[9] In a comparable situation, when U.S. Secretary of State Dulles called for a military intervention against communists in Indochina in April–May 1954, Canberra sided with London in rejecting the use of force on the grounds that it would provoke China. Minister of External Affairs Casey wrote to Dulles that Australia could go to war, but that going to war without Britain was simply "inconceivable."[10]

The map of the Canadian foreign policy debates can be stylized around the "North Atlantic Triangle," which imagined a close and interdependent tripartite relationship among Canada, Britain, and the United States.[11] A frame that lumped Canada together with two of the greatest powers in human history might appear delusional, but recall that in 1955–1956 Canada was second only to the United States in per capita income and that it had some of the world's largest banks, top-tier diplomatic corps, and comparatively large and well-equipped armed forces (the latter funded by over 7 percent of the GDP). The idea of the North Atlantic Triangle also suggested that Canadian foreign policy should aim to harmonize the Anglo-American relations so that neither the British nor the American side/angle dominated. Canadian Britishness was motivated by another factor, much as in the nineteenth century:

> Anglo-Canadians had two special incentives towards a Greater British collective identity: French and US neighbours. A strong British connection buttressed Anglo-Canadian hegemony over the Quebecois, and provided an antidote to creeping Americanization.[12]

From this perspective, the North Atlantic Triangle therefore cohered with the discourses on multiple Canadian "tensions" or "dualisms"—not just British-American and Anglo-French but also federal-provincial and East-West.[13]

Anchoring one side of the British-American continuum were "Tories," for whom it was still desirable to be both British and Canadian. On the opposite, and much weaker, side were "continentalists," for whom Canada was lucky to have the leader of the free world as its neighbor.[14] This tension emerged in countless texts in the period. For example, much like their Australian counterparts, Canadian students were taught that both the British and the Americans were their "blood brothers" and that the United States was a model of economic and political progress. But Canadians also learned that their U.S. neighbor had repeatedly invaded their country.[15] In the Australian discourse, the United States was mostly an opportunity for betterment; for the Canadians, their southern neighbor signified both an opportunity and a threat, sometimes simultaneously.

In Canada, there was a third foreign policy position, which can be called "liberal internationalism." This school of thought came from the Department of External Affairs, especially from Prime Minister Louis St. Laurent, Minister of External Affairs Lester Pearson, and diplomats John Holmes, Escott Reid, Norman Robertson, and Hume Wrong. Its main argument was that the North Atlantic Triangle, golden that it was, acted as a straitjacket. Canada, liberal internationalists argued, was a sovereign state with an interest in an "independent" foreign policy, specifically one that would avoid falling hostage to either the British past or the American-dominated future or both. For Pearson and Holmes, Canada needed to pursue middle power roles in broader communities such as NATO and the United Nations.[16] Gallup's foreign policy surveys from 1955 suggest that at least a plurality of Canadians supported NATO, the Commonwealth, and the United Nations, in that order.[17] Together with my discourse analysis, these findings lead to a conclusion that multiple discourses shaped the Canadian foreign policy process, but they all pointed out to membership in a single Anglo-led Western alliance against global communism. It was America who called the shots, yet Canadian diplomats and troops still mostly operated with their British friends overseas. Politically, the North Atlantic Triangle was in perfect balance.

SUEZ: OF BLIND LOYALTY AND PEACEKEEPING

In July 1956, Egypt's military-led government nationalized an Anglo-French company responsible for operating the Suez Canal. In the context of the Cold War, the move was interpreted as a threat to Western and, especially, British influence in the Middle East. The British government under Anthony Eden decided to resolve the problem militarily—by retaking the canal and changing the regime in Cairo. To that end, Britain forged a secret tactical alliance with France and Israel and then supplied its American and Commonwealth allies with misleading information. The invasion began on October 29, when the Israelis attacked across the Sinai. Two days later, an Anglo-French force stormed in from its staging area in Cyprus while Anglo-French representatives in the U.N. Security Council vetoed calls for a cease-fire. On November

1–2, the Americans proposed a cease-fire resolution in the General Assembly: The majority of members endorsed it, Canada abstained from the vote, but Australia opposed it.

Australia's support for Britain's illegitimate and illegal intervention in Suez was described by the Australian historian W. J. Hudson as a case of "blind loyalty."[18] From an identity-based perspective, Australia's blindness was relative. The British government in London was an extension of the Australian Self, while the Egyptian president Gamal Abdel Nasser was a petty Third World generalissimo, the poor man's Mussolini. In addition, Australia's own government was a stakeholder in the crisis. Just as he did several times during World War II, Menzies joined a British cabinet discussion of the Suez crisis in August and then, from mid-August to mid-September, led an international team of negotiators to Egypt. The prime minister saw himself a British leader, and many Australians at the time agreed.[19] Under his guidance, the Australian government decided to endorse Britain's policy of bringing the Suez Canal under international control by the first week of August.[20] Menzies did not live in a bubble. Most Australians interpreted the crisis as a blatant "confiscation" or "appropriation" of the most valuable piece of real estate in "their" British Empire. Once the fighting started, the press called for a regime change in Cairo, ignoring the fact the rest of the world cried for the war to stop. The leader of the opposition, Evatt, spoke out against the use of force in Suez but stopped short of endorsing the U.N.–brokered cease-fire.

Then, as a culmination of a seemingly more general upheaval against communism in Eastern Europe, came the Soviet invasion of Hungary on November 4. This event rendered any criticism of Britain difficult, if not impossible. In a key parliamentary debate between Menzies and Evatt over Suez on November 1, the prime minister described the Anglo-French intervention as "proper" and declared that any criticism of Britain "when Russia was on the march" in Hungary was "lunacy." The Soviets, argued the prime minister, would further exploit Western disunity. As for the U.S. opposition, both the government and the press attributed it to the momentary confusion in Washington and, in particular, of Secretary of State Dulles.[21] Not one editorial in five Australian dailies in November suggested that Britain might have facilitated Soviet oppression in Eastern Europe by weakening the Western alliance, which was a point made by Evatt in the parliament on November 8. The press also rejected rumors of Britain's collusion with Israel. "Such shabby and dishonourable plot would be so repugnant to any friend of Britain that it is difficult to believe the story has any basis" printed *The Sydney Morning Herald* on November 1. It was its Britishness that made Australia blind. On hearing the news of invasion, Menzies wrote to Eden thus: "You must never entertain any doubts about the British quality of this country."[22]

Canada's role in Suez went down in its history as the mythical "golden age" of Canadian diplomacy. Pearson's proposal to secure the cease-fire with a "truly international peace and police force" was approved in the emergency session of the General Assembly of November 3–4. In the triumphalist narrative, the proposal led not only to the resolution of the crisis but also to the institution and practice of U.N. peacekeeping. After all, Pearson later won the Nobel Peace Prize on the basis of his efforts in Suez. And yet there is little doubt the peacekeeping proposal came from the American diplomats in the United Nations. Pearson merely sold it to the right audiences, first to the U.N. secretariat and then, more critically, to the British Foreign Office.[23] Further, Pearson's diplomatic triumph was a harrowing experience for Canada at the time. In Canada's collective memory, its historical friends and allies had never disagreed so intensely and so openly, and the challenge for its government was finding a seat on the diplomatic fence. As this proved to be impossible, the government fell over to the less-popular U.S. side, seemingly turning against its European motherlands for the first time in history.[24] For the Canadian correspondent of *The Economist*, the nation's reaction to Suez "was almost tearful . . . like finding a beloved uncle arrested for rape."[25]

The Canadian press regarded the nationalization of the Suez Canal by Egypt's military junta as indefensible in light of the discourse of identity, which idolized the West, liberal democracy, and the binding contracts of capitalism. The Tories in the opposition read the crisis like the Australian government— as a rebellion by a Middle Eastern start-up against the entire Western world order.[26] The protests in the United Nations meant only that the American government resented Britain's rightful aim to reassert international leadership. As for the events in Hungary, they demonstrated that the Anglo-American disunity emboldened their enemies. Some parts of this reading resonated with a broader audience. The two invasions were seen as closely related, but the Soviet "brutality" in Hungary, explained *The Globe and Mail* on November 9, could never be compared with the Anglo-British "protection" in Egypt. Canada's national newspaper could not go so far to support the American position on Suez, but it did question the "wisdom" of the Anglo-French action. This line was picked up by the liberal internationalists in the ruling Liberal Party.

In this frame, the Anglo-French invasion was an overreaction with a potential to destroy an entire decade of efforts to build international peace *and* to contain communism.[27]

The Canadian government was careful to frame its peacekeeping proposal as a policy aimed to help Britain save face and maintain the basic Commonwealth unity.[28] Here, the Suez crisis was really about Anglo-Egyptian and Anglo-Commonwealth relations and even British politics; in other words, anything but a spat between London and Washington. This was a canny move, considering that it was not immediately obvious that Britain's Prime Minister Eden commanded no confidence of the parliament or the public, much less his own cabinet. Rather than using force to humiliate Egypt, Ottawa suggested, Britain should think about consultation, deliberation, and arbitration, especially vis-à-vis its Commonwealth allies. The frame worked because Canadians were ready to hear Ottawa criticize the British government, not Britain itself.[29]

The Globe and Mail reported on November 12 that one former British government official noted that it was Canada, not Britain, who was playing fair in Suez. Unfortunately for the Canadian government, its representatives failed to keep this frame going. Consider the special-session debate in the House of Commons between November 26 and 29 on the question of funding of Canada's peacekeeping contingent to the Sinai. The opposition parties—all of them—made a contention that the government abandoned Canada's traditional allies. The Liberals attempted to play down this particular tradition. "The era when the supermen of Europe could govern the whole world is coming pretty close to an end," said St. Laurent. Then came the predictable accusation that Ottawa was acting like "the United States chore boy," to which Pearson fired back: "It is bad to be a chore boy of the United States. It is equally bad to be a colonial chore boy running around shouting 'ready, aye, ready.'" Both responses drew ire from all Canadian audiences, even from the Liberal cabinet itself.[30] The government stumbled in this debate because it failed to appreciate that Canada still constituted itself as a halfway house between Britain and America, not as the world's peacekeeper. A state/national identity that emerged dominant from the discursive terrain at the time implied a foreign policy set in the perfectly balanced North Atlantic Triangle, yet the government's policy on Suez helped the American angle to grow at the expense of the other two. In short, for many Canadians, Ottawa's action itself was a misfit between identity and reality.

The Canadian public opinion data suggest that the country was split over Suez. In November 1956, 43 percent of Toronto respondents to a Gallup poll agreed with the Anglo-French invasion, but 40 per cent opposed it with 17 percent offering no opinion.[31] The same result came from a content analysis of the editorials and letters to the editor covering twenty six English-language dailies and three French-language dailies over the three months of the Suez crisis.[32] Despite calling its protection of the Suez Canal unwise, *The Globe and Mail* was unwaveringly supportive of Britain. Even after the British government submitted to a U.N. order to halt the fighting, Canada's national newspaper concluded on November 12: "Future historians will, we believe, applaud rather than condemn the British and French action."[33] On the same day, the Montreal *Gazette*, nominally supportive of the Conservative Party, gave the government the benefit of doubt and described Pearson's peacekeeping idea as "historic." In contrast, *Le Devoir*, like other French-language newspapers, condemned the invasion from the outset, describing it on November 3 as "inexplicable and unpardonable." The next section of this chapter will explore the influence of the Anglo-French tension on the construction of Canadian foreign policy, but note that in 1955–1956 Canada's Britishness constituted itself in relation to Quebec at home as well as to France abroad. In this discourse, the fact that the government's policy was popular in French Canada was a sure sign that it was wrong.

From a theoretical point of view, Canada's Suez policy complicates the argument about the ways in which the fit between identity and reality produces foreign policy outcomes. The concluding chapter will revisit this point. Despite the later international acclaim accorded to Pearson and other Canadian diplomats, their government's seemingly pro-American stance during the crisis turned out to be politically costly. Suez did not directly contribute to the defeat of the Liberals in the 1957 elections, but the new Conservative government under John Diefenbaker did attempt to bank on the power of Britishness at home by diverting 15 percent of Canadian imports from the United States to Britain.[34] The plan failed, as did other attempts to slow the onward flow of continental integration. As I will explore in the following section, this reality was to play a major role in the making of the Canadian policy on Vietnam.

LUCKY AND UNLUCKY NATIONS

"Australia is a lucky country, run by second-rate people who share its luck," wrote Donald Horne to his fellow Australians in 1964. Horne's *Lucky Country* lent itself to two readings. One was a scathing critique of an entrenched colonial mentality, in which Australia refused to take responsibility for its own fate and left its prosperity and security in the hands of its "great and powerful friends" and other nations. The other reading was a literalist interpretation of Australia as a success story. One Canadian official shared the latter view, with envy:

> In Australia I was enormously impressed by the cultural and economic vitality of a people who have a jaunty confidence in themselves, isolated though they are from their traditional friends. They worry not at all about the preservation of their national identity. Who could ever mistake an Australian?[35]

Compared to Australia, Canada was rather unlucky. The fact that Canada's economy ranked sixth or seventh in the world was in vain because its nationhood still seemed elusive, three years away from the national centennial. As the historian José Igartua (2006) showed, this moment of Canadian history was marked by not one, but two "quiet revolutions," one in Quebec and another in English Canada. Both were about identity.

Quebec's Quiet Revolution was hardly quiet. Text upon text surveyed for this chapter commented on the "unrest" or "changes" in Canada's French-speaking province. From the perspective of "English Canada," Quebec's revolution was welcomed because it was liberalizing and secularizing a hitherto conservative and god-loving province.[36] Not welcome, however, was Quebec's claim for full linguistic and economic equality. Worse, the revolution was giving birth to specter of secessionism, as some francophone Quebeckers were now arguing that they were not Canadians who happened to be speaking French, but *Québécois*, a North American nation long colonized by the British Empire. English Canada dismissed Quebec's newborn nationalism as "politics," even when one separatist group resorted to terrorism against Canada and "Anglo-Saxon collaborators" in Quebec.[37] One foreign policy effect of the Quiet Revolution was the signing of a cultural "entente" between Quebec and France in February 1965. The notion that French President Charles De Gaulle could play a role in Quebec's national awakening probably frightened some English-Canadians. "It should be remembered," offered the *Gazette* on October 31, "that a Franco-Russian combination has always been of one those natural alliances."

The revolution in Quebec plunged Anglophone Canada into a revolution of its own. The national identity crisis was the dominant discourse. The provincial-federal, East-West and British-American dualisms were feeding off the English-French fissure, causing the elites to ponder on the very political ontology of the state. Ralph Allen, *Maclean's* editor, suggested that the secession of Quebec would lead to a similar outcome in Canada's prairies, with the United States probably taking the entire "area between the Rockies and the Lakehead."[38] Like its French-speaking province, the rest of Canada was redefining its identity, yet with comparatively greater difficulty. A University of Toronto student conference named "What Is English Canadian?" gave an answer in a double negative: "He is not a French Canadian and he is not an American."[39] The double negative caused much frustration. According to John Conway, who appears in the second epigraph of the chapter, "If our centenary celebration is to mean anything, it must be about what we are, rather than about what we are not. And this problem of our identity we have yet to solve."[40]

The societal processes through which Australians discovered their sheer and shameful luck, while Canadians revolutionarily pondered about the absurdities of their nation-state, were reflected and reproduced in the contemporary foreign policy debates. For the younger generation, the days of British race patriotism were over, yet this generation did not include many academics as well as political leaders, such as Menzies in Australia and Diefenbaker in Canada. The attempts to revive trade links in the former metropole bore no fruit in the 1960s because London concluded that Britain's future would be best served by a bid for membership in the European Economic Community (EEC), the precursor to the EU. This turn came as a shock to the former dominions. What was shocking was not the decision to finally bury the long dysfunctional system of Commonwealth preferences in trade, so much as the British refusal to compensate Australia and Canada for their losses with a hefty severance package.[41] In the same year came the signing of the Moscow nuclear test-ban treaty, which ushered a period of Cold War détente. Here, too, Britain seemingly took an opportunity to turn away from its overseas commitments and toward its European allies. In objective terms, Britain hardly Europeanized itself then, yet both Canberra and Ottawa interpreted these changes as momentous and irreversible.[42] More importantly, it was this interpretation that threw the two Commonwealth members spinning further into the American orbit.

From the Australian perspective, Britain and America were two "great and powerful friends," both integral and positive to Australian identity. Both friends made Australia feel lucky, but only "American power" still counted against the "brooding power intelligence of the new China."[43] Thus wrote the minister of external affairs Paul Hasluck:

The War of 1939–45 taught two lessons. One was that geographical isolation was no defense. An Asian power could attack Australian territory and threaten it with invasion. That lesson has since been underlined by changes in the nature of offensive weapons. The other was that British power was not great enough at the time of a war in Europe to conduct an effective defensive war in the Far East. That lesson has since been underlined by the postwar changes in the old British Empire.[44]

Like Spender and other proponents of the American alliance in 1950–1951, Hasluck was keen to remind his audiences that it was the United States who ended up bailing out Australia in World War II. What offset the disaster of Singapore in 1942 in the Australian imagination was the U.S.–Australian victory in the Battle of the Coral Sea, which was then enthusiastically commemorated every year. After all, the United States was not only powerful but also fun. According to *Man*, Australia's newsmagazine for men, the conflict in Vietnam was the "wildest" and "whacky," "guerrilla warfare with touches of a Hollywood production," where "lovely girls and wild parties are mixed with danger." Or, in the words of one American officer: "This, man, is the way to fight a war. Nobody's ever had it so good."[45]

In 1964–1965, the obviousness and desirability of Australia's reorientation from Britain to America was constantly being forced upon the Australian audiences by many speakers, but none were as devoted to this task as the supporters of the ruling Liberal–Country Party coalition. Even Menzies, who before saw no alternatives to the old empire, now acknowledged the need for Canberra to harmonize its defense and security policies with those planned in Washington. A commitment to the United States was often framed in terms of the "domino theory." The basic idea was that the unstable Southeast Asian states were like a row of dominos: If one were to fall to communism, the rest would too. In the Australian foreign policy debate, many versions of domino theory floated around, but all led to the same conclusion: The dominos must be prevented from falling, lest Australia become a domino, too. This theory resonated with Australia's own doctrine of "forward defence," which Menzies once defined as a policy of "keep[ing] the enemy out of your country and as far away as possible."[46] The idea emerged in the 1950s, probably in the attempt to rationalize Australian deployments in the Middle East and Malaya, and subsequently became common sense. In an August 8, 1964, article on the military buildup, *The Australian* noted that the Centurion tank was a "symbol for impotence" because it was too heavy for airlift *from* the country. Forward defense denied Australia's relative isolation in favor of military interventionism abroad, but relatively few people took issue with this logic. The notable exceptions were Evatt and Arthur Calwell in the ALP opposition as well as Arthur Tange in External Affairs.[47]

The Canadian foreign policy debate in the period was almost a reversed image of Australia's. Instead of a forward defense alliance with Washington against international communism, Canada was pursuing an inward defense of sorts. "A weak and divided Canada, anxious about its present can play no worthy part in international affairs," declared Pearson, now the prime minister, in February 1965.[48] On top of the quiet revolutions at home, there was the towering presence of the American neighbor. "The problem of separate and distinctive identity [viz. the U.S.] has been with us from the beginning and, I suppose, will be with us in the foreseeable future," said External Affairs Minister Paul Martin in November 1964.[49] Anything that Canada did abroad was measured in terms of similarity/difference with the United States. In 1964, one Gallup survey captured this structural predicament well by outlining three mutually exclusive futures for Canada in the world: stay in the Commonwealth, pursue independence, or *join* the United States. Two-thirds chose either the Commonwealth or independence, while one in ten agreed to a continental union.[50]

For Canadian nationalists, the idea of an ever-closer continental unification was as disconcerting as the ongoing quiet revolutions. In the past, Canada's anti-American voices were typically Tory, but now they were coming from the political left. For example, in the parliamentary debate on the North American Air Defence Command (NORAD) in 1958, the Liberals and Progressive Conservatives, as the two mainstream parties, enthusiastically endorsed the new institution. Two smaller parties, the Farmer-Labour-Socialists and the populist Social Creditists, disagreed, arguing that NORAD would lead to loss of sovereignty to the United States. In 1964–1965, this discourse was articulated by Tommy Douglas, the charismatic leader of the New Democrats, the successor party of the Farmer-Labour-Socialist federation from the earlier period. Anti-Americanism resonated with the Canadian audiences, in part due to America's aggressive defense policies, but mostly due to its politics at home—the recent political assassinations and "racial strife." On the opposite side of the political spectrum, but without an obvious partisan representation, was continentalism, a discourse that emphasized the anticommunist, liberal, capitalist, democratic, Christian, and English-speaking unity of North America. In the context of the Cold War, for example, this discourse implied that Canada could have no better friend than the United States.

Continentalism was pervasive in the corporate and defense establishments but generally silent among politicians and academics. An exception to the latter is the aforementioned Underhill, whose *Image of Confederation* (1964) argued that Canada should stop denying its North American identities, civic and ethnic alike. It is in this context that liberal internationalism, as the middle way between anti-Americanism and continentalism, once again dominated the foreign policy debate. In this discourse, assorted continental asymmetries naturally subordinated Canada to the United States but did not make it a "banana republic." It was Holmes who explained this nuance best. Once the going got tough, he argued, Canada was the world's go-to peacekeeper.[51] In this sense, Canadian foreign policy was "modest but unique." Instead of showing force, Canada set examples: that "people of different languages and culture can coexist within a single sovereignty"; that a state can "differ from the United States without opposing the interests of the United States"; and that a former colony need not be an "eunuch state," but a middle power multilateralist, with peacekeeping and other important roles to play in the complex U.N. system.[52]

The same discourse is evident in a "white paper" on defense published in March 1964. Among other novel ideas, the document proposed leadership in U.N. peacekeeping and foreign aid and positioned the U.S. alliance as "an aspect of Canada's conviction that security lay in collective arrangements," comparable to NATO. This was a rather weak description of a bilateral arrangement, which controlled Canadian airspace, defense production, and most of its strategic defense planning and claimed the defense of the entire Northern hemisphere. The dominance of liberal internationalism agrees with Robert Bothwell's interpretation of Canada–U.S. relations at the outset of the Vietnam War: "For Canadians, relations between the two countries were not a means of expressing similarities but of defining and even amplifying differences."[53]

VIETNAM: OF DESPARATE GAMBLES
AND BENEVOLENT NEUTRALITY

Compared to the Suez crisis, the war in Vietnam had a longer and more complex history from both the Australian and Canadian perspectives. These countries already had their military personnel committed to the theater of operations. In 1954, Canada joined tripartite international commissions for Indochina, whose task was to supervise truce and new political boundaries in the region following the French colonial withdrawal, including a division of Vietnam into communist North and pro-Western South. The other two members of the international commissions were communist Poland and nonaligned India, which made Canada the sole representative of the Western bloc.[54] In 1964–1965, Canada's 200 soldiers and diplomats in and around Vietnam were therefore observers, though not peacekeepers trying to separate two warring sides in the post-Suez U.N. sense of this role. In contrast, Australia's contingent consisted of a platoon of military advisors (since 1962) and an air transport squadron (since August 1964), and its purpose was to help the United States strengthen the defense capabilities of South Vietnam.

Australia and Canada's subsequent choices in Vietnam were mostly determined by these prior commitments: Canberra joined the United States in its military campaign against communists, while Ottawa maintained its observer neutrality. But despite differences stemming from the basic roles accorded to them in Indochina, the Australian and Canadian governments shared one overarching concern, and that was to manage their great and powerful American friend. The more the Johnson administration moved to escalate and Americanize the war in 1964–1965, the more it asked for help from its allies. In February 1965, Johnson asked for "more flags," meaning more military commitment from more allied states. By July, he was asking for anything from diplomatic support to "technical advising" and logistics to "deterrence" to, ultimately, "combat" or "operational" assistance. The political subtlety of this menu of choices was heightened by a palpable possibility that the United States would go for a "maximum air war" and even a "nuclear castration" of North Vietnam.[55]

The Australian government went well beyond the call of duty. In December 1964, it came out alone in encouraging U.S. bombing of North Vietnam over negotiations; in April 1965, it placed an infantry battalion under U.S. command; a month later, it even amended Australia's recent and controversial military conscription bill in such way that it would enable Australian conscripts to serve in Vietnam. Menzies's cabinet repeatedly considered policy options that fell short of committing ground troops, yet it decided to fight alongside the United States. The decision was heroic considering that Australia faced an ANZAC dilemma–style problem at the time or, to borrow from Peter Edwards and Gregory Pemberton, the "two allies and two conflicts" problem.[56] Vietnam was America's conflict, while Malaysia–Indonesia confrontation was Britain's. The doctrine of forward defense suggested a commitment to both, but Australia had only three infantry battalions available for overseas service. Britain's conflict was a familiar commodity, considering that

Australia already fought and defeated communist guerillas in Malaya in the 1950s and that it kept a battalion there, as a part of a Commonwealth reserve asked to protect the international shipping lane in the Strait of Malacca.

What made this conflict zone even more salient was the behavior of Indonesia's President Sukarno. From the Australian perspective, Sukarno was as unpredictable and as aggressive as Egypt's Nasser was in Suez, which was equal if not worse to the behavior of communists in Hanoi and Beijing. By taking over Dutch New Guinea in 1962, Sukarno first dangerously pressed against the Australian colony of Papua New Guinea. He then turned against the newly formed federation of Malaysia, which culminated in a border clash between Australian and Indonesians troops in October 1964. And most worryingly, Sukarno approached China in November 1964, a move that confirmed old fears among the Australian elites about the inevitability of the "Jakarta–Peking axis." Just as Johnson was calling for help in Vietnam, the entire "corridor" or "arc" to Australia's "near north" was starting to look like another iron curtain. This particular threat loomed large in the Australian "official mind" until September 1965, when a military coup against Sukarno led to a realignment of Indonesia with the Western bloc.

The conflicts in Malaysia and Vietnam both involved a weak Western ally trembling before an aggressive, pro-Chinese dictatorship and its insurgent proxies. In this sense, Menzies's deputy wrote to British Prime Minister Wilson, that the conflicts were "part of a common pattern and a common threat."[57] But in no way were they comparable in terms of their intensity. From a materialist perspective focused on military capabilities, geography, and behavioral records, Sukarno's Indonesia was significantly more threatening to Australia; indeed, the Malaysia–Indonesia confrontation tied down twice as many allied troops as the Vietnam conflict. In November 1964, a regularly scheduled defense review indeed identified Indonesia as Australia's main threat and called for conscription.[58] On November 10, Menzies spoke in the parliament vaguely about conscription as a "continuing requirement to make our forces available for cold war and counterinsurgency tasks," but, on the next day, the *Sydney Morning Herald* concluded that Australia was "preparing against war with Indonesia."

Five months later, Australia was officially fighting two wars with equal zeal. Canberra sent an infantry battalion in January to Malaysia and another, in April, to Vietnam. To understand this shift, let us begin with the foreign affairs and defense committee (FAD), Australia's top decision-making body made up of five or six cabinet ministers plus the representatives from the military. In mid-1964, Hasluck, plus the defense minister Shane Paltridge and the chiefs of staff committee Frederick Scherger were the hawks on Vietnam, while Prime Minister Menzies and his deputy John McEwen (who was also the trade minister and the leader of the Country Party) were the skeptics.[59] Hasluck was the most vocal, having all but proposed the Vietnam intervention scenario to the Australian public as early as June 1964. According to one counterfactual analysis, if one of Hasluck's predecessors had been at the helm of the ministry of external affairs, Australia would have sent its forward defense units only to Malaysia, not to Vietnam as well. Casey, who held office from 1951 through 1960, reportedly believed in the Sino-Vietnamese rivalry, not the domino theory, while his successor Garfield Barwick resigned in April 1964 partly because he believed that forward defense should not go past Malaya and Borneo.[60] Critiques of the domino theory, as implied in the notion that North Vietnam's Ho Chi Minh was communism's "new Tito," existed in the Australian foreign policy discourse, but only on the margins.[61] As for Barwick's limited forward defense idea, a look across the Gallup opinion polls suggests that it would have had much more considerable traction in the foreign policy debate.[62] With a Casey or a Barwick in the FAD, Canberra might have well ended up fighting one, not two, wars in 1965.

These counterfactuals underestimate the resonance of frames speaking to the desirability of America's strong presence in Asia that go back to the ANZUS debate in 1950–1951. Once it became clear that the United States crossed the point of no return in its commitment to Vietnam, Hasluck and other hawks carried the day. The key event occurred in the first week of August, 1964, and it involved the infamous naval confrontation between North Vietnam and the United States in the Gulf of Tonkin and the subsequent bombing of the former by the latter. In the extended parliamentary debate on August 11–13, Hasluck made an argument that the use of force had "no current alternative . . . to check the downward thrust of militant Asian communism."[63] In this frame, the bombing campaign suggested not simply that Hanoi was indeed militant but more importantly that Washington was now fully committed to the containment of communism on the Asian mainland. Now compare the framing of an objectively similar event involving enemy militancy, but not the U.S. ally. In September, Sukarno escalated its policy of confrontation with Malaysia by landing its paratroopers on the Malaysian peninsula. A U.N. Security Council resolution, vetoed by the Soviets, deplored Indonesia's action, and the Western bloc protested in unison. Here it was Britain who threatened a punitive counterattack. To test Indonesia, a Royal Navy squadron announced a passage through the waters claimed by Jakarta. The incident, dubbed the Sunda Straits Crisis, was resolved when Indonesia allowed the squadron to pass, though not via the desired route. That the Sunda Straits and Tonkin incidents had a lot in common was not lost on contemporary Australian observers, yet one difference was crucial. For the government and the media, in contrast to the American punishment of North Vietnam, a British attack on Indonesia would have been counterproductive.[64]

Between Australia's two great and powerful friends in 1964–1965, the United States was significantly greater and more powerful. As Scherger later reflected on Vietnam: "It never was conceivable to us that America would lose—no way."[65] The realm of the conceivable was shaped by factors other than simple military bean counts. According to John McEwen, who played the triple role of the trade minister, Menzies's deputy, and the leader of the Country Party, the cabinet's Vietnam decision was "an act of faith."[66] In this view, the alliance with the United States was not only a meaningful insurance policy but also a commitment to friendship. Consider the language of Menzies' famous announcement of the Vietnam decision to the parliament on April 29:

> The takeover of South Vietnam would be a direct military threat to Australia and all countries of South and Southeast Asia. It must be seen as a thrust by Communist China between the Indian and Pacific Oceans . . . We have decided—and this has been in close consultation with the Government of the United States—to provide an infantry battalion for service in South Vietnam . . . alliances, as well as providing guarantees and assurances for our security, make demands upon us.[67]

The prime minister ended his speech with a reading of President Johnson's letter, which said that a commitment "proves again the deep ties between our two countries in the cause of world peace and security." The opposition did not buy it. On May 4, Calwell suggested that the decision to go to war was based "on three false assumptions: An erroneous view of the nature of the war in Vietnam; a failure to understand the nature of the Communist challenge; and a false notion as to the interests of America and her allies." In other words, the ALP held the conflict was primarily a civil war; that communism was a political, not military problem; that the United States could easily end up a loser like France; and, most importantly, that there was direct threat to Australia and that Calwell invoked the official positions of Britain and Canada as evidence that alternative policies of support were possible. Menzies responded by implying that the ALP propagated shameful free-riding. "American soldiers from the Middle West can go and fight and die in South Vietnam, but that is not for us," quipped the prime minister.

Once the language of "guarantees and assurances" turned into the language of duty, the debate was practically over. Overwhelmingly, the press agreed with the prime minister. Save for one, all of the editorials surveyed in the week after Menzies's announcement commented on the close links between the intervention in Vietnam and the American alliance, both in the sense that the benefits of the latter outweighed the pitfalls of the former, and in the sense that it was Australia's duty to help its friend. A *Canberra Times* editorial concluded on May 1 that Australia "got what even Hitler feared, a war on two fronts. It is a desperate gamble." Exchange Vietnam for Suez and the United States for Britain, and there is another case of Australia's "blind loyalty" in the twentieth century. Some of the language Menzies used to frame Australia's stance on Vietnam is indeed reminiscent of the old times. Speaking at a party rally in Sydney in April 1965, the prime minister described the U.S. intervention as "the greatest act of real courage since Britain stood alone in the Second World War."[68] Later, he wrote that "from the outset of American military operations against aggressors in Vietnam I found it impossible to contemplate that Australia could allow the United States to 'stand alone' in that enterprise."[69] In 1954, Casey explained to Dulles that going to war without Britain was inconceivable. A decade later, it was inconceivable for Australia to stay out of an American war, even if it looked like a "desperate gamble."

Canada, too, was given ample opportunity to gamble on Vietnam. At various points in this period, Johnson's continual calls for help prompted Pearson's cabinet to consider an option of withdrawing from the moribund international commission. Each time the cabinet concluded, and then duly explained to various White House officials, that Canada's observer role in Indochina was far more valuable to Western interests than any other form of assistance it could provide to the war effort itself. Among themselves, Canadians reasoned, also correctly, that continuing participation in the commission removed "pressure for direct Canadian involvement in the Vietnam situation."[70] Here was a general rationale for peacekeeping, which Ottawa subsequently deployed many times to its advantage. Conversely, Washington and other Canadian allies found that Canada's peacekeeping claims were an excuse to avoid more difficult conventional operations.

As it turned out in Vietnam, America's problem with Canada was not inadequate involvement but inadequate talk. Just as the Australian government was signaling readiness to commit combat troops to Vietnam, the Canadian government decided it was time to open up a debate on the direction of the war. It was in the midst of the bombing campaign phase code-named Rolling Thunder, on April 1, 1965, that Pearson gave a speech at Temple University in Philadelphia. In that speech he called for "a measured and announced pause" in the U.S. assault of North Vietnam. Like other Canadian officials at the time, the prime minister was careful to endorse the American goals in Vietnam and focus his critique of the American means only on the new bombing campaign. But these nuances were lost. Other allied leaders spoke against the bombing, but rare was a foreign official who dared question American foreign policy on American soil while America was at war.[71] The rest of the story was revealed decades later: When the two leaders met at Camp David the day after the Temple speech, Johnson took Pearson away from his entourage and then shouted at the prime minister for "pissing on the neighbor's rug."[72]

Pearson's Temple University speech is evocative of the broader ways in which Ottawa attempted to distance itself from the Vietnam War. The Canadian government called for diplomatic solutions and on top of that insisted that its observers in Indochina had to uphold objectivity, balance, and fairness. This rhetoric caused dismay and frustration in Washington. Secretary of State Dean Acheson described Canadian diplomacy as the "stern voice of the daughter of God."[73] The Canadian diplomat Holmes was less sarcastic. For Americans, he later wrote, Canada was "a tiresome and self-righteous nag."[74] And yet, there are also good reasons why the historiography on Canada's Vietnam experience tends to revolve around the so-called complicity thesis.[75] Behind the official rhetoric, Canada generally supported the American war effort. More than a few Canadian manufacturers were happy with an increased demand for products from south of the border, while survey research data suggests that the Vietnam War was no less popular in Canada than in the staunchly pro-American Australia.[76] Further, much like those Australian diplomats who sent all-important ANZUS documents to their British counterparts in the 1950s, the Canadian staff in the Indochina supervisory commissions shared their private information with the American embassy officials in Saigon. As historians have shown, these practices were not only "cultural" but also a matter of policy. For one, it was on the explicit (and secret) orders from Ottawa that the Canadian diplomat Blair Seaborne went on five missions to Hanoi between June 1964 and June 1965, thus maintaining the sole communication channel between it and the Americans. Seaborne continued to make his trips even when it became clear that Washington was not interested in diplomatic solutions but in field intelligence.[77]

From these observations, it follows that Canada's Vietnam policy was another case of "benevolent neutrality" in the history of relations among core Anglosphere states. As did the United States during the South African War, Canada experienced a clash of identities during the Vietnam War. In short, the discourse of continentalism implied that Canada was primarily a U.S. ally in the war against communism, while liberal internationalism and anti-Americanism argued that Canada was primarily an observer and peacekeeper, but a warrior. Rather than resolving this ambiguity, the Canadian government embraced it. The peacekeeper identity dominated the formulation and public debate on the war, while the ally identity dominated the policy implementation stage in Vietnam. According to Douglas Ross, the prowar position was made outside the parliament, mostly by anticommunist hawks who argued that peacekeeping was meaningless when it clashed with the interests of Canada's Cold War allies.[78] This frame did not fit with the revolutionary processes at home. It was through relating to, and accommodating, Quebec's Quiet Revolution that the Canadian elites moved to define themselves as a unique nation with unique tasks on the world stage, such as peacekeeping and middle-power mediation.

All of these roles were embraced by the minority Liberal government led by Pearson, the golden diplomat from Suez. In an illustrious liberal internationalist fashion, the Canadian government held on to Canada's preset peacekeeping role in Indochina. In internal and public deliberations alike, Pearson expressed his desire for a negotiated settlement in Vietnam, as did most of his cabinet ministers. Notably, no official described the conflict as a civil war or questioned the U.S. assistance to South Vietnam. Probably the most anti-American in the cabinet was Finance Minister Walter Gordon, though in this period his contributions to the foreign policy debate concentrated on the Americanization of the Canadian industry.[79] Foreign Minister Martin anchored the pro-American side of the cabinet, yet, he, too, generally argued for less violence and more diplomacy.[80] Overall, the Liberals appeared eminently moderate in the Canadian parliament, where members of the official and unofficial opposition frequently engaged in anti-American tirades. The same can be said with respect to segments of the mainstream media as well.

In comparison to their Australian counterparts, the Canadian Broadcasting Corporation (CBC) and *The Globe and Mail* were more critical about the U.S. intervention in Vietnam, especially with regards to the presence of so-called American advisers. In March 1965, for example, the CBC reported on the U.S. shipment of chemical weapons to the South Vietnamese army and made an analogy to Canada's World War I experience, when its troops were the target of German mustard gas. The erroneous report was later retracted, but it speaks to a tendency among Canadian elites to moralize over the Vietnam War.[81] As Bothwell notes, and as the subsequent chapter will show, "moralism and moralizing are part and parcel of liberal international behavior," historically shared by Canada, Britain and the United States alike.[82]

Liberal internationalism dominated the Canadian debate on Vietnam in Canada, but not in Indochina among Canadian soldiers and diplomats there. Observer impartiality was the official line, but it was continentalism that fit with everyday practices, such as drinking in the air-conditioned GI bars or taking advantage of the free transoceanic transportation provided to Canadians by U.S. military.[83] Two decades of the continental defense integration progress—which included ABC military standardization programs—meant that Canada's armed forces became special Canadians: "If there were a segment of the Canadian population immune to anti-Americanism, this was it."[84] The same can be said about some diplomats.[85] No less important from the ground perspective of South Vietnam, American power did not look overwhelming to Canadians; if anything, the communist side appeared stronger until the spring of 1965. This frame of the United States as the underdog in Vietnam never resonated with the audiences in the Canadian media space, but it was standard fare in Australia.

The ambiguities of Canadian policy might have been more pronounced in Indochina, but they were more fundamental and more complex than simple political and cultural disagreements between assorted bureaucratic units.[86] The ambiguities were not absolute either because the peacekeeper and the loyal ally did not necessarily contradict each other. In the latter sense, the Vietnam War was reminiscent of the Suez crisis. The Canadian government desperately wanted its ally to seek peace when the ally was impetuously going for war. But, unlike in Suez, the government did not pay a price for its policy. Rather than seeing ambiguity as something to be corrected, most Canadian elites embraced it. After all, the taproots of this ambiguity permeated the dualistic Canadian society, especially at the time of two quiet revolutions.

Consider the growing importance of Quebec in Canadian foreign policy. Since they had been introduced to Canada in the 1940s, public opinion data have shown how the French-speaking province has long skewed Canada's national average to the left on many issues, including world affairs. That said, and with exceptions, every time Ottawa moved to support the wars waged by Canada's great and powerful friends in the Anglosphere, significant numbers of francophone Quebeckers would show their displeasure, thus causing the question of national unity to spring to the top of Canadian foreign policy concerns. The Quiet Revolution in the 1960s made Quebec an even stronger factor in Canadian politics. One ambitious Canadian politician memorably explained it in 1968: "In terms of realpolitik, French and English are equal in Canada because each of these linguistic groups has the power to break the country. And this power cannot be claimed by the Iroquois, the Eskimos, or the Ukrainians."[87] The ebb and flow of the Anglo-French accommodation has varied over time, and so have its consequences for Canadian foreign policy, but a predilection for nonviolent options was almost always among them. Peacekeeping, Canada's legendary twentieth-century contribution to modernity, was popular among Canadians partly because it was politically fitting for the dualisms and tensions at home.

From the perspective of the Anglosphere core as a racialized club, Canada's membership was at once sustained and undermined by the tension between French and English Canadians. In the 1960s, the two groups made each other meaningful not only in linguistic or more broadly cultural terms but also in racial terms. That Canada was a unique condominium made up of two distinct and rather immutable European peoples was evident anywhere from history textbooks and newspaper cartoons to the reports on the work of the Royal Commission on Bilingualism and Biculturalism. Before Quebec's Quiet Revolution, the hegemony of English Canada was taken for granted at home as well as abroad. In the aftermath of the Suez crisis, for example, Egypt refused to accept the Queen's Own Rifles of Canada as a bona fide peacekeeping infantry, as opposed to a reminder of the British invasion force. This rebuke compelled Pearson to later spearhead a successful effort to change the national flag such that it would better reflect Canada's unique identity.[88] And it was this new Canada that in 1970 became one of the founding members of the International Organization of the Francophonie, the French Commonwealth. Arguably, much like Britain's turn to Europe, Canada's discovery of its inner and outer "Francosphère" has influenced the subsequent patterns of international conflict/cooperation as much as various continuities within the Anglosphere.[89]

THE DEPUTIES

In the attempt to recount one story of the Anglosphere in international relations, this chapter has considered the divergences of Australian and Canadian foreign policies in Suez and Vietnam. During the Suez crisis, the dominance of British race patriotism implied Australia's loyalty toward Britain. This loyalty is historiographically seen as "blind," but at the time it resonated with the discourses and debates on the Australian Self. By the time of the Vietnam War, this type of loyalty was transposed onto the United States. Australia followed the United States into Vietnam despite being bogged down in a similar conflict in Malaysia. As for Canada, its loyalty to Britain in Suez was overruled by a liberal internationalist government, whose representatives framed Canada as a unique player in world affairs. The unwillingness to support the motherland constituted a misfit with Canada's Britishness, so the government framed its policy as a temporary disagreement with the British government under Eden, not a divergence of national interests between two independent states. Canada found itself in a similar position during the U.S.–led intervention in Vietnam. Like in Suez, Ottawa never publicly condemned the goals of its belligerent ally, but its call for more diplomacy and less violence drew ire. In this case, the politically relevant Canadian audiences approved the government's judicious distance. In retrospect, the success of both of these policies had much to do with the circumstances beyond the control of its advocates in Ottawa. As Marc O'Reilly noted on the case of Suez, such an important intermediary role within the North Atlantic Triangle never presented itself to Canada again.[90] Similarly, the progression of the war in Vietnam came to vindicate the liberal internationalist discourse in the Canadian foreign policy sphere.[91]

Australian and Canadian security cooperation with the United States has generally followed the pattern set in the Vietnam War. Australia's heroism has continued: Its government sent troops to every major U.S.–led military intervention since 1965. This record—always more political than military—has now become the standard frame in every meeting between Australian and American officials. In comparison, Canada has continued to pursue ambiguity: No foreign military is as integrated with U.S. forces as Canada's, yet the Canadian government never fails to downplay this fact at home and abroad.

The divergence between Australia and Canada vis-à-vis the U.S. alliance is structurally rooted in the relationship between geography and national identity. To use an old adage, if Canada has been a "regional power without a region," then Australia has had to be a regional power with too big a region. But geography is not destiny. As the last two chapters have shown, Australians often worried more about the Middle East than their Asian "near north." Since the 1980s, they have decided to stop worrying and learned to love Asia, but they again started worrying about the Middle East in the 1990s and 2000s, mainly out of the desire to "upgrade" ANZUS.[92] This dance will probably continue so long as Australian identity continues to be coconstituted with the Anglosphere. Arguably, Australia's geography will become its destiny only once Canberra moves to embrace Asia the way London has embraced Europe since the 1960s.

Geography is one reason why Canadians became peacekeepers, not warriors like Australians. Once the United States gave up on the idea of annexing its northern neighbor, sometime in the latter half of the nineteenth century, geography ceased to be a source of Canada's worries. Recognition that the United States cannot defend the Northern America without also automatically defending Canada began to be formally institutionalized in 1940, with the signing of the Ogdensburg agreement and the establishment of the Permanent Joint Board on Defense.[93] The two counties have been joined at the geostrategic hip ever since: They have maintained a joint defense command, a common defense industry and interoperable forces, which means the Canadian military has come to depend on the United States for strategy and military doctrine, material procurement, and professional training.[94]

This integration—and the next chapter will examine its economic aspects—has produced one of the most mature security communities in the world. From a realist perspective centered on defense, Canada has been a free rider since the mid-1950s. Whatever the ride, it has been bumpy. For the past six decades, Washington has nearly always maintained that Canada's defense spending was "too low," while Ottawa has nearly always tried to point out that the American military complex was "too much." This dynamic, too, has generally amplified what Martin called the "problem of distinct and separate identity" in 1964–1965. Expressed through another old adage, Americans were proud of who they were (Americans), while Canadians were proud of who they were not (Americans). One Canadian Self–Other tension begat another: If English Canada agonized about the dominance with the U.S. Other, then French Canada agonized about the dominance of English Canada. Combined, the sum of these tensions has led to a pattern of ambiguity in Canadian foreign policy.[95] So rather than assuming the role of America's "deputy sheriff," as some Australians declared themselves in early 2000s, Canada underplayed its role in *Pax Americana*. Canada's tensions at home and ambiguities abroad are self-reinforcing and, a constructivist would add, constitutive of Canadian agency on the world stage.

Compared to the periods examined in the previous chapters, in the middle decades of twentieth-century Anglosphere, racism was on the wane. This is not to say that the identities constitutive of the Anglosphere were not racialized, both at home and abroad. As this chapter has shown, Australians feared Asian Communism not in ideological, but in racial terms. Nominally a Cold War ally, Indonesia was widely understood as another China—as a populous, collectivist, and decidedly non-Western dictatorship with a large Communist Party and an even larger army, which was sooner or later poised to attack Australia. Yet it was in this period that the Anglosphere began to define itself in explicitly antiracist terms. One of the key processes that brought about this change was the rise of apartheid South Africa. Washington scaled down its defense cooperation with Pretoria in the early 1950s for the same reason it attempted to build a pluralist "Pacific Pact"—to show Asian and African nations that the United States was at least as progressive as the Soviet Union on the question of race in world politics. In 1960, Canada was the first "old" Commonwealth nation to side with the "new" Commonwealth in pressing for Pretoria's expulsion from that club. As time went on, the rest of the Anglosphere community came to define itself against South Africa. It was this interaction that helped established the idea of the "international community" and the concomitant expectation that rogue governments could not hide behind state sovereignty. Arguably, the forms of liberal internationalism that developed in the post–Cold War period greatly owe to the moral victory of the antiapartheid campaign, which various Anglosphere agents appropriate as their own.[96]

Liberal internationalism developed hand-in-hand with multiculturalism, an idea that liberal values of freedom, democracy, and equality should apply to ethnically defined groups of people.[97] This particular Anglosphere story falls mostly outside the scope of my genealogy, but I wish to note that the versions of multiculturalisms that emerged in Australia and Canada were direct reactions to various racist Others, among whom lurked numerous dark shadows from the shared Old Commonwealth past.[98] The reactions were slow moving and, at first, invisible, yet momentous for the history of the Anglosphere. In the area of immigration control, for example, whites-only British stock-preferred policies introduced in the 1880s were discontinued in 1967 in Canada and in

1973 in Australia. In both countries, non-Europeans came to make up the largest newcomer group in late 1990s. In sharp contrast to the nineteenth century, the processes of "new" immigration and de-Anglicization of core Anglosphere societies have been self-reinforcing thanks to multiculturalism.

Critical in the making of an antiracist, liberal-multicultural Anglosphere was the creation of the distinction between ethnicity and race. Victoria Hattam has argued that these two categories form part of the same "associative chain," in which race is fixed to body, blood, and hierarchy, while ethnicity is rooted in language and religion (or, broadly, culture), which then gives it a sense of pluralism, equality, and fluidity.[99] The chain not only gives meaning to both categories, but it also acts as a carrier of old ideas. From this point of view, while ethnicity has emerged as the preferred term in most Anglosphere societies, its use implicitly conveys meanings long consigned to history. In the post–quiet revolutions Canada, for example, English and French Canadian ceased to be understood as racial, but as cultural or even just linguistic referents. Yet these new and infinitely more pluralist meanings have continually served to privilege and protect some identities over others, such as European over indigenous, Métis, and American; federal over regional, national, and supranational; or bicultural over multicultural, intercultural, or transcultural. In short, the race-ethnicity distinction might have helped to rewrite, but not eliminate or even significantly reconfigure, racialized identities. I will return to this proposition in the concluding chapter.

5 EMPIRE, IRAQ, AND THE "COALITION OF THE WILLING"

> *We do think the same, we do feel the same, and we have the same—I think—sense of belief that if there is a problem you've got to act on it.*
> —Tony Blair in a BBC documentary, September 8, 2002.

> *We're not the same.*
> —Jean Chrétien, interview in *Maclean's*, December 30, 2002.

IN THE ANALYSIS OF THE RUN-UP to the U.S.–led military intervention in Iraq from the perspectives of Britain and Canada, this genealogy comes to its last case study. The intervention began on March 19, 2003. On March 18, British Prime Minister Tony Blair announced to the House of Commons that Britain was going to war against Iraq, a rogue state in possession of weapons of mass destruction (WMD) and ties to international terrorism. Blair said: "Iraq is not the only part of this threat. But it is the test of whether we treat the threat seriously . . . It will determine the pattern of international politics for the next generation." The prime minister underlined that the purpose of the intervention was not only disarmament but also the removal of Saddam Hussein, Iraq's long-time dictator. On March 17, Canadian Prime Minister Jean Chrétien made the opposite announcement in his House of Commons. In response to a question posed by an opposition MP, he said, "If military action proceeds without a new resolution of the Security Council, Canada will not participate." He also added that his government was against the idea of regime change: "If we change every government we don't like in the world where do we start? Who is next?"

The British-Canadian divergence over Iraq is puzzling considering that their governments—Blair's Labour and Chrétien's Liberals—faced nearly identical structural and contextual conditions. First, both countries were such long-standing American allies that the military and defense establishments saw no alternative to building greater interoperability with U.S. forces, both within NATO and through ABCA standardization programs.[1] Further, the governments led by both prime ministers had previously supported a U.S.–led intervention against Hussein's Iraq: in 1998, Operation Desert Fox was a punitive action carried by American and British air forces and supported mainly by an ABCA naval task force. Next, both London and Ottawa spared no diplomatic resources in trying to get the U.N. Security Council to pass a resolution authorizing the disarmament of Iraq, while not a single editorial in the mainstream press asked their respective governments to throw in its lot with France, Germany, and other allies, who opposed the military solution.[2] Once the status quo, which was the continuing containment of Iraq, became increasingly unlikely, both London and Ottawa faced an option of backing the United States politically, but not militarily. The majority of the forty-five members of the anti-Iraq coalition, which U.S. Secretary of Defense Donald Rumsfeld dubbed the "coalition of the willing," in fact supported the U.S. troop invasion not by sending troops but by expressing willingness to see the war happen. Arguably, not unlike during the Vietnam escalation in 1964–1965, nonmilitary support of the U.S. cause in Iraq was justifiable, considering that both Britain and Canada had made prior, and major, commitments to protect American interests elsewhere.

Perhaps most important, the antiwar sentiments and arguments were remarkably similar between Britain and Canada. Throughout the period under study, public opinion polls found that between 40 and 60 percent of respondents—including a majority of Labour voters in the British case—disliked the intervention, even if a (second) U.N. resolution on Iraq materialized, as well as, in even larger percentages, U.S. President George W. Bush.[3] Both countries also saw mass protests against the war. On February 15, at least a million Britons hit the streets in protest, as did over 200,000 Canadians. Political commentators in both countries agreed that Hussein was a brutal tyrant but doubted American estimates of Iraqi military capabilities, especially on the WMDs. Many suggested that the real rationale for the war was the control of Iraq's oil.

And yet, in spite of all these similarities, London and Ottawa chose very different policies. Rather than sending a combination of commandos plus air and naval support, the British government authorized Operation Telic, which at 46,000 troops was the third largest deployment of British forces since World War II. It was a heroic overcommitment. In what follows, I will show how London framed this policy as consistent with both "Atlanticism" and "liberal internationalism," two powerful but separate discourses in the British foreign policy debates. In a critical rhetorical move, it was Blair who framed Britain as a pivotal partner to the American "force for good," which had a right to the "will of the international community" on Iraq. On the other side of the Atlantic, history examined in the previous chapter repeated itself. As in 1964–1965, a Liberal government decided to sit out an American war, while its first minister refused to act as a cheerleader. When a reporter asked Chrétien, on March 28, 2003, whether he was "for or against" the ongoing U.S.-led invasion of Iraq, the prime minister responded with a "maybe."[4] Using a historical-comparative perspective, I will demonstrate how a coalition of "liberal internationalism" and "anti-Americanism" once again shaped a policy that ambiguously distanced Canada from its best friend, closest ally, and biggest trading partner. Here my analysis will end with a critical discussion of liberal and constructivist perspectives on the Canada–U.S. relationship.

THE BEST IN THE WEST

In 2002–2003, Britain and Canada self-identified as capitalist, liberal, and multicultural and, as such, among the few most desirable places to live in the world. There was little condescending dominance, however. The government was rapidly losing power to globalization and, on the inside, to the private sector and the media. Much anxiety was caused by the talk of public service reform, which covered "medicare" in Canada and, in Britain, the entire "1945 welfare state." Elsewhere, public authority clashed with an ever-greater demand for individual freedom and collective rights, as reflected for example in the debates over drug legalization.

On multiculturalism, both societies defined themselves against their racist pasts, but Canadians were slightly more upbeat about their future. Most typically, the Canadian elites understood that their society, at various stages of history, consciously embraced immigration and globalization and so ethnic, religious, and regional diversity. In September 2002, the government's Speech from the Throne committed to "strengthen the bonds of shared citizenship."[5] The receding threat of Quebec separatism doubtless fit with the narrative, too. British texts were less celebratory. London was recognized as a multiethnic and multiconfessional haven, comparable to no other city in the word, save for New York. In this city of cities, it was "cool" to be "second generation" or "mixed" and to consume chicken tikka masala, a hybrid dish approved by a Labour government official.[6] On the whole, however, Britain agonized with its cultural diversity. The main themes were the devolution, or quasi-federalization, and the struggles to share citizenship with various racialized Others, known under the rubric of the 2001 Bradford, Burnley, and Oldham riots. The leaders of ethnic minorities argued against the word *English* (but not the word *British*),[7] while government, namely the Cantle Report and the home secretary David Blunkett, called for "community cohesion," "core values," and "managed migration."[8]

Britain and Canada were both moored in the West, in the sense that its Others were the "developing world," "former Communist regimes," the Cold War–era South American military juntas, as well as the perennially tumultuous Balkans and the Middle East.[9] Among these, by far the most oppositional Other was Islam. This particular relationship was racialized and civilizational and, as such, difficult to accommodate in the multicultural context at home. Text upon text in this period associated Islam with terrorism, corruption, superstition, extreme misogyny, fatalism, and other seemingly immutable features. The key to understanding Islam in this period was 9/11, which was code for terrorist attack by Al-Qaeda fanatics on the United States and the subsequent beginning of a Manichean clash between liberty and tyranny. The British and Canadian media followed the American lead by labeling this clash the "global war on terrorism" or "war on terrorism" (WOT), but usually with the quotations marks in place. The main frontline was in Afghanistan, where the U.S.–led forces, which included British and Canadian troops, occupied Kabul, the capital city, and fought Al-Qaeda and Taliban enemies in the east of the country. Not unlike in the Cold War, British and Canadian societies understood that it was important to fight fire with fire, not for the sake of their own survival, but also, quite selflessly, for the survival of the rest of the West and the rest of the "international community."

In both Britain and Canada, the United States was understood as the world leader and the best friend, yet most texts negatively and ironically depicted American culture (for example, simple-mindedness of Hollywood, monotony of CNN), political economy (such as ceaseless and swelling consumerism, depressing inequalities), and politics at home (including ungainly President Bush, parochial Congress) and abroad (for example, superpower, military powerhouse, peacemaker, or world's police). Canadian texts were significantly more anti-American, which was also true in comparison to Canada of 1964–1965. Once again, the neighbor to the south underwrote Canada's prosperity and defense but actually threatened Canada's sovereignty and identity. On their part,

British texts posited greater comfort and equality vis-à-vis the American Other. In talent and popularity, British celebrities were on a par with their American stars (while their Canadian counterparts "must wear name tags"). The British Empire was consigned to the dustbin of history, but Britain held on to a permanent seat in the U.N. Security Council. In a typical statement made by Prime Minister Blair: "We are not a superpower today, but we can act as a pivotal partner . . . Our past gives us huge, perhaps unparalleled connections with many different regions of the world."[10]

In another case of a core Anglosphere state/nation struggling with its geographical location, the dominant discourse of British identity regarded Europe, then synonymous with the EU, as more negative and more distant than the United States. The newspapers and newsmagazines surveyed in 2002–2003 summarily ignored the presence of thousands of armed Americans on British soil but could not stop publishing stories on the pathologies of the EU. On the Eastern enlargement, the media welcomed the EU's attempt to assimilate postcommunist Others, but more than a few voices expressed fears about factories moving east while Eastern Europeans moved west. The Convention on the Future of Europe in Brussels was out of control. On defense, the proposed EU force was regarded as a paper tiger, in need of U.S. support. And with respect to the euro, the media was pleasantly surprised by the EU's smooth turn to a single currency but typically argued in favor of "keeping the pound" or, in another popular motto, "one currency, one government." Against this picture, the Eurobarometer surveys in the period showed that most Britons preferred Europe over America most of the time and in most areas.[11]

The government, self-styled as New Labour, was on the side of Euroskeptics, too. For example, most British elites understood that Chancellor of the Exchequer Gordon Brown saved his prime minister from the mistaken notion of taking the euro across the English Channel. From the perspective of the discourses of British identity that dominated the period under study, governing Britain nearly always meant a certain distancing from Europe. Most obviously, New Labour was attractive precisely because it claimed it could steer the "Third Way," a mythical middle road between state-sponsored and free-market varieties of capitalism.[12] As Andrew Gamble suggested, the Third Way in economy was what the "bridge" was in foreign policy—a metaphorical *via media* between Europe and America, two political, social, economic, cultural and, indeed, ontological referents for Britain at the turn of the millennium.[13]

The bridge was a powerful frame in British foreign policy debate because it comfortably centered Britain in the mid-Atlantic, closer to Bermuda than to Calais, but without sustaining an obvious hierarchy or even a dichotomy between Europe and America. It was Blair who set off the bridge metaphor in 1997: "There is no choice between the two. Stronger with one means stronger with the other . . . We are the bridge between the U.S. and Europe." This school of thought in British foreign policy is usually known as Atlanticism. In this analysis, Atlanticism went against Britain's European identity in the sense that it implied that Britain should embrace a united Europe through a special relationship with America, not vice versa.[14] My survey of the House of Commons debates on foreign policy suggests that Atlanticism was the default position for both Labour and Conservatives, the largest opposition party. Considering the way they lined up to vote in favor of the war in March 2003, the Tories were probably more gung-ho about the special relationship than was the Blair government. David Reynolds described this consensus in the following words: "Thirty years after withdrawing from east of Suez and joining the European Community, Britain still often behaves as if the Atlantic Ocean is narrower than the English Channel."[15]

The liberal internationalist idea that their state should help other people in the world, in anything from fighting terrorism to reducing global poverty, was shared between British and Canadian discourses. British liberal internationalism had expansive ideas about global governance and the betterment of the international society of states, which was in line with Britain's pivotal and well-connected role in the United Nations, the IMF, NATO, the Group of Eight (G8), and the Commonwealth.[16] In this discourse, the defining moment was Blair's famous speech to the Chicago Economic Council in April 1999. The speech justified NATO's air campaign over Kosovo in terms of a "new doctrine of the international community," which rejected U.N.–based principles of noninterference in favor of internationalism and humanitarianism. Blair subsequently fine-tuned his international vision, but the basic argument remained the same: An interdependent, globalized world blurred the distinction between a foreign policy driven by values and one driven by atomistic national interest. Similar views were expressed by numerous Labour and Liberal Democrat MPs, public servants from International Development, Foreign and Commonwealth Office, Defence, think tanks like the Foreign Policy Center, and across the British media.[17]

Numerous contradictions between British and American policies existed—on the Kyoto Protocol or on the International Criminal Court and Israel/Palestine, for examples—but the government argued that none of these put liberal internationalism and Atlanticism at loggerheads. The United States, as Blair argued in January 2003, was still a "force for good" overall:

> I am not surprised by anti-Americanism, but it is a foolish indulgence. For all their faults, and all nations have them, the U.S. are a force for good; they have liberal and democratic traditions of which any nation can be proud. Quite apart from that, it is massively in our self-interest to remain close allies. Bluntly there are not many countries who wouldn't wish for the same relationship as we have with the U.S., and that includes most of the ones critical of it in public.[18]

The framing was broad enough to target Atlanticists, liberals, realists, and moralists alike. By remaining close to the United States, Britain won the right to partake in the decisions concerning the entire planet, including, above all, the decision on who is good and who is evil. Like the bridge metaphor, the phrase "force of good" was coined in the first New Labour government to describe Britain, but eventually Blair came to use it to refer to the United States and, in fact, to the AASR—echoing the turn-of-the-twentieth century trans-Atlantic discourses of Anglo-Saxon moral superiority.[19] What made the leadership of Anglo-America appear so self-evident this time was not the racialized liberalism practiced by the fraternal association of the English-speaking peoples, but a set of universal liberal principles.

More so than Blair's general ruminations on global morality, what united liberal internationalism and Atlanticism was his government's framing of the WOT as a long-term process of reordering the world in a liberal image. Here, the enmity of Al-Qaeda was directly comparable to the enmity of contemporary rogue states as well as past totalitarian regimes. This narrative came close to the voices of neo-conservative America and predictably opened the government for comments and criticism coming from across the political spectrum. On the right, "liberal imperialists" argued that the United States should take cues from the most enlightened and, indeed, humanitarian aspects of Britain's imperial past.[20] On the left, "Marxist-feminists" critiqued the entire liberal-capitalist model, focusing the public's attention not only on the "root causes" of terrorism but also on the soak-the-poor effects of globalization, irresponsible corporate behavior, and assorted forms of misogyny. Being "good at force," from this point of view, was usually the opposite of being "a force for good."

In Canada, the default position on foreign policy was liberal internationalism, but it differed from Blair's version in important respects. For one, virtually all Canadian texts acknowledged Canada's mid-size capabilities, which implied that Ottawa should not be everywhere or do everything but that it should rather pursue "niche diplomacy" and other comparative advantages in the United Nations, NATO, G-8, the Asia Pacific Economic Cooperation, the Francophonie, and other international forums. So while not as pivotal as Britain, Canada was still confidently called itself the "principal" or at least "relevant" power, "integrator," "consensus-builder," "value-added nation," and "assertive globalist."[21] Then, much as in 1964–1965, Canadian liberal internationalism was premised on independence and sovereignty, once again defined as difference vis-à-vis the American Other. Good liberal internationalists in the ruling Liberal Party and the media understood that a consensus-building, peacekeeper Canada distinguished itself from the United States by default. Similarly, independence was always enabled by multilateralism, meaning cooperation with actors other than the United States. British liberal internationalism was silent on this subject, which is hardly surprising considering that its sovereignty was threatened by the EU, not the United States.

What is more surprising is the status of military force in Canadian liberal internationalism. Traditionally, this discourse had supported the diplomatic model for crisis management, set long ago under Pearson.[22] In this discourse, Canada was a "civilian" power that fought only as a last resort and only with its friends and allies, multilaterally, and within international law, like in Afghanistan. The Kosovo intervention was merely an exception that proves the rule. Among British liberal internationalists, this was a minority position represented by the nonmainstream Liberal Democrats, namely, their leader Charles Kennedy and foreign affairs spokesperson Michael Moore. Yet Canada, too, saw a liberal internationalism that came closer to Blair than to Pearson. Under the label "human security," this discourse was introduced in the Canadian debate by the former Liberal foreign affairs minister Lloyd Axworthy in the second half of the 1990s. It was Axworthy who, much like Blair, gave a speech during the Kosovo intervention that suggested that military force can be used to protect human security.[23]

This radically internationalist and humanitarian understanding of world affairs called for the broadening and deepening of international law and institutions, increased development assistance, and coalitions with like-minded international actors, such as Norway or the International Committee for the Red Cross. Axworthy retired from politics in 2000, but his ideas about Canada as a "soft" or even "moral" power permeated the debates in 2002–2003. On the one hand, Foreign Minister Billy Graham appropriated the successes of the international antilandmine treaty and the "responsibility to protect" (R2P), an idea that the international community should always act to protect civilian populations from large-scale harm. On the other, there were critics who pointed out gaps between moral rhetoric and reality, the latter being Canada's dwindling investment in various aspects of foreign policy.[24]

As in 1964–1965, the alternative to liberal internationalism was "continentalism." This discourse, typically associated with military and business establishments, specified a Northern America in which American dominance and Canadian independence were not mutually exclusive. Multilateralism was naïve or hypocritical: Had Canada been a "superpower," argued one *Globe and Mail* commentator on January, 16, 2003, it would have not "ignore[d] its national interest." Second, continentalism was the most logical option in light of the deep, broad, and persistent integration in commerce and defense between two counties, especially in the post-9/11 era.[25] And last, the best way to match the liberal internationalist rhetoric to the global reality, continentalists posited, would be to deepen the alliance with the United States. Like British Atlanticism, Canadian continentalism imagined foreign policy as a trade-off between autonomy and influence: Being close to America provides Canada with leverage that it otherwise does not have in the world. More ambitious continentalists argued in favor of the "big idea" or the "grand bargain," which meant the dismantling of the Canada–U.S. border and the creation of an EU-like "North American community of law."[26]

Liberal internationalism and continentalism offered different ideas on Canada's position on the Iraq War. For the former, an independent Canada bent on U.N. multilateralism needed to sit out the war. In accordance with the latter, Canada should act in unison with the southern neighbor. In a backward reading of history, the dominance of liberal internationalism in the Canadian parliament and the media prevented Canada's participation in Iraq, yet days before the Americans dropped their first bombs on Baghdad, Ottawa was officially undecided on the question of the war, while Canadian diplomats searched for a "compromise solution" that aimed to merely postpone the invasion until early April.[27] The following section will examine how different events in 2002–2003 brought pressure to bear upon the framings and counter-framings of America's Iraq policy.

WOT WAS HAPPENING TO AMERICA?

In early 2002, both Britain and Canada militarily supported U.S. operations in Afghanistan, which included combat against the Taliban resistance. British and Canadian contingents—respectively, 5,000 and 2,000 troops—were large by any measure. In February 2002, Ottawa pledged to basically double its original commitment, in line with the expansion of the mission of a new, NATO-based peacekeeping task force, which later became one of the arguments for nonparticipation in the Iraq invasion. Indeed, by dispatching extra troops to strengthen its Afghan mission in March 2003, the government at once tied its own hands and symbolically freed up U.S. troops for Iraq.[28] On its own, this decision was not difficult, although one major-general resigned in protest against what appeared to be a willful overstretch of Canadian Forces. Most of the world lined up behind the U.S. intervention in Afghanistan for two reasons. First, though the odious Taliban regime had collapsed, the Taliban rebels were thought to be protecting Osama bin-Laden, the Al-Qaeda leader and the mastermind behind the 9/11 attacks. Second, the entire international community agreed to help with the problems of Afghan state building and development, such as democratic elections or heroin trade. In both Britain and Canada, most of the opposition, the media and the surveyed public therefore backed this war, though not without an occasional apprehension. "Britain did not do very well in its first three Afghan wars," *The Times* wrote on May 12, "It remains to be seen whether . . . it will fare better in its fourth."

A toponym that sparked a major debate over this war, and the WOT more generally, related to a place not in Afghanistan but in the Caribbean. This was Guantanamo, America's Cuban navy base, where the U.S. military was "processing" certain "captives from the war" and "unlawful combatants." Once it was revealed that British citizens might be among these captives, questions ensued about the legality of detention and treatment under international law. The early debate centered on the 1949 Geneva Convention, the power of special military tribunals set up to impose sentences (specifically, whether America's death penalty could apply outside civilian oversight) as well as the historical and political status of Guantanamo in the United States. These American practices did not sit well with the discourses of British and Canadian identity. Participation in the U.S.–led mission in Afghanistan, argued *The Globe and*

Mail, could lead to a possible "conflict of interest" with international law.[29] In January 2003 came the news of torture (or "violent interrogation") and the outsourcing of torture through "rendition." *The Economist*, no enemy of the Bush administration, placed America's new counterterrorism measures in the history of failed homeland security projects, including the torture of Guy Fawkes, Britain's famous seventeenth-century terrorist. Even in the 1970s, the newsmagazine suggested, the British government never treated the Irish Republican Army (IRA) terrorists in such unacceptable manner.[30]

Canadians were even more critical, as evidenced in the growing media space granted to the International Red Cross, Amnesty International, and Human Rights Watch on the subject of the WOT. What made the U.S. case infinitely more difficult was the so-called Tarnak Farm Incident of April 18, when friendly fire from an American F-16 killed four and wounded eight Canadian soldiers during their training exercise near Kandahar. On the day of the incident, Bush had five public appearances but failed to communicate on the incident. The next day, *The Globe and Mail's* banner headline read: "A Nation's Grief Turns to Anger." Bush apologized later that day. On April 22, a columnist in the same newspaper later suggested that the incident "really wasn't much of a story. Yet it ended up embarrassing the President of the United States." The story in fact continued in the Canadian media for months. The first-cut media reports, always in search for poignant ironies, considered the semantics of the word "friendly fire," the absence of Canadian casualties in combat since Korea and, last but not least, Bush's "insensitivity," "reticence," "spite," and "indifference." Follow-up reports continued to question the U.S. military: Why were the pilots "part-timers"? Should they face a full military court martial? Why did they call one of them "psycho"? Were the bombs "authorized"? (The analyses went as far as counterfactuals in which a Canadian fighter plane dropped a bomb on U.S. troops: Would Canadian pilots be extradited?) As the story continued to unfold, in which Canada's status in the U.S. probe was read as that of a supplicant, not a respected friend and ally. The event correlated with a spike in the anti-American sentiments.[31]

By mid-2002, hitherto separate criticisms of U.S. counterterrorist campaign and of the Bush administration had begun to merge together. What greatly enabled this process was the publication of two U.S. security policy statements: the National Strategy for Homeland Security (NSHS), published in July, and the National Security Strategy of the United States of America (NSS), published two months later. The first document called for a greater securitization of the American homeland: tighter borders, expanded role for military forces, new secrecy laws, new special counterterrorist teams, and citizens' antiterrorist surveillance. The second made a moral case for unilateralism, free trade and free markets, preventive/preemptive war and the continued primacy of the United States in the world.[32] In no uncertain terms, the Bush administration thus identified American interests (law and order, multiculturalism and, above all, hegemony), American friends (such as Canada and Britain) and American enemies (Iraq, Iran, and other rogue states).

To most British and Canadian commentators, these documents, together with the publication of the leaked draft of "Patriot Act II," became the proof that the U.S. Other was distancing itself from its closest friends and allies. On the NSHS, typical was a comment in *The Scotsman* on July 17:

> The irony in the creation of a million or more state-registered informers is that the US could find itself being compared to Saddam Hussein's Iraq, Nicolae Ceaucescu's Romania, or the former East Germany, where millions of ordinary citizens were in the pay of its secret police, the Stasi.

On a freedom–security trade-off defined by the Bush administration, the British and Canadian Selves choose the side of freedom. A reduction of civil rights and legal protections, in this frame, constituted not only a short-term victory for the terrorist enemy but possibly a long-term one. As for the NSS, the doctrine of preemption, argued *The Independent* on November 9, was not only on "legally dubious" ground but was also stretching the limits of what is politically and morally legitimate, even under post-Kosovo definitions of legitimacy. Others suggested that the doctrine was hypocritical, while some (Canadians) added that American friendly fire incidents in Afghanistan might be related to the "shoot first, talk later" philosophy of the Bush administration and, within it, the mythical "neoconservatives."[33] The left-leaning media in both countries summoned the idea of the American empire, best exemplified in a series of historical comparisons published in *The Guardian*.[34]

Sympathetic critics downplayed the significance of the NSHS and NSS, arguing that the policy statements were temporary glitches in the American political system and that they would never be implemented as policy, much less redefine that familiar and still desirable American way of life. Supporters of America's security reforms, like the editors and commentators in Britain's *Daily Telegraph* or Canada's *National Post*, were in the minority. Critically, the British government, at least the prime minister, came out in support of U.S.

policy statements. Blair's speeches from the period implicitly linked America's new doctrine of preemption to his own 1999 interventionist doctrine, thus legitimizing the former in the eyes of at least some liberal internationalists in Britain and elsewhere.[35] For most liberal internationalists, especially those in Canada, no such link existed. Even those who believed that the use of force can be a force for good concluded that the Americans did not understand or did not care about human security or R2P; indeed, it was one thing to lead the international community and quite another to engage in imperialism.

With each subsequent piece of news—Guantanamo, torture, friendly fire, citizen surveillance, the NSS—the power of the discourses of identity that emphasized difference vis-à-vis the American Other increased and, in turn, raised doubts about U.S. leadership in the world. As the next section will show, Ottawa's framing of its position on the Iraq question in terms of independence, international law, and multiculturalism was effective precisely because it resonated with a more general attempt of the Canadian Self to distance itself from the American Other. Between the two national contexts, liberal internationalist framing served contrasting purposes—prowar in Britain, antiwar in Canada. Another difference was the Blair factor. Though no less shaken than Canadian continentalism by the unpopular words and deeds of the Bush administration, British Atlanticism was kept alive by the rhetorically skillful prime minister and his team.

THE MEANINGS OF FRIENDSHIP

The Iraq War has been such a divisive event in world politics that it has invoked comparison to both Suez and Vietnam, two bywords for the greatest Anglo-American imperial follies of the twentieth century.[36] A compare and contrast might serve as a quick review of the previous chapter in this book. Like in Vietnam, America's pursuit of "more flags" met with mixed results in the case of Iraq; here, too, most of American allies—traditional or potential, formal and informal—puzzled over the need for such costly endeavor. Washington did slightly better with its core English-speaking allies this time: Australia joined again, and Britain replaced the tiny New Zealand. Britain, as in Suez, coalesced with an ally to topple an Arab dictator by force. This time, the ally was the United States, not France, yet this did not make the British experience any less difficult. As for Canada, it merely replayed its Vietnam role: The Canadian military kept away from the shooting, while the government officials ambiguously pontificated on the wisdom of the war.

The talk of empire as well as Suez and Vietnam analogies were pervasive in the British and Canadian debates on the run-up to the Iraq War. The American war drums were hit in January 2002, when President Bush described Iraq as a member of the enemy club labeled the "Axis of Evil." The speech took many by surprise in Britain, even those who might have logically expected that the United States, as a "force for good," would clash with the forces of evil. Most commentators dismissed it as a new form of electoral pandering for midterm congressional elections.[37] Canadians were bemused that one of them, Bush's speechwriter David Frum, claimed the authorship of the phrase.[38] As the year progressed, the war drums become louder. Major U.S. troop movements in the Gulf were justified by self-defense. According to the Bush administration, Iraq possessed WMDs and was planning to put them to multiple uses, including punishing the rebel Kurds, coercing the Arab neighbors and, most alarmingly, arming Islamic terrorists groups such as Al-Qaeda. Preemptive military action, argued U.S. officials, was an imperative not only to disarm Iraq but also to replace Hussein's dictatorship with a democratic regime. On September 20, *The Times* suggested that the rationale for war should be "weapons, not regime," while, on October 4, *National Post* argued for "regime change, too."

The British decision to go to war was made as early as April 2002, at a meeting between Blair and Bush that took place at the latter's private ranch in Crawford, Texas. (What remains unclear at the time of this writing is whether the prime minister made British support conditional.) Blair reportedly stated after the meeting: "We're not going to be with the other Europeans. Our policy on Iraq has always been different to them. We've always been with the Americans on this one."[39] A taste of what was to come took place in June 2002, when the Anglo-American air campaign codenamed Operation Southern Focus began to destroy select ground targets in Iraq. As the campaign progressed, London and Washington harmonized their language on the Iraq problem more and more. Between August and February, Downing Street issued four much-publicized documents, which cumulatively built the case for war against Iraq: First it was the WMD threat, then regime change, then the potential cooperation with terrorist groups, and finally, the need to enforce the "will of the international community" (presumably by coercion from the ground, not simply from the air). Among the government representatives, Blair was the foremost hawk on Iraq. The prime minister framed the policy situation in the language of liberal internationalism, which gave legitimacy to any anti-Iraq policy aimed at removing Hussein from office.[40] And when pressed about the inherent selectivity of the doctrine of preemptive interventionism, Blair would give a response he successfully used in the debates on the Kosovo intervention in 1999—"when you can, you should."[41]

When he could, Blair also gave a specifically Atlanticist twist to his liberal internationalist frames—the notion of shared responsibility. In a liberal internationalist reading, shared responsibility was consistent with the idea of Britain as a "pivotal partner" in the world, but in an Atlanticist reading it meant "influence" in Washington. In the prime minister's own words: "I will tell you that we must stand close to America. If we don't, we will lose our influence to shape what they do."[42] This idea was expressed by virtually every member of the Blair government, including top ministers as well as national security advisor David Manning, chief of staff Jonathan Powell, and Blair's spinners Alastair Campbell and Tom Kelly. The media backed the latter frame, too. For example, *The Observer* observed on February 2, 2003, that "Blair knows that Bush is creating the New World Order. And Blair knows that, in order to be of it, you have to be in it." His contemporaries have given Blair much credit for persuading his audiences about Britain's shared responsibility, yet the idea was already ingrained among the British elites.[43] What Blair accomplished was the blending of liberal internationalist and Atlanticist definitions of shared responsibility, such that being pivotal to the progress of the world became synonymous with being pivotal to the progress of the Bush administration.

The problem in this framing was its misfit with U.S. unilateralism, which was often expressed as a neo-conservative principle. Like their Canadian counterparts, British liberal internationalists were believers in the U.N. process or, at the very least, in large international coalitions with claims to collective legitimacy. The White House was so contemptuous of this process that the long search for U.N. resolutions, which started in September 2002, was in fact led by the British government. Without London, Washington would have failed in getting even the first (or "initial") U.N. Security Council resolution against Iraq on November 9—the famous resolution 1441. The decision gave Hussein one "final opportunity" to let U.N. weapons inspectors into Iraq and surrender WMDs. Resolution 1441 was better than no resolution, but it was too ambiguous on whether Hussein's noncompliance would imply automatic war. And so, the British diplomats were sent to work again and stopped only days before the invasion. In January, Blair was still confident that U.N. authorization was forthcoming. An unnamed government minister told the press: "The government's policy can be summed up in two words—United Nations.

Stick to the United Nations and there will be less trouble, or even no trouble at all."[44]

The same idea was shared, and sometimes publicly expressed, by several cabinet ministers. In mid-August, the British press reported on a "cabinet rift" on Iraq between majority hawks and minority doves, the latter defined by their pro–U.N. stance, but not necessarily pacifism.[45] As for Labour itself, it was dovish: In October, the annual party conference endorsed a resolution on the need to follow the U.N. route with regards to Iraq. In the British parliament, the pro–U.N. position was often an antiwar position. As such, it was articulated by the Liberal Democrats and some "rogue" elements in Labour, among the Tories, and by the Scottish and Welsh nationalists. Indeed, what significantly defused the Iraq debate in the House of Commons was the unflinching Atlanticism of the Conservative Party, whose leader Iain Duncan Smith was as gung-ho to see Hussein go as anyone in Washington. For Blair, notes Dan Keohane, this meant a fortuitous "buffer of about 20–25 percent for his Iraq policy."[46]

As skilled as Blair was in linking Atlanticism and liberal internationalism together, the war was still a hard sell to some of his audiences. In September, Labour split over a parliamentary motion considering Britain's involvement in a possible military conflict against Hussein's Iraq. On March 17, the day before the House of Commons vote on the war, leader of the chamber Robin Cook resigned, prompting what was perhaps the first standing ovation in Westminster history. In one of the most effective counterframing moves, Cook turned Blair's "when you can, you should" argument against the idea of a well-armed, threatening Iraq: "Ironically, it is only because Iraq's military forces are so weak that we can even contemplate its invasion."[47] And on the fateful parliamentary vote on March 18, more than a third of MPs from Blair's own party defied him by voting in favor of an antiwar amendment, an event Andrew Gamble described as the "largest rebellion in the history of the Labour party."[48] The defiance was meant to be symbolic. In the subsequent prowar motion, the majority of rebellious backbenchers abstained, giving it a pass.

In his defense of the war vote, Blair declared that "partners are not servants, but neither are they rivals." The statement arose in the contexts of the accusations that the prime minister was the "U.S. ambassador to the world," "Bush's Foreign Minister," and, least charitably, Bush's "poodle." Blair dismissed these criticisms using various frames, but most typically he spoke of the commonality of the Anglo-American positions on Iraq. In an interview to *The Guardian* on March 1, he retorted: "It's worse than you think. I believe in it. I am truly committed to dealing with this irrespective of the position of America."[49] Biographers of Blair—as well as the official government inquiries—have so far bought this argument, which tends to metaphorically peg the prime minister as a watchdog rather than a lap dog.[50] Part of the evidence no doubt lies in the zeal with which he ensured Britain's overcommitment to Iraq. Reportedly, the idea of backing the United States nonmilitarily was presented to Blair "six or seven" times in the run-up to the war, including by Bush (in private) and Rumsfeld (in public) in March.[51] Blair rejected all proposals, explaining that his views on military interventions were shaped by values and convictions, not short-term politics. Notably, the prime minister said the same thing about each of Britain's five interventions during his rule—two in Iraq and one each in Sierra Leone, Kosovo, and Afghanistan.

Timothy Dunne has argued that the Iraq War "reaffirmed the vice-like grip of Atlanticism on Britain's identity." Dunne also offered a counterfactual:

> Had key ministers in the UK government believed in internationalism, then, at a minimum, it would have made its support for the United States conditional upon a consensus in the Security Council as well as upon indicators of significant support from other multilateral institutions.[52]

In my interpretation of the British debate on Iraq, key ministers—including, importantly, the second-in-command Brown[53]—did in fact believe in internationalism or at least expressed these beliefs in front of various audiences. If anything, liberal internationalism was more salient than Atlanticism. The "vice-like grip of Atlanticism" obtained only when the Blair government merged the two discursive positions. Indeed, the NSS-style argument that the post–9/11 world demanded considerable flexibility over nineteenth-century laws and institutions of the international community was also Blair's. In this analysis, the prime minister was spectacularly successful in reframing the unpopular American doctrine of preemption as the more familiar doctrine of the international community, which he introduced in 1999. Conversely, what was missing for the critics were the counterframes, which would have pointed out to, as Dunne called it, the "fundamental incompatibility between Atlanticism and internationalism."[54]

In the Canadian debate, too, there were attempts to frame the Iraq intervention in liberal internationalist terms. On October 4, a *National Post* columnist thus explained the need to oust Hussein: "Immanuel Kant, William Gladstone and Woodrow Wilson would have approved. So should we.

So should progressives everywhere." There were also attempts to frame the intervention Blair-style, as a shared responsibility. Consider a passage from a foreign affairs column in *The Globe and Mail* on November 15:

> Jean Chrétien told an interviewer that Western arrogance helped to bring on the terrorist attacks. If only we stopped abusing the poor, he suggested, such attacks might abate. Contrast that position to Tony Blair's; the British Prime Minister made it plain from the start that his country would be in the front lines against terror—not just because of its friendship with the United States, but because Britons themselves were at risk.

In contrast to the British case, the attempt to introduce the discourse of liberation to Canada's Iraq intervention debate was a flop. Some corners of the Canadian media were prowar, notably *National Post*, but the majority were not.[55] More typically, the commentators and editorials expressed hope that the military confrontation would be avoided and, more ideally, that Canadian diplomats would find a U.N. route to peace, like in Suez. "The last time the world faced a crisis like this, a Canadian found a way out," wrote a *Maclean's* columnist on February, 24, 2003. In the parliament, the prowar position was held by the right-of-center Canadian Alliance. The party leader Stephen Harper, together with Stockwell Day, Peter McKay, and Jason Kenney, vociferously criticized the Chrétien government on Iraq, first for dithering and then for turning against Canada's "traditional and historical allies." The pattern of referencing of Canada's Anglosphere identity reached a dubious height in Harper's House of Commons statement on March 20. As the Canadian media later discovered, instead of composing yet another statement on the subject of the Iraq War, Harper's speechwriters simply copied an old speech—one Australian Prime Minister John Howard gave to his parliament two days earlier.[56]

To make his points, Harper could have just repeated the select passages from Blair's House of Common statement on March 18. That particular mixture of British Atlanticism and liberal internationalism would have probably resonated better in the Canadian context. And yet, any attempt to fix Canada as a progressive interventionist or an Anglosphere shareholder would have probably failed before the Canadian audiences. Like in the Vietnam case, the liberal internationalist discourse in the Canadian foreign policy debate was made and remade primarily in relation to the present-day United States, not the negative and distant Others in Asia or in the international past. In

2002–2003, this discourse was indeed solidified through the dominant inter-pretations of America's conduct in the WOT. Arguably, the opportunity for a discursive coalition between human security talk and continentalism was probably lost in September 2002, with the publication of the NSS. With every subsequent word and deed toward the rest of the world, the Bush administra-tion weakened the continentalist camp in Canada and, conversely, strength-ened the anti-Americanist one.

In light of this dynamics between identity and reality, it is unlikely that any Canadian politician or pundit could have successfully argued, like Blair did in Britain, that the United States had a right to impose the "will of the international community" in Iraq. Axworthy, whose views on humanitarian military interventionism in 1999 mirrored Blair's, took a rather pacific stance on Iraq in September by writing an article entitled "Make Sense, Not War."[57] Michael Ignatieff, then a Harvard professor whom the Canadian media always included in their top "who's who" lists, in fact argued in favor of liberal wars, yet his contributions to the Iraq debate were pitched to American, not Cana-dian audiences.[58] But even if a liberal-interventionist Axworthy or a liberal-imperialist Ignatieff had been a cabinet minister, it is far from certain that Canada would have joined the U.S.–led coalition of the willing.

Chrétien made Canada's official position clear only days before the inva-sion, but various types of evidence suggests that the Canadian government decided to sit out the Iraq war as early as February 2002, when they tied their hands with a renewed military commitment to Afghanistan. In parliamentary debates and other public engagements, most Liberals, including most cabinet ministers, openly expressed their reservations about the war. Finance Min-ister John Manley and former Finance Minister Paul Martin, who acted as the prime-minister-in-waiting at the time, occasionally suggested that all op-tions were open. In reality, the only pro-American hawk was defense minister John McCallum.[59] In the rest of the House of Commons, MPs from the three smaller opposition parties followed the lead of the Liberal majority; in gen-eral, the centrist Progressives Conservatives were more reserved, while the New Democrats and the nominally separatist Bloc Québécois were more anti-American than the ruling party.[60]

Canada's nonparticipation in Iraq was made possible though a mixture of liberal internationalist and anti-American frames. As in the British con-texts, the most common were diagnostic and prognostic frames, according to which the invasion was either unnecessary, given the absence of evidence on the WMDs, or premature, given the absence of a "war resolution" from the U.N. Security Council. But the most effective frames were identity claims with regards to the U.S. Other. Much like their colleagues from the two left-leaning opposition parties, some liberal MPs argued that the cross-border differences were unbridgeable on Iraq. For Liberal MPs like Brent St. Denis, John Cannis, Janko Peric, and Yvon Charbonneau, Canadian policy on Iraq was not a function of the U.N. involvement, but of the degree of Washington's unilateralism, hypocrisy, and bullying. In this line of argumentation, Canadian independence sometimes became a function of outright defiance of the American neighbor. Using some very undiplomatic language, Carolyn Parish and Natural Resources Minister Herb Dhaliwal expressed Canadian foreign policy against Bush and even Americans in general.[61]

Other Liberals, especially cabinet ministers and those in the parliamentary foreign relations committee, were more careful with their identity frames. Foreign Minister Graham was the most diplomatic. In one parliamentary speech, he quoted Bush's 2003 State of the Union address, in which the president stated that the American government responds to the American people, not to other states. Here, Graham underscored a functional similarity: "Canadians expect no less from their government. And why would Americans expect less of us than they expect of themselves?"[62] Two weeks later, he claimed alliance and friendship:

> I think we should be where we are, have our policy, which is to support the multilateral system with good arguments and to say to them, "We're staying put. And you're better to have an ally and friend that debates frankly than to have someone who says yes, sir."[63]

In both statements, Graham articulated Canada as independent and equal to the United States. By implication, Ottawa could not only make its own policy (or nonpolicy), but it could also deliberate, disagree, and, ultimately, stay the course in the face of the superpower pressure. Herein lays an important theoretical lesson. In Britain, claims of similarity and friendship with the United States led to claims of shared responsibility and, ultimately, legitimized British support of the Bush administration. In Canada, the same claims legitimized distancing from Washington. The fact that they were both meaningful to their respective audiences shows why it is important to account for the discursive topographies in specific national-historical contexts first before moving to analyze the ways in which foreign policy elites argue to make or break the fit between identity and reality. In substantive terms, this analysis suggests that a combination of liberal internationalism and anti-Americanism was so strong an undercurrent that even a Blair would have not been able to send Canada to the war in Iraq.

ASYMMETRIC INTERDEPENDENCE
AND THE HOLMES PARADOX

The previous chapter described Canadian policy on the Vietnam War escalation as ambiguous. The same can be said about Canadian policy in the run-up to the Iraq War.

While Ottawa consistently supported the U.S. desire to disarm Iraq, its prime minister questioned the American conduct of the WOT, preemption, regime change, and even the mainstream theories on the causes of Islamic terrorism. Similarly, the Canadian government valiantly committed to Afghanistan yet gave somewhat half-hearted blessings to their allies in Iraq once the shooting started.[64] Like in the Vietnam case, Canadian ambiguities were related to the domestic politics on federal-provincial and Quebec versus the rest of Canada dimensions. For one, the government's pandering to the antiwar and anti-American sentiments probably helped the Liberal Party of Quebec to win the provincial election in April 2003.[65] And yet, much as in the Vietnam era, the primary source of the ambiguity in Canadian foreign policy was the tension between English Canada and the American Other. What the foreign minister Martin identified in 1964–1965 as the "problem of separate and distinct identity" still existed sixty years later.

Like then, this problem needed not necessarily be solved. Consider a prowar argument that was occasionally advanced by the Canadian Alliance MPs, business groups, some academics, and the premiers of Alberta and Ontario. By taking part in the U.S.-led coalition of the willing, in this view, Ottawa would protect its valuable (nearly) million-dollars-a-minute trade with America. Conversely, by saying no the United States over Iraq, Ottawa was risking punishment and thus jeopardizing Canada's prosperity.[66] This line of reasoning, in fact, was perfectly in line with a liberal IR perspective on complex interdependence, a feature of the global society in which each state is dependent on other states. According to Robert Keohane and Joseph Nye, power relations among states are differentiated by resource asymmetries.[67] In this model, the Canada–U.S. dyad stands as a paradigmatic case of asymmetric interdependence, whereby Canada is highly vulnerable to U.S. pressure. Asymmetries exist in defense, justice, and other areas, but liberal theories of interdependence typically focus on commerce.[68] Here is how Chrétien described Northern America in his speech to the Chicago Council on Foreign Relations on February 13, 2003:

> In 2000, Canada bought more U.S. goods than all 15 countries of the European Union combined and three times as much as Japan. Thirty-eight U.S. states count Canada as their largest export market, including the state of Illinois. In turn, Canada exports more to Illinois alone than it does to the entire European Union.
>
> Energy security is fundamental to American prosperity. We supply the U.S. with 94 percent of your natural gas imports. Close to 100 percent of your electricity imports. And 35 percent of uranium for nuclear power generation.
>
> In 2002, Canada supplied the U.S. with 17 percent of its imported crude and refined oil products—more than any other foreign supplier, including Saudi Arabia. Canada's oil sands contain 2.5 trillion barrels of oil, of which 315 billion barrels are recoverable with current technology. This surpasses the oil reserves of Saudi Arabia.

As important as Canada was to the United States, the United States was significantly more important to Canada. To capture the fundamentally asymmetric nature of the Canada–U.S. relationship, Chrétien could have also mentioned that 85 percent of Canadian trade went south, while 25 percent of U.S. trade went north; and that about 35 percent of Canada's GDP was purchased by the Americans, while less than 3 percent of U.S. GDP was bought by Canadians. Indeed, the prime minister could have said that Canada was so dependent on its neighbor that the United States was probably more important to the Canadian economy than any single actor in Canada itself, including its government. If liberals are correct about the link between asymmetries in interdependence and exploitative bargaining, on Iraq, the United States could have used or threaten to use economic pressure to bring Canada in line. The Economist seemed to recognize this potentiality on March 15, 2003: "How could the superpower's neighbour and biggest trading partner be against?"

In the end, Canada was against and the American economic pressure or punishment never materialized.[69] The Bush administrations, as well as some members of Congress, duly expressed their disappointment over Ottawa's decision to sit out the war, but the Congressional cafeteria never renamed Canadian bacon "freedom bacon," as it did with French fries. Much as in the case of

New Zealand's unexpected diffidence over nuclear cooperation in 1985–1986, the United States let its asymmetrically interdependent partner off the hook. The U.S–Canada relationship may indeed be a poster case for liberal theories of complex interdependence, yet these specific outcomes can be better explained by a constructivist perspective, according to which interdependence and collective identity are self-reinforcing.[70] Collective identity does not imply harmony. Security communities like the Canada–U.S. relationship or the Anglosphere community are at once characterized by cooperation as well as by conflict, such as border and trade disputes or the unexpected defections from a seemingly common cause. Yet, unlike in other interstate relations, conflict in security communities is subjected to certain rules that prevent it from spiraling out of control. These range from highly legalized rules international arbitration, as in free trade agreements, to practices such as bargaining strategies ("will help in Afghanistan instead"), apologies ("we are overstretched") or rebranding (for example, "friend, not an ally").

Here we come back to practices, which can be defined as social structures inscribed in mind and body that drive social action. As a number of constructivists have pointed out, identities and practices are mutually constituted and self-reinforcing: Who we are shapes what we do, while what we do shapes who we are.[71] On the basis of the evidence presented in the previous chapter, I can confirm that practices need not be institutionalized or even clearly articulated in intergovernmental deliberations. In the U.S.–Canadian interactions over Vietnam and Iraq, the most effective security community-sustaining practices are transgovernmental, intermestic, transnational, and civilizational. Following Ted Hopf, I might even add that practices are the most effective in keeping the community together once they had evolved into *habits*, those unreflective responses to the world that guide most human action most of the time.[72] From this perspective, every security community is simultaneously a power hierarchy, but the more its collective identity is enacted through representations, practices, or habits, the lower the likelihood that the more powerful side will pressure, punish, or otherwise use the extant asymmetries to its advantage.

Habits of cooperation might explain why the United States was so lenient to Canada's defection from the coalition of the willing. Writing during the Vietnam War, no high point of Canada–U.S. harmony, Holmes observed what he called a "paradox":

Canada, though closest of the allies to the United States in geography and culture, has a record of more independent thought and action than more distant allies. So unquestioned is the mutual commitment of the North American partners that Canadians often feel more assured in their diplomacy than, say, Australia or Germany.[73]

Assurance is certainly the correct word to describe the way in which the government dismissed its critics, who argued that nonparticipation in Iraq would lead to an economic punishment by the United States.[74] A policy situation similar to this one, in fact, took place during the escalation of the Vietnam conflict. After years of laborious negotiation, the two countries were on the verge of signing a "historic" agreement on the integration of their automotive industries; indeed, the "Auto Pact" was to Northern America what the European Coal and Steel Community was to the EU. The two interactions occurred in parallel, yet resentment over the Canadian position on Vietnam never compelled the Johnson administration to use the pact as a bargaining chip or a punitive tool.[75] As in 2003, in 1965, too, Canada's dependence on the U.S. economy had no direct bearing on the continuity and change in U.S.–Canadian security cooperation.

The "Holmes paradox" has been subject to two mutually inclusive explanations, good management and the invisibility hypothesis. According to the first, Canada has been one of the most consistently successful foreign lobbies in U.S. history: "Canadian leaders have a narrow margin of manoeuvre, that they utilized with extraordinary skill," wrote Henry Kissinger in his memoirs.[76] According to the second explanation, rewards and punishments need visible targets, but, as far as Washington is concerned, Canada tends to be invisible.[77] Prime facie, this was true in June 2003, when one official report on the Iraq war recognized the contribution of the Canadian air force. On June 24, *The Globe and Mail* published an editorial entitled "War? What War?" Later, Washington admitted that it had confused Canada's participation in America's two wars.[78]

Both of these explanations are consistent with aforementioned constructivist teachings. Countless practices and habits of Canada–U.S. cooperation that have taken place at the intergovernment, transgovernmental, and intermestic levels for decades have watered down America's proclivity for preemptive, punitive, and other forms of coercion, exploitative bargaining, and other Hobbesian policies. Even policies associated with face-saving are relatively absent from the American behavior in the Northern American security community. It is important to note that from the perspective of practices and habits, these absences need not be a function of collective identity, but rather of "commonsensical" and "self-evident" interactions. In this sense, the Canadian ally might be effective and/or invisible in Washington not because Canada is an extension of the American Self, like Ohio or Oklahoma, but because of the long, uninterrupted history of peaceful practices and habits. After all, the Canada–U.S. special relationship evolved over time, but it never experienced a crisis comparable to the one that disrupted the AASR in Suez. Constructivist hypotheses on the force of practices and habits in security communities need further study, and to that end I propose that international peace might be the strongest in the communities once structured by representations and inarticulate know-how of shared racial and postracial origins.

To do justice to this proposition, one would of course have to reverse the claim made in this book and examine the ways in which the practices and habit of cooperation among English-speaking peoples have maintained a racialized identity in world politics. The evaluation of this proposition would require a different theoretical framework and another book. (As I posited in the introductory chapter, in the constructivist and post-Humean ontology of causation, discourses and practices are mutually constituted or caused, yet must draw a line between what we are trying to explain and what explains it.) For now, we could suggest that the Holmes paradox is a testament to the power of collective identity, rather some mind-bending principle that can be grappled with but never resolved. Canadians—like Australians in fact, though not always like Germans—feel more assured in their diplomacy vis-à-vis the United States because their powerful neighbor has long treated them as mostly friends and partners, as opposed to rivals, enemies, barbarians, savages, or some other negative and distant Other.

The same dynamics operate in the rest of the Anglosphere core, and not just among old Commonwealth nations.[79] In the middle years of the twentieth century, the AASR emerged as security and economic hierarchy, but this process occurred in the context of discourses, practices, and habits of collective identity. Hence, as in the Canada–U.S. case, Britain yields authority to the United States, which, in turn, does not abuse its power over Britain. For example, despite repeated U.S. requests for British military or at least political assistance during the Vietnam War, London never sent even a "platoon of bagpipers," as Johnson once memorably put it.[80] The disagreement did not lead to strained relations. Washington continued to help London in nuclear research and defense as well as by supporting Britain's beleaguered pound. Security-economy linkages did play a role,[81] but, as I have suggested in Chapter 3, strategic bargaining always and by necessity takes place in a social contexts shot through with intersubjective meanings. In this sense, Britain and Canada are neither "dependencies," "satellites" of the American empire, nor are their leaders "poodles" or "lap dogs" of American presidents but are co-owners of a community—indeed, usually known as the "international community"— that happens to be centered on Washington.

In the next chapter, I will consider how collective identity operated in the AASR during the Suez crisis, which stands out as a single case in which the United States directly used economic coercion against another core Anglosphere friend and ally. Here, a brief epilogue to the Iraq War is in order. Once the U.S.–led invasion force swiftly made its way to Baghdad, the public opinion across in many countries swung in favor of the war. As the invasion force found no WMDs and as it became evident that the problems of the occupation in Iraq would be many times greater than those in Afghanistan, the support for the war dissipated, equally swiftly. Official inquiries and related public spectacles ensued. Already by the mid-2000s, even top government experts agreed that the war was unnecessary or that it was counterproductive to the WOT.[82] Bush was reelected in 2004, but many critics argued that Iraq already made him the worst president in American history. Chrétien and Blair were both forced out of office by the members of their political parties, in 2003 and 2005, respectively. Both departures were framed by Iraq, and in this picture only Chrétien looked good.

As in the historical cases examined in the previous chapters, as well as in the case of the Iraq War, the Anglosphere community arose in both unity and discord, within and across states, nations, and societies. Most obviously, the war produced the Anglosphere through the way American, British, and Australian forces jointly forced their way into Iraq in March 2003. Other countries were willing to send their soldiers to fight, yet the Anglos bore the brunt of warfare—precisely as in Afghanistan. These militarized images of the Anglosphere alliances, forged against the wishes of the old imperial rivals (remember the "non-nein-nyet" coalition in Iraq?) inspired more than a few Anglophone conservatives and neoconservative thinkers to revisit the idea of Greater Britain. The term *Anglosphere* emerged in this context. James C. Bennett, the American entrepreneur and intellectual, wrote two books on the Anglosphere, arguing that revolutionary developments in communication and transportation had finally made it possible for globe-spanning Anglophone societies to establish a "network commonwealth" of liberal democracy, free trade, and labor movement.[83] The British historian Robert Conquest proposed—dreamily, he admitted—a "political association" of English-speaking states.[84] These proposals merely picked up where Churchill, Chamberlain, and Carnegie left off, yet they intrigued serious readers, starting with *The Economist*.[85] As with the term *Greater Britain* in the 1900s, the use of the term *Anglosphere* might have passed its high mark in the 2000s, but what is remarkable is a certain continuity and persistence of this discourse:

> Grandiose fantasies of Anglo-Saxon unity and superiority continue to exert their mesmeric power, shaping visions of a future world order, and drawing people back into the dangerous orbit of empire.[86]

6 THE ANGLOSPHERE AND ITS LIMITS

All the people like us are We/And every one else is They.
—**Rudyard Kipling, "We and They," 1919**

Questions of identity may insinuate their way into all forms of politics, but all forms of politics are not about questions of identity.
—**Gearóid Ó Tuathail,**
"Dissident IR and the Identity Politics Narrative," (1996)

During the past three centuries the spread of the English-speaking peoples over the world's waste spaces has been not only the most striking feature in the world's history, but also the event of all others most far-reaching in its effects and its importance.
—**Theodore Roosevelt, *The Winning of the West*, Vol.1 (1889)**

RUDYARD KIPLING'S EARLY-TWENTIETH-CENTURY poetical reflections on a binary logic to cultural, civilizational, and imperial interactions capture the politics of identity, which has been the conceptual and theoretical foundation of this genealogy. We–they dynamics have indeed been borne out in each of the preceding chapters, even if my story is more complicated than simple Anglos-versus-the rest binarizations would allow. I have indeed argued that the Anglosphere came into existence through a variety of social and political inclusions and exclusions on multiple levels of analysis—at home, abroad, and in-between. The special relationships that crisscross the putative core of this community were once based on claims of shared Anglo-Saxonism, while today they rest primarily on claims of liberal internationalism.

As identity alone does not and cannot capture all relevant questions and answers in the study of world politics, I will now relate my Anglosphere story back to IR, both theoretically and substantively. My goal in this chapter is to clarify and elaborate the main strengths and weaknesses of my arguments, findings, and puzzles. I will begin with a short overview of the theoretical argument made in the book and then move on to engage select IR theories on hegemony, appeasement, balancing, the Kantian peace, security communities, hierarchy, empire, networks, and power. Here, I will evaluate various knowledge claims, which may be regarded as alternative, complementary, or otherwise relevant to the story told in previous chapters. Where appropriate, I will also make a note of further research areas and, indeed, policy relevance of my findings. The very last section will include a brief reflection on the future of the Anglosphere.

HISTORICAL FITS AND MISFITS

This genealogy has made a case that the history of the Anglosphere cannot be understood without a reference to the legacies and shifts in Self–Other relations inside and outside the territorial boundaries of its five core states. The theoretical framework developed in this book to explain the impact of these legacies and shifts on international conflict/cooperation has proven useful, at least on balance. According to the main proposition, foreign policy was expected to follow the debates that fit between the meanings of state/national identity and experienced reality. The proposition is borne out in the majority of case studies. First I found that British foreign policy toward the United States twice changed because its expression did not fit the dominant discourse of identity—once in each of the two Venezuela crises (Chapter 2). These two misfits were productive of a long-term transformation in which the main rival evolved into a close cousin and, in some contexts, the most reliable strategic partner. With each new international event, the Anglo-American rapprochement strengthened. In supporting Britain's military campaign against the Boers, however, the U.S. government faced a different misfit—this time between America's anti-imperialist, Anglophobic identity on the one hand and Washington's benevolent neutrality toward London on the other hand.

In the case of ANZUS (Chapter 3), I discovered that the events in Korea and Malaya greatly helped the Australian and New Zealand governments deal with an apparent misfit of joining an alliance without Britain. The motherland was excluded only after Australian and New Zealand elites successfully convinced their audiences—and some American ones—that British exclusion would be only nominal and that all four English-speaking powers would anyway form a common front against any type of Asian expansionism. In the Suez crisis (Chapter 4), it was Canada who experienced a major misfit between its dominant Britishness and the government's decision to side against Britain. To legitimate its policy, the government Britain's own action as un-British—which proved fitting only once the "Suez Tories" in London fell from grace. Conversely, the Australian decision to unconditionally support the Eden government went down in history as a case of "blind loyalty." During the escalation of the Vietnam War in 1964–1965, Australian and Canadian policies both resonated with their mainstream discourses of identity. Both states saw each other as sovereign and independent, but while the Australian government defined independence as the ability to help America first and Britain second, its Canadian counterpart framed independence as uniqueness and, more explicitly, difference vis-à-vis the United States. In Iraq (Chapter 5), Britain's decision to participate in the U.S.–led "coalition of the willing" did not obviously resonate with the dominant discourses of Britishness at home, but the government framed its policy in line with two of them—liberal internationalism and Atlanticism. In Canada, the same foreign policy debate and the decision to sit out the war served to confirm the dominance of liberal internationalism and anti-Americanism.

The majority of the case studies support the proposition on the productive role of the fit between identity and reality. According to the framework developed in Chapter 1, debates among the foreign policy elites were expected to shift policy in the face of a rhetorically demonstrable misfit. This occurred in the British debates in Venezuela I and Venezuela II, as well as with the United States in Venezuela I. Anomalously for my proposition, policy failed to shift in spite of the demonstrable misfit in three as well: the United States in the South African War, Canada in Suez, and Britain in Iraq. In each of these three cases, the government stood its policy ground against significant opposition across their country's foreign policy elite and wider society. In each case, hitherto new frames were deployed to legitimate the policy choice. U.S. support of Britain against the Boers held in part because its proponents framed it in terms of a racialized hierarchy in which British Anglo-Saxons by evolutionary necessity bested South African Boers.

In Suez, the St. Laurent government argued the leaders of Canada's motherland(s) were mistaken but essentially redeemable. The attempted framing of Canada as an independent country and a good international citizen fell flat because it implied that the country was no longer British, which is what most Canadian audiences rejected. And, in Iraq, Britain's choice to participate in the war held against all kinds of demonstrated contradictions, mainly because Prime Minister Blair and his closest team managed to sell the idea of the Anglo-American moral legitimacy to the most important audiences—the cabinet, Labour, Parliament, and a significant section of the British media.

These anomalous cases demonstrate various limitations of my theoretical framework but also suggest areas for further theorization of identity, arguing, and foreign policy. One proposition is that the more unified the elite, the more authoritative their ability to promote their ideas and actions. The next theoretical step would be to refine the framework such that it includes more situational, institutional, and social factors that enable and encumber foreign policy debates that lead to international conflict/cooperation.[1]

The theoretical and methodological framework has been useful in shedding light on the rise of the Anglosphere in international relations. The Anglo-American "great rapprochement" was largely a product of Anglo-Saxonism, a profoundly racialized discourse of identity that called for peace and cooperation between the American and British empires. In making the rapprochement possible, Anglo-Saxonism also influenced several subsequent developments in international conflict/cooperation, thus recasting history in ways that are still felt today. Most important among the consequences was the slow and unsteady growth of the AASR. In the first three decades of the twentieth century, relations between two English-speaking empires oscillated between close friendship and occasional rivalry. But what prevented Britain and the United States from choosing the opposite sides in World War I were fin-de-siècle developments, namely, the construction of Hun Germany.

As I said in the introductory chapter, the story of the rise of the English-speaking peoples to global dominance has often been told through various liberal "progress" narratives—rags-to-riches, revolution-to-rapprochement, autocracy-to-democracy, racism-to-multiculturalism, colony-to-nation, or imperial-war-to-international-law. Some of the narratives can be found in my book, too, particularly those on the death of the British Empire and the rise of the politics of cultural recognition and redistribution in Britain and Canada. To the extent that these narratives are attentive to mutual contradictions and to the fact that all social systems are open, progress narratives can indeed be helpful in showing how the English-speaking peoples emerged from the discourses, practices, and habits based on the idea of race as a biological fact and then evolved into an antiracist community. We could also suggest that this emergence was shaped by a misfit between liberal identities and illiberal realities. In late nineteenth-century Britain and the United States, illiberal realities such as the dispossession of indigenous and colonial populations, racial segregation, or racist immigration controls were explained away as philosophical "dilemmas"—freedom versus order, liberty versus empire, or ethics versus evolution. As the abstractions become crises of political authority, these dilemmas were resolved, one by one, in favor of the liberal commitment to equality and inclusion of all people, not just certain white propertied men. The human rights revolution that in the mid-twentieth century—a product of decolonization, civil rights movements, second wave feminism, and other forces—in fact overturned the ideas of natural inequality on a global scale. Today, all core Anglosphere states and societies define their liberal identities, not simply against present authoritarian Others but also against their own racial past.[2]

The mainstreaming of antiracism—the introduction of legislative, political, and other measures against racism—has had a paradoxical effect of reifying racialized structures of meaning. Instead of reducing race talk, national census-style racial categories have contributed to it, in addition to hardening the ongoing confusions over the race/ethnicity distinction. The political elites around in newly constituted liberal-multicultural Anglosphere democracies embraced cultural diversity, but not so tightly as to irrevocably upset the "traditional" cultural hierarchy, which has long kept the descendants of historical Anglo-Saxons on the very top. As critics of liberalism pointed out, half a century of national and international antiracism has not radically changed the structures and processes of separation, inequality, privilege, and domination established in the bygone age of biological races, formal empires, and scientific racisms. Analytical constructs such as "cultural racism," "differential racism," "postbiological neoracism," "raceless racism," and "racism without races" have been recently developed precisely for the study of these unhappy continuities.[3]

Whether, or to what extent, these "new" racialized discourses, practices, and habits are brought to bear on the foreign policy elites in the English-speaking world is a question that requires theoretical refinement and further research. My discourse analysis of British and Canadian identities in 2002–2003 suggested that racialized meanings might have been at play in government-sponsored efforts to reframe official multiculturalisms in terms of "shared citizenship" and "civic values" or "managed migration." The idea that multiculturalism should be predicated on individualism and secularism resonated with the audiences, reinforcing Islamophobia and related worries about minority segregation, "disloyalty," and "unrest."[4] What did not resonate with the public was Chrétien's offhand remark that terrorism might have "root causes." Instead of generating a debate on the legacies of empire and structural exploitation in world politics in Canada's foreign policy debates, the remark was dismissed as pathetic anti-Americanism and unnecessary pandering to the political and cultural left.

But what about the exceptional rise of Barack Obama to the American presidency in 2009? According to *The Economist*, "When they voted to send a black man to the White House at the end of 2008, Americans performed one of the most remarkable acts of rebranding in the history of their remarkable nation."[5] If the words and deeds of the Bush administration in the WOT caused anti-American sentiments to rapidly rise around the world, the arrival of Obama had the opposite effect. But the term *rebranding* implies change in style at the expense of substance. This is particularly relevant on the issues of race. The media's focus on Obama's blackness—over liberal, cosmopolitan, urban, and many other markers that could have been used to describe him— testified both to the persistence of black/white racialization and to the invocation of a new America, variously described as hybrid, global, cosmopolitan, postracial, postracist, postethnic, "browned," or "majority-minority."[6]

At the time of my writing, this new America is still a mirage, and it might never arrive. What works against it, first, is any number of latest American and international reports on racial discrimination in the United States. Second and related, America's "race relations" are still interpreted on the black/ white axis, which tends to solidify the status quo. Recall that the 2000 census introduced the new "multiracial" option, yet all but 2.4 percent of Americans declared as members of a single race, while eight in ten Hispanic Americans self-identified as white, thus entrenching America's old racialized hierarchy.[7] And third, vagaries of history and geography have so far dashed hopes for a postracial future: Many examples from South America and elsewhere imply that hybridity does not necessarily lead to the disappearance of the ideas, practices, and habits of privilege and protection based on race.[8] Allow me the freedom to paraphrase Marilyn Lake and Henry Reynolds: White men have long been in retreat, but they made so many false starts and reached so many dead ends in the past that one should wait a little longer before celebrating the collapse of the "global colour line."[9] From this point of view, the Anglosphere's past, too, has not yet passed.

ANGLO-SAXONS AND REALISTS

Realism assumes an international system marked by Hobbesian anarchy, defined as the absence of authority above the level of sovereign states, where security is scarce and self-help is the norm. The most elegant realist theory is structural realism. Here, the structure of international politics mainly arises from the differences of material capabilities and only among chief states, known as great powers. In offensive realism, one version of this theory, the overweening influence of material disparities is modified by geography, particularly by the so-called stopping power of water. John Mearsheimer famously argued that "island great powers" like Britain behave differently than "continental great powers" like Germany, which still behave differently from "regional hegemons" like the United States. In the dog-eat-dog world of great power rivalry, hegemony of any kind is the safest position and arises only due to the systemic inefficiencies such as "buck passing" (waiting for someone else to balance bids for hegemony). In the last 200 years, the sole great power to pull off a lasting regional hegemony is the United States, which did it by outsmarting European balancers, particularly Britain.[10]

Colin Elman has recently expanded Mearsheimer's theory to specifically deal with the puzzle of American hegemony in the face of European determination to prevent it. In Elman's interpretation, American hegemony was a magnificent fluke due to contingent "local considerations" such as the "improbable" absence of European balancers in North America.[11] In the Louisiana Purchase of 1803, his main case study, Elman discovers that a confluence of rising security concerns in its own region prevented France from holding onto the Louisiana territory and thus thwarting America's westward expansion. The same explanation applies to Britain. "If France had not sold the territory," counterfactually reasons Elman, "it is very likely that an Anglo-American alliance would have followed."[12] Could it be instead that Britain failed to check America's rise because its leaders thought that the world was big enough for two Anglo-Saxon empires?

Bradford Perkins, the historian who coined the term *great rapprochement*, described the Anglo-American relationship in the period of the Louisiana Purchase as the "first rapprochement."[13] It is indeed possible that some version of Anglo-Saxon identity—expressed perhaps exclusively through nonverbalized practices—might have contributed to this rapprochement as well. This time the enemy Other was France, as demonstrated by the dynamics of a small-scale Franco-American war of 1788–1800 (known as the "quasi-war," "pirate war" or "half-war").[14] The military and paramilitary battles in the Atlantic that occurred over the French attempt to hurt Britain by harassing its commerce with the United States saw a great deal of seemingly spontaneous and effective Anglo-American cooperation against French warships. The same pattern emerged at various points in the nineteenth century, especially in the Asia-Pacific in the period between the Treaty of Wangxia of 1844, America's first diplomatic agreement in Asia, and the Spanish-American War. Once again, this type of Anglo-American security cooperation was never formalized and almost never acknowledged by state representatives, yet the practices such as the sharing of information, ammunition, and supplies or the escorting of each other's merchant convoys were arguably outside the norms guiding relations among comparable imperial navies.[15]

In Chapter 2, I argued that Anglo-Saxonism profoundly shaped British appeasement policies in the 1890s. Now I wish to suggest that similar processes might have shaped Anglo-American relations earlier in history. Prima facie, the outcome of the War of 1812, in which neither side could decisively defeat the other on both land and at sea, created mutual deterrence. In a realist interpretation, this situation benefited the United States in the long run, as its power in the region grew faster than Britain's. According to Kenneth Bourne, already by the second third of the nineteenth century, London began to appease the Americans to avoid war, as evidenced by the concessions it made over Maine, Texas, Oregon, and Mexico.[16] The appeasement thesis, so popular as it is in diplomatic history and in IR, might be severely overdrawn.[17] The Webster-Ashburton treaty that settled the northern Maine boundary not only "broadly favoured the British," but it also removed a joint transborder security problem posed by the irredentism of the Patriots and their Anglophobic supporters in the United States.[18] Maine was the easy border dispute compared to Oregon, which then described an enormous chunk of North America west of the Rockies and sandwiched between the Mexican and Russian empires. Here, Britain was weaker than the United States by any realist measure, and yet the 1846 settlement came to favor London. The European empire kept a greater part of Northern America for itself (that is, Canada was larger even after America's purchase of Alaska); won an "Asian trade route" for its colonists, including the navigation rights on the Columbia River; and retained the rights to a naval base at Esquimalt.

America's diffidence in Oregon might have been influenced by "local considerations," namely the looming war against Mexico in 1846. If so, the realist explanation is challenged by the fact that the U.S. empire acted as an appeaser, not the appeasee. Another challenge arises from the aforementioned Canadian Question. The Alaska purchase rendered the United States a noncontiguous state and created several boundary disputes with the British empire, yet the

United States never once tried to abrogate the Oregon settlement and take over the Northwest Pacific coast. Would the situation have been different had Canada been a part of a non-Anglo empire? This might be unanswerable, but note how, in the case of the Texas annexation, the British elites maintained that Anglo-Saxon Texans "naturally" belonged to the United States, as opposed to Mexico.[19] An *Economist* editorial from the 1850s frames this argument thus:

> You cannot forever uphold the semi-civilised, semi-Spanish, degenerate Mexicans or Nicaraguans—with their effeminate habits and their enfeebled powers—against the hasting, rushing, inexhaustible energies of the Anglo-Saxon Americans. Criminal, course, violent as they often are, it cannot be denied that they rule and conquer by virtue of superior manhood . . . Central American people and *exploité* by Anglo-Saxons will be worth to us tenfold its present value.[20]

Using similar language, a New York Times editorial in 1860 expressed hope that Americans and British would "more clearly understand in the future that the 'manifest destiny' of the two great Anglo-Saxon Empires is not antagonistic, but points to the accomplishment of the same high purposes—the extension of freedom and the spread of civilization."[21]

The content, contestation, and resonance of Anglo-Saxonism has doubtless wildly varied between Britain and the United States and across the long nineteenth century, but its influence on transatlantic conflict/cooperation was no doubt significant. On the basis of the preceding interpretation, I therefore propose that America's rise to regional hegemony was facilitated not only by geography or localized inefficiencies of European balancing, but also by Anglo-Saxonism—or some functionally equivalent set of racialized ideas and practices that glued the two English-speaking empires together. If proven correct, this hypothesis would not render the offensive realist account invalid, but it would greatly complicate its narratives of America's lucky rise to hegemony.[22] From this perspective, a critical case for both realist and constructivist explanation concerns the transatlantic politics of the American Civil War. For realists, British nonintervention poses a puzzle: If there ever was a strategic opportunity for the European empire to reverse its putative North American losses, it was in 1861–1862, yet London kept its neutrality in the conflict.[23] For constructivist theories emphasizing racial identity, British policy also constitutes a puzzle, considering that London now faced two sets of American Anglo-Saxons—the Union and the Confederacy.[24]

There is also a theoretical point to be made about the logic of appeasement. Consider the paradigmatic Munich case. Even realists would agree that Britain's appeasement of Nazi Germany failed because of the fundamental differences of identity: A status quo power could never appease a revisionist power bent on overturning the entire world order. In contrast, Britain's appeasement of America in Venezuela I succeeded because the two powers regarded themselves as Anglo-Saxon empires, not rivals. One U.S. newspaper argued in January 1896 that London's decision to appease Washington had no *realpolitik* overtones: "No American has dreamed of attributing this to cowardice."[25] In turn, it might be that the policy of appeasement is likely to succeed precisely when it is *not* understood as appeasement but rather as some sort of reciprocated restructuring between state actors who already share something in common.

But what about the fact that Britain and the United States kept planning for war against each other until the eve of World War II? A skeptical realist would doubtless point out to the famous color-coded scheme, in which U.S. war planners regarded the British Commonwealth as a potential enemy: Britain was "Red," Canada "Crimson," Australia "Scarlet," and New Zealand "Garnet."[26] Further, in 1921, an increasingly independent-minded Canada decided to design its "Defence Scheme Number 1," which was plan for a preemptive attack on its southern neighbor, targeting Albany, Minneapolis, Seattle, and Great Falls, Montana. On the one hand, the presence of these plans constitutes evidence against the argument that the AASR emerged in the 1890s. On the other hand, however, war plans do not speak for themselves in the sense that they are commissioned for pedagogical purposes as well as for strategic planning.[27] More important, if war plans were *the* smoking gun, the balance of evidence probably works *against* the realist argument.

In my own survey of the extant British war plans from 1894–1896, which included Colonial Office and War Office papers (which further included military and naval intelligence departments plus Admirality), I mostly found documents concerning other European empires. Rare mentions of the United States related to its navy, which was described as a nonenemy, both in terms of capabilities and "intentions."[28] On the U.S. side, war planning took place at the Naval War College; then, after the Spanish-American War, at the War and Navy Departments, and the U.S. Army College; and finally, in the early 1900s, at the Joint Army and Navy Board. According to Steven Ross, the United States had a plan for an invasion of Canada, possibly written by Mahan, in 1892.[29]

American planners outlined another during the first Venezuela crisis, but a full strategic plan for war against the British Empire was drafted only in 1910. It is indicative that the subsequent color-coded schemes did not single out Britain as more dangerous than Germany (Black), Japan (Orange), or France (Gold) and that the first "two-ocean" plan was directed against a potential Spanish–Japanese coalition, not against the actual British–Japanese alliance.[30]

My main criticism of realism goes against its old motto, authored by Talleyrand, Palmerston, De Gaulle, Acheson, Kissinger, and many others, which says that nations have interests, not friends. This genealogy suggests otherwise. In addition, consider an analysis set in a different ontological, epistemological, and methodological context. In a preliminary statistical analysis of a sample of American interventions from Korea to Afghanistan, I found that U.N. authorization and English language were the two most influential factors shaping the multilateral make-up of U.S.–led military intervention.[31] From this perspective, the very first "coalition of the willing" emerged in the Korean War, where Britain and neo-Britains, plus ten other nations, joined a U.S.–led war against common enemies. In this post-1950 trend, when the chips are down, Australia, Canada, New Zealand, and, especially, Britain are more willing to fight alongside the United States than randomly selected formal allies, democracies, and other Western states.

Realist teachings on the significance of geography and military capabilities were borne out in this analysis as well: All being equal, the closer the state to the target of the intervention and the more it spent on defense that year, the more likely it is to participate in a U.S.–led war. Interpreted differently, relatively isolated and poorly armed Canada and New Zealand were less prone to help the United States than was Britain. The arguments made in the book accord with this reading but add that geography and military capability are always discursively shaped. Should Europeanism come to dominate British foreign policy debates, Britain, too, could decide to "disarm" and/or "hide" in its region, much as Canada and New Zealand have done, according to realists. Some other parts of my story also accord with realism. As I have shown in Chapter 2, for example, turn-of-the-twentieth-century American and British empires waged imperial and colonial wars overseas partly because their elites argued that they lived in a Hobbesian world characterized by constant competition among slowly evolving racial groups. This world has disappeared: Social Darwinist foundations of race are gone, formal imperialism, and colonialism are now illegitimate and "great power wars" no longer occur. What has not disappeared is the American empire, which can now be defined as an international hierarchy in which American political authority sits against a variety of nested, consenting, and segmented peripheries.[32] The notion that U.S. special relationships with Australia, Britain, Canada, and New Zealand are also imperial relationships is evidenced from Chapters 3 through 5. Each of these four friends and allies, while independent and sovereign in principle, is dependent on the United States on the basis of two mutually inclusive sets of factors: discourses, practices, and habits of collective identity on the one hand and asymmetric exchanges of rights and obligations in security, economic, legal, and other relations on the other hand.

In the historical-comparative terms, however, these patterns of dependence are exceptional, too: Doubtless, the American self-restraint has always been greater in relations with Canada and New Zealand than with Grenada, Iraq, and other actors situated in various imperial peripheries. This exceptionalism arises from collective identity and is expressed through claims of collective legitimacy. In 2003, for example, the Bush administration and the Blair government framed their decisions to go to war against Iraq as legitimate by referencing each other as "forces for good." Herein lays a theoretical point about the English-speaking alliance as an arm of the American empire: The former is more helpful to the latter in terms of collective legitimacy than in terms of the willingness of Australians, Britons, Canadians, and New Zealanders to fight and die for the imperial cause. Put otherwise, various perspectives on the hierarchical and imperial orderings of political authority international relations are in many ways consonant with realism, but they are also equally consonant with liberal and constructivist theorizations of security communities. What ultimately limits realist contributions to this research agenda is an ontology that treats identity as parasitic on the material world and tends to conflate power with material resources and direct behavioral outcomes, as in the "classical" view that power is a relationship of influence between actor A and actor B.[33]

RACE AND THE KANTIAN PEACE

Liberals, like realists, believe that the global society is mostly composed of sovereign, territorial states, but they treat relations among them as predominantly Grotian or Lockean rather than Hobbesian. Here, states still live in anarchy, but they also share certain institutions, norms, laws, and other inventions that make their life easier. As a paradigm, constructivism arrived on the scene in the 1990s as a foil to both liberalism and realism. Its main argument is that anarchy is not an iron cage, but, in Alexander Wendt's words, "what states make of it." Constructivists thus rejected realist and liberal assumptions on the existence of a presocial global society and argued that the world is neither exclusively Hobbesian nor predominantly Lockean or Grotian. Rather, constructivists proposed, multiple worlds were possible, including a Kantian one.

Liberals and constructivists have both investigated the causes and conditions of the Kantian world, in which states work together to maintain peace and achieve other mutually beneficial goals. For liberals, the Kantian peace, which they also call the liberal peace, is caused by three factors: transnational interdependence, international law and institutions, and democratic institutions and norms.[34] In Chapter 2, I have briefly discussed the liberal argument that democracies never or almost never fight each other. As Michael Doyle has assiduously pointed out, the "democratic peace" thesis constitutes but one leg of the liberal tripod—the Kantian peace always goes in joint sufficiency with interdependence and institutions.[35] From this point of view, the Anglosphere appears as a typical Kantian "zone of peace" or "pacific union": The special relationships that crisscross its putative core are indeed characterized by high interdependence, high institutionalization, and at least a hundred years of perpetual democratic peace.

Constructivists, too, have read *The Perpetual Peace*, Kant's main text on international politics.[36] Rather than denying the joint impact of interdependence, international institutions, and democracy on peace and cooperation, constructivists emphasize their nonmaterial dimensions. In this view, the Kantian peace—like any other international order—follows Self–Other relationships among states: Friends will cooperate more or less automatically, rivals will cooperate much more judiciously, and enemies will almost certainly fight. The main difference between the liberal and constructivist understandings of Kantian worlds therefore hinges on the understanding of identity: Whereby liberals tend to read identity in terms of a fixed regime type (democracy), constructivists like to emphasize the historical and geographic variability as well as dynamism of identity formation.[37] Compare liberal and constructivist readings of the Kantian peace against the history of Anglo-American relations. According to liberals, the ebb and flow of Anglo-American conflict/cooperation in the long nineteenth century was mostly shaped by democratic norms and institutions as well as by the mutual perceptions of "liberalness."[38] Liberals argue that respect for contracts and transparency inherent in both identity and behavior of British and American democracies minimized the threat of cheating or the need for armed enforcement in various intramural settlements in the period. Anglo-American disputes—related to anything from Civil War damages to Oregon, Venezuela, or Alaska boundaries—were therefore overcome because London and Washington opted for legal and binding procedures for international conflict resolution that were a familiar feature of the liberal-democratic order at home. In this reading, liberalness can be regarded as a continuous variable, ranging from "low" in the War of 1812 to "high" during the "great rapprochement."

This genealogy disagrees with the liberal interpretation of history. The origins of the Anglosphere are racial, rather than liberal-democratic. As I have shown in Chapter 2, the American and British empires learned how to cooperate once they became convinced they were led by the people of the same race—a collective identity was created under conditions of exclusion and oppression of non-Anglo-Saxons. Consider a paired comparison of America's territorial expansion policy in the aftermath of the Texas Annexation. In the northwest (Oregon), the United States peacefully settled its territorial disputes with the British empire; in the southwest (Mexican Texas), it went to war with Mexico. From the perspective of Washington, there are four cross-case similarities: the territorial dispute, temporal proximity (the disputes were nearly simultaneous), commercial interests (a trade route to Asia), and even a general foreign policy orientation (the Manifest Destiny). Liberals would argue that the variation in the outcome must be a function of regime type—Britain was a democracy, Mexico was not. According to Maria Fanis, the liberal hypothesis falls short because there is no evidence to suggest that American elites differentiated British North America from Mexico primarily in terms of democracy and perceptions of liberalness.[39] According to her analysis, a much stronger explanatory variable is Anglo-Saxonism: It was collective identity that implied cooperation with the racially similar Britain and conflict against the racially different Mexico. In short, the Kantian peace between the American and British empires was racialized, not simply liberal-democratic.

The theoretical point is twofold. First, in comparison to realists, liberals have been far more attentive to the role of nonmaterialist factors in world politics. What they failed to recognize is these factors must be theorized as they emerge within their specific historical and geographic contexts. A particular problem in the liberal program on the Kantian peace was a tendency to project the democratic present backward through time such that democracy assumes a transhistorical and immutable quality. True, qualitatively oriented researchers have long argued that democratic institutional features mean different things in different historical contexts: hence a recent tendency to break a hitherto single variable of democracy into types and subtypes such as centralized/decentralized, social/liberal, elitist/nonelitist, and pacifist/militant.[40] At the same time, even the most historically minded liberals have shied away from conceptualizing regime type in cultural dimensions as well (for example, Anglo-Saxon democracy). Historicization also implied the role of learning and socialization. In liberal accounts of the Kantian communities, the conditions under which democracies learn from experience that other democracies prefer peace over war are typically left implicit. For many constructivists, benign or virtuous cycles of socialization are central—state actors become socialized into the peaceful and cooperative practices such that they make them part of their state/national identity, and that identity in turn sustains an interest in peace and cooperation as an end in itself.[41] Learning is part of this process: If states believe that a friendly relationship will last and behave accordingly, they are less likely to feel sensitive to threats and, in turn, are less likely to pursue precautionary policies that could undermine the relationship itself. The result is a benign cycle of ideas and actions.

The last sentence leads to the second theoretical point on security communities: What is a benign cycle for some states may be a vicious cycle for others. Liberals theorize interaction because of the dyadic focus of their research agenda on the Kantian peace.[42] From the perspective of constructivist ontology, however, interaction is not simply a relationship between two independent units; rather, to say that identities are interactive is to say that identities are constituted in the sense of X being impossible without Y (for example, East/West, rich/poor, Maori/Pakeha). Here, one of the main insights in Kant's *Perpetual Peace* arguably concerns the constitutive link between the international system of states on the one hand and state identity or behavior on the other. For Kant, perpetual peace would be established only when liberal republics become dominant in the international system of states. Further, liberal ends, Kant accepted, might be pursued by nonpacific means. In the liberal idiom, this insight is regarded as methodological; for constructivists, however, it is ontological. In the words of Tarak Barkawi and Mark Laffey, Kantian "zones of peace and war are not separate and discrete phenomena explained by the presence or absence of liberal institutions within states but effects of mutually constitutive international political, social and economic relations."[43] In this view, democracy and liberalism cannot be divorced from the ideas and practices of empire and imperialism, in which liberal ends are systematically pursued by illiberal means. The Kantian peace is thus recast as the "imperial peace" or the "Western peace."[44]

Barkawi and Laffey have also pointed to the question of race as another problem in the liberal reading of the Kantian peace.[45] Following the dominant school of thought political theory, liberal IR indeed tends to extol Kant as the defender of freedom, world peace, constitutionalism, human rights, and other liberal virtues.[46] But these ideas do not exhaust Kant's thought on world politics. In *The Observations of the Feeling of the Beautiful and Sublime* (1764) and, especially, *Physical Geography* (1802), Kant strongly propagated white male supremacy, according to which white women were passive subjects and Asians ("yellow Indians"), Africans ("Negroes"), and Native Americans ("Americans"), in that descending order, were half-subjects.[47] The immediate reaction, of course, is to relativize Kant's racism both against history ("all eighteenth-century European men of letters were so prejudiced") and against the rest of the philosopher's opus ("Kant is a force for good overall").[48] Yet liberals must be careful not to dismiss this critique too quickly. First, if the historical context is the ultimate arbiter of politics and ethics, then it follows that the liberal creed might always be less universal in practice than hitherto advertized by some liberals.

Second, and more important, Charles Wade Mills, Robert Bernasconi, and other philosophers of race have acknowledged what is at stake in fixing the "real Kant." If race and racism are our historical keys to interpreting the meaning and context of Kant's thought, then they are likely to become our keys to re-reading "our conventional narratives of the history and content of Western philosophy," starting with liberalism.[49] Arguably, this rereading has already begun. Kant is now beginning to be read as one of the first European theorists of race, while strong arguments are being made that his political philosophy emerged in and through tensions between humanism on the one hand (for example, human freedom, universality, and equality) and racialized and gendered "deviations" from humanity on the other.[50] This critique stems from, and deepens, the old licking of liberalism for its double standards on the question of membership in the political community, which says that all liberal communities draw a hard and fast line separating groups of people in matters of political authority.[51] What is new is an emphasis on racialization: Starting with aforementioned W. E. B. DuBois, critical race theorists have argued that the line of membership in a liberal community is always a "color line," at least in part.[52] Not only can those of the "wrong" color—or wrong markers of their daily experience—not participate in the community as free, self-governing individuals, but the liberal community is likely to govern them by illiberal means.[53]

A recognition of the racialized dimensions of liberal political communities is relevant for IR because it suggests that it is possible to theorize and analyze not only the imperial peace of the Western peace but also the "racialized peace." To be sure, the global society has doubtless undergone dramatic shifts away from race and racism such that racializations on the historical scale are no longer possible. And yet, the logic of racialization suggests that the exclusionary and discriminatory practices hitherto associated with the biologically untenable concept of race might still continue in the guise of ethnicity, culture, values, institutions or language. In mid-1960s, for example, Australia and Canada self-identified as liberal democracies in which the autonomy of all individual was protected by a state whose power to rule was systematically checked by the rule of law. Yet both polities treated their indigenous populations as political, cultural, economic, legal, and/or social outsiders. By the turn of the twentieth century, sovereign authority in Anglosphere states had become infinitely more open in access and membership, yet racialized lines were arguably still in existence, most obviously in the case of illegal immigrants or the Muslim minority. Elements of such racializations were present in international conflict/cooperation as well. In the middle decades of the twentieth century, many political elites in core Anglosphere states were all too keen to draw a hard-and-fast line between the new and old Commonwealths while, in the 2000s, a similar line obtained between the "forces of good" and the "Axis of Evil." In Chapters 2 and 3, I have suggested that cooperation between and among select English-speaking democracies was impossible without some degree of exclusion of other entities, including other democracies, like Wilhelmine Germany in 1902 and the Philippines in 1951. Here, liberalness was framed as subordinate to racialized identities. According to David Haglund, even France, that veritable birthplace of modern democracy, was actively alienated by the Anglos in the early postwar years.[54]

Arguably, even the present-day NATO is characterized with similar self-other dynamics. Consider an observation by Christopher Hitchens, whose ethnographies of the AASR and the Anglosphere are legendary:

> This long arc of cooperation means that a young officer in, say, a Scottish regiment has a good chance of having two or even three ancestors who fought in the same trenches as did Americans and New Zealanders. No military force evolved by NATO, let alone the European Union, can hope to begin with such a natural commonality.[55]

The talk of "natural commonality" was indeed present in Britain's Iraq debate, when the government framed its willingness to go to war in precisely these terms. In Canada, Canadian Alliance MPs also used this frame, but their goal was to criticize the government for turning its back to its traditional friends and allies. For the military and defense establishments in the Anglosphere, these meanings are carried by the term *interoperability*. In a passage taken from Britain's white paper on defense from December 2003:

> Our Armed Forces will need to be interoperable with US command and control structures, match the US operational tempo and provide those capabilities that deliver the greatest impact when operating alongside the US. Continuing exchanges with the US on issues such as rapid deployment planning, developing doctrine and concepts, and new technologies, will remain important.[56]

Similar language can be found in the equivalent documents of Australia, Canada, and New Zealand.

Viewed in terms of semiformal ABCA standardization programs, interoperability goes back to World War II, but recent developments have harmonized the militaries of core Anglosphere states to an unprecedented level. According to Thomas-Durell Young, ABCA armies—to say nothing of other services—have now developed a capability for both joint and combined operations, which is the new world standard for multinational military cooperation. The same can be said about the legendary Echelon network and even with regards to coordination of efforts in drafting new laws of war manuals.[57] All of these developments, as Young has observed, have little to do with "mutually held threat perspectives" and everything to do with shared culture:

> To be blunt, to date, such important Western allies as France, the Federal Republic of Germany, and Japan are simply not given the breadth of access to

information and low-level, but important, decision-making opportunities by the United States as are its Anglo-Saxon brethren.[58]

The talk of "natural commonalities" can also be found in the efforts to distribute the costs of lavish defense spending across around the Anglosphere. In a testimony before the U.S. Senate Armed Services Committee in March 2006, the British arms procurement minister Lord Peter Drayson argued that one of the main benefits behind the quarter-trillion-dollar Joint Strike Fighter project was to "ensure that future generations of U.K. and U.S. servicemen and women can continue to stand shoulder to shoulder in pursuit of common goals."[59]

Every one of these feedback cycles between ideas and actions is virtuous for the mythical Anglosphere core but vicious for its significant Others, beginning, say, with British Europhiles who might argue that Britain should build nuclear, airlift, and sealift capabilities within an EU military-industrial complex. What is more significant is that the discourses, practices, and habits of "natural commonalities" in security cooperation also create "natural" enmities. The terrorist attacks of 7/7 in London were perpetrated by British Muslim citizens who justified their acts as a response to the U.S.–led WOT, which they interpreted as a clash of two *ummahs*—the Islamic world on the one hand and the Anglosphere and the West on the other. To the British government and the rest of the world, the bombings were an attack on civilization and, especially, on British multiculturalism. It might be no huge stretch to propose that benign cycles of ideas and actions that produce the Anglosphere also produce similar, but extremely vicious, dynamics with potential to undermine the British state, nation, and society.[60]

Relevant to this extrapolation are recent policy ideas concerning global networks and the "league of democracies." The former refers to the informal transborder institutions directed at producing joint goods, as in Bennett's vision of the Anglosphere as a "network commonwealth." In Britain, the idea of networks was introduced in a 1997 report by Demos, a New Labour think tank, under the slogan "Hub UK—Britain as the world's crossroads." In 2009, the Labour government resurrected it, arguing that the "bridge" metaphor was "good [but] never quite right" and that Britain better resembled a "global hub, plugged into the networks that matter . . . We have global assets. A global language. Global businesses and NGOs. And global networks."[61] In the same year, Anne-Marie Slaughter, who later became a policy advisor to U.S. Secretary of State Hillary Clinton, observed that a networked world gave America a distinct "edge" thanks to a combination of liberal appeal, economic prowess, youthful demography, cultural diversity, and other factors that no other society in the world can match.[62]

The idea of the league of democracies, also known as the "concert of democracies," emerged in the 2000s and has been advanced by liberal thinkers like Slaughter, neoconservatives like Robert Kagan and, reportedly, even by some political advisors to Obama. The idea is reminiscent of Clarence Streit's "union of the democracies" with an expanded reach, now covering the "United States and its democratic partners in Europe *and* Asia." The league, its proponents argue, would not only "institutionalize and ratify the 'democratic peace'," but it would also serve humanity as a permanent taskforce for tackling problems such as climate change and global poverty. Indeed, thanks to its relative "efficiency" and "legitimacy," the league of democracies could also act as "an alternative forum for the approval of the use of force in cases where the use of the veto at the Security Council prevented free nations from keeping faith with the *aims* of the U.N. Charter."[63]

Conceptually, politically, and normatively, the "league of democracies," with its Greater British historical echoes, coheres with Blair's "global alliance for global values," namely the values of "liberty, democracy, tolerance and justice."[64] Even the discourse of civilizations is here. According to Michael Clarke, Blair's vision referred to a "world in which there was a clash, not *between* civilisations, but rather *about* civilisations; about the willingness to embrace a liberal democratic capitalist world order on a globalised scale."[65] Clarke's point can be applied to the policy discourse on cross-cutting networks: Here, too, the implied goal is the spread of liberal values and institutions aimed at realizing various zones of peace, though not necessarily of the Kantian sort. Both projects might be regarded as exclusionary and hierarchical in the sense that they promise to solve problems through nested clubs, one waiting room at a time. The networked world is typically envisioned as a globe-spanning English *Sprachraum*, which is already a hierarchical arrangement composed of many shifting "nodes" and a few fixed "hubs."[66] Non-Anglophone and, indeed, illiberal networks belong to a different world.

Similarly, the raison d'étre of the self-appointed league of democracies would not be democracy per se but the specific version of the liberal, capitalist international order centered on Washington, D.C., much like in the era of Churchill and Streit. Here, the degree of historical change in this club will depend on the membership status of the "great democracy" of India, to use a phrase Churchill used to reserve only for Britain and the United States, just like its continuities depend on the threatening presence of more-or-less familiar outsiders—various "Islamic," "sovereign," "consultative," "Bolivarian," and "people's" democracies. Once a mere jewel in the British crown, India is now a self-driven locomotive of the global economy and a much-coveted member of any democratic league.[67] Indeed, the Obama administration held its first official state reception in November 2009 for India's Prime Minister Manmohan Singh. At the arrival ceremony, Obama underscored a "common story," that of two nations "who struggled to break free from an empire" and build democratic republics committed to "liberty, justice, equality" at home and abroad, as well as to each other.[68] So re-centered, the league of Euro-American-Asian democracies might yet become the most successful of visions in the modern tradition of articulating *An*global governance.[69]

THE POWER OF TALK

In terms of the discourses, practices and habits of an Anglo collective identity in international relations, Suez, Vietnam, and Iraq are bywords for disagreements, disunity, and divisions. Let us focus on the Suez crisis. According to a standard (and unusually anthropomorphized) account of this crisis, in making a secret deal with France and Israel to attack Egypt, Britain deceived the United States, its principal friend and ally. Angry at what it saw as betrayal, the United States reacted by launching a holier-than-thou diplomatic campaign against Britain in the United Nations, followed by a decision to pull the plug on British finances and oil supply. Humiliated and hurt, London backed off and ended its intervention in Egypt.

On the surface, the outcome appears to be consistent with realist predictions, in the sense that a use of direct and material force in the form of economic sanctions against a less powerful state (or empire) achieved the effect desired by a more powerful state (or client). In fact, so successful was the United States in its policy that its leadership (or imperial overlordship) was never again challenged by Britain. And yet, realists would be mistaken to dismiss the idea of the AASR as a sporadic mirage in a permanently Hobbesian world. Cooperation, even in Kantian security communities, does not imply harmony. Indeed, the Suez crisis went down, as the American president Eisenhower called, as a "family spat."[70]

International crises like the Anglo-American clash over Suez are plainly rare. Within long-standing security communities, they are exceedingly rare, and when they occur, they do not spell the end of the community.[71] Security communities are in fact produced through cooperation as well as contestation (the latter goes not only for diplomacy among member states but also, as I have argued, in foreign policy debates within them). American economic sanction over Suez caused no anti-American jingoism and minimal resentment in Britain; in fact, many British elites preferred the policies of the Canadian and even American governments during the Suez crisis to the one held by their own government. Had British elites interpreted America's attack on its economy in 1956 as an attack on the British state or nation, rather than on the Suez Tories, international relations would probably have taken a different historical turn. France, the other great power belligerent and America's second-closest European ally, read the lessons of the Suez crisis very differently. Already in 1957, France pushed for European integration, ostensibly away from the American empire. Here, it is also worth noting that Washington "detested" French imperialism more than the British version of the same.[72]

The Anglo-American relations over Suez demonstrate the counterfactual validity of security communities but also confirm the notion that security communities are also imperial communities. The theoretical framework evaluated in this book was based on a view that power lies in discourses that produce meanings, as in the claim that the fin-de-siècle Anglo-American rapprochement was made possible by a discourse of identity that produced the American and British empires as two branches of a single Anglo-Saxon race. Understood in terms of productive power, the United States rules in the Anglosphere core not simply by negotiating and renegotiating imperial contracts with Australian, British, Canadian, and New Zealander clients but mainly through the discourses of collective identity—here I later added practices and habits—that produce a community in which the United States acts as the "leader," while others follow, variously, as "supporters," "friends," "allies," "deputy sheriffs," and "forces of good."

From this perspective, salutary is Janice Bially Mattern's analysis of the Suez crisis, in which she has shown how empires are maintained not only by military and economic force, as realists or liberals argued, but also by "representational force."[73] Here, Suez was primarily an intergovernmental and transgovernmental contest between Washington and London over how to "fix the meaning" of the events surrounding the invasion of Egypt. The crisis ended once American representational force overpowered that forward by the Suez Tories in London. Translated into the theoretical language used in this book, Suez was a framing war. The Eisenhower administration framed the British-led military intervention against Egypt as un-British, which then resonated not only in the "international community" (that is, the U.N. General Assembly), but also in Britain itself. In brief, Britain abandoned its mission because Washington helped create a major misfit between British identity and reality.

Bially Mattern's account stands out as a rare attempt in IR theory to situate classical and productive conceptualizations of power in a single explanatory framework. Power to control discourse and win debate is indeed an important element in the life of security communities because it serves to reestablish disrupted or even broken identities. From this perspective, whenever they face a misfit, members of the community will resort representational force to produce (or re-produce) identities most in alignment with their own. The wartime AASR therefore collapsed in November 1956 but was quickly rebuilt on new, more clearly American, terms.[74] Bially Mattern is correct to point out that security communities are harmed by breaks in the practices on which collective identity rests—nonviolence, consultation, compensation, and, ultimately, state sovereignty. But I have two reasons to be skeptical about the implication that security communities can be talked in and out of extinction by specific government representatives in specific situations. In 1956, the AASR had been between one and six decades old, in the sense that political actors could successfully claim tradition, history, and collective memory in front of their audiences. The AASR was also remarkably broad and deep in terms of various transatlantic flows. Here, too, collective identity went hand in hand with integration and interdependence but not necessarily as a single identity. In Chapter 5, I suggested that different issue areas are characterized by different linkages and, indeed, different discourses of identity. From this perspective, the term security community tends to be a misnomer: In 1964–1965, Canada and the United States created the Auto Pact but bickered over Vietnam. It could be that two communities, one in security, the other in commerce, were operating according to significantly different logics—discursive, practical, or habitual. Canadian historians who have spent equal time studying security and economics in U.S.–Canada relations have indeed concluded that, in Bothwell's words, "Politics was politics, and trade was trade."[75]

This discussion leads to both substantive and theoretical propositions. First, because the Anglosphere identity might operate differently in different areas, it is possible for national elites to simultaneously argue for seemingly contradictory policies, such as being pro–U.S. in trade but anti-American in international security. This also means that multiple worlds are possible, both within national debates on foreign policy and in international conflict/ cooperation. For example, the British and Canadian elites debated war and peace in Afghanistan, Iraq, and elsewhere in 2002–2003 against what they saw to be a complex world characterized by Kantian zones à la Anglosphere or the West, Lockean, and Grotian emphases on state sovereignty and international law and Hobbesian fears of terrorism. In short, future constructivist research would do well to explore the condition under which security community can be simultaneously Kantian in security, Lockean in trade, and Hobbesian in international sports competitions. The second point is that security communities do not depend on a single debate or a single set of practices; rather, they are simultaneously produced across issue areas, which might give them extraordinary resilience. A policy-relevant conclusion is that peace and cooperation rooted in collective identity are more enduring than the same processes locked in by international institutions alone. Arguably, because the structures that can make or break the Anglosphere are intersubjective, even the abolishment of NATO, ANZUS, or NORAD would not constitute a death blow to the community. Conversely, we should expect security communities like the Anglosphere to collapse only when *most* discourses and *most* practices in *most* issue areas collapse. This outcome is rare but not impossible; the American Revolutionary War and the American Civil War are examples of such collapses, even if these cases refer to "amalgamated" as opposed to "pluralistic" security communities.[76]

Bially Mattern's idea of "representational force" is a reminder that the social construction of reality is always a political construction of reality as well, such that talk is never purely rational as in the Habermasian ideal of a single, overarching, and universal code of action. Put otherwise, the classical power of A to influence the behavior of B is as constitutive of security communities as are deliberative validity claims. According to the case studies covered or alluded to in my book, the United States indeed won in numerous disagreements or disputes with other states. For example, against initial British desires, the United States achieved arbitration in Venezuela I and II, peacekeeping in Suez and war without U.N. blessing in Iraq. But the United States did not automatically get what it wanted, certainly not when it wanted it. In virtually every case covered in the book, the arguments made by the weaker side had an impact on U.S. policy. As I have shown in Chapter 3, even the very junior Anzacs were able to get the United States to shelf its original plans for a broader Pacific pact. With respect to the theories on democratic alliances and security communities, my analysis suggests that multilateralism, close consultation, and, indeed, argumentation may therefore serve as both constitutive and regulative norms.[77] In turn, I join the chorus of calls for further conceptual and theoretical work on the relationship between classical and productive forms of power in world politics. From the perspective of the Anglosphere agenda, particularly desirable would be a consideration of the ways in which the relationships of influence are affected by collective identity, namely how discourses, practices, habits, and many-sidedness of "friendship" between A and B circumscribes the power of A over B.

As Jennifer Mitzen has shown, talk has a double effect in the global society because it shapes individual foreign policies as well as what she calls "transnational public spheres."[78] A policy-relevant finding is that states and other actors can talk themselves into patterns of war and peace more effectively and more often than some IR theories allow. In this sense, the process and outcome of framing wars in politics are always significant. What wins hearts and minds, for example, are frames that successfully link events, policies, and institutions to identity. Policy makers should therefore pay attention to the ways Self–Other relations are understood and debated across various communities in international politics, including their own society.

Policy makers should also understand that Self–Other relations are always constitutive. Within security communities, members are expected to treat each other as friends; by default, this also means that relations with outsiders must be less than friendly. Consider the Anglosphere, the West, the EU, "transatlantic community" or the "international community." Political actors speaking on behalf of these five worlds always exclude the "rest" as competitive, hostile, rogue, backward, or otherwise different. Each of these Self–Other relationships entails politics and policies that may be less productive of peace than claims of friendship, alliance, and partnership. For example, the "war/ peace" relationship legitimizes the use of force and other predatory policies, not trade and tourism, yet it also carries basic respect for sovereignty and human rights, which may be reflected in the treatment of prisoners of war. In comparison, the "civilization/barbarism" relationship legitimizes terrorism, guerilla warfare, permanent occupation, or torture.

Reframing is easier than changing policy, but the latter is usually impossible without the former. In January 2009, American President Obama was asked by Al Arabiya, an Arabic TV channel, if the phrase "global war on ter-ror," the infamous WOT he inherited from Bush, was too confused with the war on the Muslim world. In February, the International Commission of Ju-rists asked the Obama administration to discontinue the use of the phrase, as did some military officials from the Pentagon. By late March, the United States was no longer fighting the WOT, but an "Overseas Contingency Opera-tion."[79] The Obama administration was right to conclude that what "we" say about "them" is always consequential, but if this history of the Anglosphere is any indication, finding a frame that would lead to cooperation depends less on political communication advisers and much more on a broader and more sustained readiness of the Self to listen to its significant Others and accept mutual differences as well as ongoing asymmetries.

THE PATHS AHEAD AND THE GRIP OF HISTORY

As a security community, the Anglosphere has a number of important qualities—imperial, liberal, transnational—but this genealogy has argued that the most important quality of all is its racialized history. For one, the origins of this security community are racial. Without Anglo-Saxonism there could have been no Greater Britain, no "great rapprochement," and no AASR. And without the AASR, there could have been no ANZUS, no NORAD, and no proclivity to rally behind the U.S. flag in the post–World War II (and post-Suez) era. The feedback loop of ideas and actions that produced this iden-tity in international relations was set in motion with the first reification and sedimentation of meanings on the state, empire, nation, and race; by the time this genealogy picked up the story, its subjects—Anglo-Saxons, Americans, the British Empire—had been taken for granted.[80] Could the Anglosphere be-come so reified and sedimented one day?

A historical institutionalist would describe the Anglosphere as path de-pendent, which means that initial conditions (that is, ideas about Anglo-Saxon supremacy) constrained later developments (that is, Anglo-American coopera-tion).[81] Put differently, various internal and external interactions made (that is, "great rapprochement") as well as unmade (that is, Suez) the Anglosphere, but each subsequent transformation was shaped by the last in such a way that the dis-courses, practices, and habits of this security community still resemble the discourses, practices, and habits of Dilke's Greater Britain or Churchill's English-speaking peoples. While usually not indexed as a theoretical building block in the agenda on security communities, path dependence is implicitly present in the logics of learning and socialization. Once again, according to basic identity theory, identities are produced and reproduced through self-reinforcing cycles of ideas and action; the more benign the cycle, the more peaceful and cooperative the outcome.

Like genealogists, institutionalist theorists of path dependence, too, agree that nothing is deterministic, inevitable or preordained—every social system is subject to multiple realizability. It is only by looking back that we can identify self-reinforcing and path dependent historical processes, which suggest that once ideas, practices and institutions—interoperability or intelligence-sharing network—start down a certain route, it is difficult to change course, even if some powerful actors were disposed to do so.

What does this mean for the Anglosphere and its agential potential in world politics? The glue that keeps the Anglosphere together in international relations will be subject to a combination of "exogenous" and "endogenous" tensions. The former include anything from new technologies to demographic and environmental shocks, flu pandemics, or even hard-hitting economic depressions. As Bell, Belich, and others have shown, what made Greater Britain possible in the nineteenth century were improvements in transportation and communication like the steamship or the telegraph. In the 2000s, argued Bennett, the Anglosphere was united by the Internet, and in the future, to borrow ideas from science fiction writing on the Anglosphere, this role might be played by nanotechnologies.[82] The "endogenous" tensions are related to what Alexander Wendt calls "deindividuation."[83] The Anglosphere community rests on a collective identity, not a single identity; therefore, the idea that the English-speaking states would voluntarily surrender their individuality for the purpose of creating a political association is madcap.

At the same time, the tension between incorporation and individuation is a real macrohistorical process, which is reflected in IR debates on the nature of agency in world politics. IR theory has traditionally focused on the political order developed in, and imposed by, Europe since the seventeenth century. In this ontology, political authority mostly rests with sovereign states—spatially demarcated units who recognize each other's centralized juridical supremacy within, though not beyond, the territorial borders. In the theoretical framework developed and evaluated in this book, I have accorded agency to elites within states as well as to states themselves. States are indeed agents: They are (like) people in the sense that they have identities, interests as well as capacities for debating over various courses of action and acting on the basis of these debates.[84] As for the entities located above and across the state level—empires or transnational networks, for example—my theoretical framework has treated them as contexts (material, institutional, discursive, practical) within which state actors would act.

Predictably, my genealogy has greatly complicated my theory. In my case studies, I have discovered no shortage of multiple, intersecting, and overlapping structures of political authority other than states/nations—empires and networks as well as races, civilizations, and multinational corporations. In the nineteenth century, the Anglosphere "acted" through bankers, gold miners, and naval persons and through coalitions of the willing in the twenty-first century. Agency can indeed be conceptualized and theorized differently. All centralized and formally unitary organizations whose identities are greater than the sum of their constituent parts, like Canada, the EU, and, at times, the United Nations or NATO, can be regarded as corporate agents. Conversely, collective agents are decentralized groups of formally independent state and nonstate actors who cooperate on a regular basis on specific tasks like the contact groups for Balkan peacebuilding or Namibian independence.[85]

This broader conceptualization of agency is useful in thinking about the future of the Anglosphere. Let's go back to that scenario in which a "political association" of the English-speaking peoples would rule the world or at least a large part of it. In terms of its breadth, this particular Anglosphere would easily surpass most current regional organizations because it claims not a single geological landmass but a combination of language, values, and institutions, whose reach is global or at least multiregional; in fact, this entity could become a pluralist and a loosely coupled civilization based only on the multidialectism of the English language. As for its depth, this Anglosphere would institutionally model itself on the U.S. federation, possibly on the eighteenth-century British Empire as well.[86] For the conservative historian Andrew Roberts, there are indeed already so many continuities and similarities between *Pax Britannica* and *Pax Americana* that future historians will treat the English-speaking peoples as a "single historical entity," à la republic-cum-empire of Rome.[87] Roberts's teleological principle calls for at least one more analogy—a future *Pax Indica* as the Byzantine arm of the Anglophone Rome, which would claim unity of not millions, but billions, of people. Of course, the ultimate teleology is the world state in which English would be the new Latin.[88]

From a perspective that assumes continuing individuation of its core members, the future of the English-speaking peoples looks different. Here, further collectivization would be stymied by the discourses of American isolation-ism (or hemispherism), Australian Asia-Pacific regionalism (or globalism), British Europeanism (or little Englandism), and Canadian or New Zealander anti-Americanism (or Métissage). The case studies in this book have already captured the potential of at least some of these ideas to affect international conflict/cooperation. It is therefore easy to imagine a combination of endog-enous and exogenous developments that would comprehensively dereify and desediment the Anglosphere and so consign it to this history of forgotten empires. Australia's next push into Asia—or Asia's pull of Australia—might be permanent. Britain might dissolve into several provinces of a federal EU. Canada and New Zealand might come to identify with transcultural or hybrid identities that would vigorously negate old ethnolinguistic connections. And the United States might discover that it really belongs to the Hispanosphere or to the new world–American civilization. If the latter set of scenarios seem less convincing to you than the rise of a new Rome, this might be because you have read this Anglosphere story backward and found yourself nostalgically pausing over Churchill's line from the beginning: "If we are together, nothing is impossible."

REFERENCE MATTER

APPENDIX

NOTE ON PRIMARY SOURCES

THE HISTORICAL RECOVERY OF IDEAS—as well as practices and habits—has been a long-standing problem philosophical and methodological for both historians and social scientists. Foucault famously challenged genealogists to "read everything" in generating their archives. There are many cases of Herculean efforts undertaken by solo researchers to recover pieces of history. For example, in his historical reconstruction of French ideas circa 1899, Marc Angenot told his "story of the year" from an archive of 1,200 books, 150 daily newspapers, and 400 periodicals.[1] My genealogy was less ambitious. To tell six stories of the year from five national perspectives, I relied on fifty books, forty daily newspapers, and eighty periodicals. In the end, the archive of primary source texts subjected to analysis came to consist of nearly 3,000 discreet units, ranging from a short newspaper article to a novel: 800 for Chapter 2, 500 for Chapter 3, 900 for Chapter 4, 700 for Chapter 5. This appendix describes the sampling strategies I used in accessing data in each chapter.

As I explained in Chapter 1, I executed my case studies in three analytical steps, each corresponding to a level of the content and contestation of identity: society, debates, and decision. The selection of texts in steps one and two was based on circulation, region, ownership structure, and political or ideological orientation. (These dimensions are referenced in social history and in the standard guides on national literatures). I excluded publications the contemporaries regarded as extreme and thus unrepresentative of the discourses and debates of interest. For example, for the British archive on Venezuela II, I excluded the pro-American *The Spectator* and the anti-American *Saturday Review*. Because documentary sources like these favor the voices of journalists, an attempt was made to mine letters written by more ordinary citizens ("letters to the editor") wherever possible.

This type of historical research has become easier in the digital age.[2] To generate a basic archive of newspaper and newsmagazine articles, I started with the electronic, full-text, word-searchable online databases. Apart from randomly chosen dates of publication, these searches helped me get a handle on special coverage of major events, defined deductively, using common historical knowledge (for example, Election + 1894), whereby texts on intramural foreign relations (for example, "Corinto Occupied") were excluded from the archive analyzed in the first step.[3] Where sources were nondigitized and/or where the digital search yielded small and/or biased samples, research proceeded with the help of a microfilm reader at one of five libraries: Ohio State (Columbus, OH), Griffith University (Brisbane), Libraries and Archives Canada (Ottawa), the National Library of Australia (Canberra), and the British Library Newspapers (London).

To identify the bestselling works of fiction and nonfiction, I consulted the contemporary book review sections in the newspapers and periodicals as well as cultural histories. Where weekly best-seller lists were not available or ambiguous, I consulted newspaper and newsmagazine reviews of "books in most demand." For the historical period examined in Chapter 6, the bestseller data was readily accessible online. For British bestsellers, data came from Nielsen BookScan (formerly Whitaker BookTrack; no equivalent in Canada at the time) as well as from the lists in *The Guardian* and *The Times*. For Canada, I consulted the weekly rankings in *Maclean's* and *The Globe and Mail*, as well as the latter's annual pick of the hundred "best and influential books of the year."

Chapter 2 looked at the texts produced and consumed by the Anglo-American elites at the turn of the twentieth century, focusing on the years 1894 and 1900 (both January to December). The first analytical sample began with a series of keyword searches in standard online databases of historical newspapers and newsmagazine. To diversify this sample—and to minimize the bias in favor of *The New York Times, Nation,* and *Harper's* in the U.S. sample and *The Times* in Britain, I read *Literary Digest* and *Public Opinion* (which were particularly diverse as they contained summaries of editorials and articles from various regions in both the United States and Britain) and three British broadsheets: *Westminster Gazette, The Manchester Guardian,* and *The Morning Post.* The archive of periodicals included *Atlantic Monthly, Contemporary Review, Economist, Fortnightly Review, Forum, Harper's, National Review, Nineteenth Century* (and *Nineteenth Century After*), *North American Review, Observer,* and (*American Monthly*) *Review of Reviews.* A few of these publications specifically catered to transatlantic audiences.[4]

The second step was to consider texts left by foreign policy officials. These can be loosely grouped into public (party platforms, legislative debates, public memoranda, speeches, and publications by foreign-policy decision makers dealing with things foreign) and private (correspondences, diaries, and inner government documents such as the memoranda prepared for cabinet meetings, minutes, and personal notes—texts that were not publicly available at the time). Both types of sources from this period are available in multiple formats. I read British government records at the National Archive at Kew, either in print or the microform.[5] Additional data on the Venezuela crises came from the contemporary journalistic coverage, using the techniques described in the preceding paragraphs. In this chapter, as well as Chapters 3 and 4, particularly useful was the popular *FRUS—Papers Relating to the Foreign Relations of the United States.*

Chapter 3 focused on the trans-Tasman texts from the Long 1950 (January 1950 to February 1951). The Australian sample included a dozen newspapers and newsmagazines: *The Advertiser* (Adelaide), *The Age* (Melbourne), and *The Argus* (Melbourne, defunct since 1957), *The Canberra Times, The Sydney Morning Herald, Australian Journal* (defunct since 1962), *Australian Quarterly* (defunct since 1967), *Man: Australian Magazine for Men* (defunct since 1974), *Walkabout* (defunct since 1974), the special "70-year Pageant" Number of *The Bulletin* (February 1), and literary magazines *Southerly* and *Meanjin*. In terms of published works of fiction and nonfiction, analyzed were Nevil Shute's *A Town Like Alice*, Frank Hardy's *Power without Glory*, Frank Clune's *Ashes of Hiroshima*, and John Tierney's (aka Brian James's) *The Advancement of Spencer Button.* The New Zealand sample included one (literary) magazine, three books (two histories and one young adult novel), and four main dailies, respectively: *Landfall*, William Pember Reeves's *The Long White Cloud* (1950 reprint), Harold Miller's *New Zealand*, Colin Rich's *Teko-Teko in Waitomo, The Dominion* (Wellington), *The New Zealand Herald* (Auckland), *The Otago Daily Times* (Dunedin), and *The Press* (Christchurch).

For foreign policy, I used the same newspapers and newsmagazines but without randomization. This archive was augmented by a reading of specialist magazines such as *Current Notes on International Affairs* (Canberra). For the ANZUS negotiations, I combed through published documents like *FRUS, DNZER,* and *Documents on Australian Foreign Policy: The ANZUS Treaty, 1951,* as well as various private and public documents deposited the National Archives of Australia in Canberra and the National Archive in Kew. In the Australian National Library, paper collections of Percy Spender (MS 4875) and Robert Menzies (MS 4936) were particularly useful. The same goes for two secondary sources, Ian McGibbon's *Unofficial Channels,* a collection of the correspondence among New Zealand's four diplomats responsible for ANZUS, as well as for David McIntyre's *Background to the Anzus Pact*, which covers the treaty from its blueprints, through all drafts, and ends with a look of the diplomacy and politics of signing and ratification.

Chapter 4 looked at Australia and Canada from two temporal perspectives, 1955–1956 (March 1955–November 1956) and 1964–1965 (March 1964–July 1965). The Australian archive followed the pattern explained earlier, but I expanded it to include the following periodicals: *The Advertiser* (Adelaide), *The Age* (Melbourne), *The Argus* (for

1955–1956), *The Australian* (Canberra, for 1964–1965), *The Canberra Times*, *The Sydney Morning Herald*, *Australian Journal* (for 1955–1956), *Australian Quarterly*, *Man: Australian Magazine for Men*, *Meanjin*, *Overland*, *Quadrant* (for 1964–1965), *Southerly* and *Walkabout*. For books in 1955–1956, I leafed through Alexandra Hasluck's *Portrait with a Background* and a university-level textbook edited by Gordon Greenwood, *Australia: A Social and Political History* (reprinted until 1975). My 1964–1965 archive included Donald Horne's *Lucky Country* (then running as a feuilleton in *The Australian*), Henry Johnston's *My Brother Jack*, and the paper edition of John O'Grady's (aka Nino Culotta's) *They're a Weird Mob*.

In Canada, the English-language texts were selected from *The Globe and Mail* (Toronto), *The Toronto Star*, *Montreal Gazette*, *Canadian Dimension* (for 1964–1965), *Canadian Home Journal* (for 1955–1956), *Chatelaine*, and *Maclean's*. For French Canada, I read *Le Devoir* (Montreal), *Le Magazine Maclean* (for 1964–1965), and *La Revue populaire* (for 1955–1956).[6] In term of the book archive, for the first period, I read volume two of Donald G. Creighton's biography of John A. Macdonald; Pierre Berton's *Golden Trail: the Story of the Klondike Rush*; Malcolm Ross's collection of essays, *Our Sense of Identity*; the proceedings of the Conference of Canadian Writers in Kingston; and three history textbooks used in the primary and secondary education curricula in several Anglophone provinces: *Canada in the Western World*, *North America and the Modern World*, and *The Story of Canada*. My 1964–1965 archive built on W. L. Morton's *The Kingdom of Canada*, Frank Underhill's *Image of Confederation*, Margaret Laurence's *Stone Angel*, Hugh MacLennan's *Two Solitudes* (because it had just become available in French and was again popular) and the advanced high school textbook by Kenneth W. McNaught, and Ramsay Cook, *Canada and the United States*. For foreign policy debates, I analyzed specialist publications and the Australian and Canadian Hansards (quotations of parliamentary speeches are from lower chambers, except where otherwise stated). For the Suez and Vietnam decisions, I relied on voluminous secondary sources, but I also reviewed the cabinet memos and the prime minister's papers kept at aforementioned national archives and libraries.

Chapter 5, covering Britain and Canada, from January 2002 to March 2003, began with a selection of three nonfiction best sellers shared between two national archives: Michael Moore's *Stupid White Men*, Margaret MacMillan's *Paris 1919* (published in Britain as *Peacemakers*), and Roy Jenkins' *Churchill*. Then I expanded the British archive to include two history textbooks, one nationally used high school advanced-level "core" text (Walsh 2001) and another a history of London for children (Bailey and Maynard 2000). I combined these with Iain Sinclair's travelogue of sorts *London Orbital* and three fictional novels: Allison Pearson's *I Don't Know How She Does It*, Ben Elton's *High Society*, and Zadie Smith's *The Autograph Man*. For the British press, I sifted through *The Daily/Sunday Telegraph*, *The Economist* (Britain section only),

The Guardian/Observer, The Scotsman (Glasgow), *The Independent, New Statesman, The Times,* and *The Spectator.* I completed my archive with a selection of texts on the British identity authored by the Home Office and the Institute for Race Relations, a London think tank.

My Canadian media archive covered *The Globe and Mail, The National Post, Le Devoir, Maclean's,* and *L'actualité.* For books, I read Carol Shields's *Unless,* as a best-selling novel published by a Canadian author in the period under study, and a selection of short stories from *The Journey Prize Anthology.* Then I followed up with one primary school history textbook, Cruxton and Wilson's, and two high school history textbooks, Newman's and Fielding and Evans's (both were in circulation in most provinces and were available in French, though not part of the Quebec curriculum) and Hacker's national history for children as well as *How to Be a Canadian,* the best-selling satire by the Ferguson brothers. Last, I considered the government word on national identity by drawing on a few parliamentary statements as well as on the publications by Citizenship and Immigration Canada.

For foreign policy debates, I read the periodicals, the parliamentary debates, and select specialist publications. With respect to the last source, I combed through texts published by the following London-based foreign policy think tanks: the Foreign Policy Centre ("Reports"), the Royal Institute of International Affairs (*International Affairs, The World Today*), the International Institute for Strategic Studies (*Adlephi Papers, Strategic Comments, Survival*), the Institute for Public Policy Research ("Reports"), the Royal United Services Institute (*RUSI Journal*), the Oxford Research Groups ("Briefings"), and the Centre for Defence and International Security Studies at Lancaster University ("Bailrigg Papers"). For Canada, I read *Canadian Foreign Policy, International Journal, Études internationales, Policy Options,* and the 2002 issue of *Canada among Nations* as well seven recently or contemporaneously published books on Canadian foreign policy.[7]

To trace British and Canadian decisions on Iraq, I relied on a combination of press conference transcripts, press briefings, parliamentary debates, publicly available interviews, and freshly written insider accounts. Perhaps more than any recent war, Iraq has received an avalanche of journalistic accounts, often written by the individuals who happen to be more on the inside of the political process than some elected representatives. The British side of the war, in particular, has been well researched. While most internal government documents will be hidden from the view of the public for another three decades, I was able to use data from leaked documents as well as from memoirs and diaries published by four cabinet ministers (Blunkett, Campbell, Cook, Short) and five official and/or semijudicial inquiries (Hutton, Butler, the Intelligence and Security Committee, the Foreign Affairs Select Committee, and Chilcot).[8] Unless otherwise noted, I retrieved the British government documents, including various speeches and the texts authored by the government bodies such as Policy Planning

Staff in Foreign Office from one of the standard websites (fco.gov.uk, pm.gov.uk, publications.parliament.uk, number-10.gov.uk) in the period between February 2004 and July 2005. I similarly retrieved Canadian government documents (parl.gc.ca, pm.gc.ca, and dfait-maeci.gc.ca) in the period between December 2002 and January 2004.[9] For the Canadian perspectives on the Iraq decision, I relied on the memoirs by Prime Minister Jean Chrétien and his advisor Eddie Goldenberg as well as on confidential interviews with officials in the Privy Council Office and the departments of National Defence (DND) and Foreign Affairs and International Trade (DFAIT).

NOTES

Chapter 1: What Is the Anglosphere?

1. The term went from a science fiction novel in 1995 to a think tank in 1999 and then to the media and academia in 2000s. It entered the *Shorter Oxford English Dictionary* in 2007 (Browning and Tonra 2009; Vucetic 2010).

2. Churchill 2002 [1956–1958]. The latter epigraphs are from Jenkins (2002). On the "Churchill cult" in the English-speaking world, see Hitchens (2004) and Gilbert (2005).

3. See, inter alia, Ferguson (2002), Mead (2007), and Roberts (2006).

4. Quotations are from Carr (2001 [1939]: 80, 74–75).

5. On the concept of identity in IR, see Abdelal et al. (2009), Hopf (2002), Mitzen (2006), Ó Tuathail (1996), and Wendt (1999). On constructivism in IR, philosophy, and metatheory, see Wendt (1999); cf. Guzzini and Leander, eds. (2007) and Wight (2006).

6. Compare Adler and Barnett (1998: 39), Deutsch et al. (1956: 5), and Williams (2001: 538–543).

7. See, inter alia, Barnett (1998); Brysk, Parsons, and Sandholtz (2002); Cohen (2008); and Gong (1984).

8. For notable exceptions, see Bellocchio (2006), Bially Mattern (2005), Haglund (2005, 2006), and Shaw (2007).

9. Bennett (2004, 2007), Conquest (2005), and Windschuttle (2005).

10. Here, the idea of the Anglosphere is a call for the creation of the "Anglo-Saxon Ummah" (Muthyala 2005: 1260, cf. Monbiot 2005). On the political and normative liabilities of the word "Anglo," see Belich (2009: 58–65), Parekh et al. (2000: 38–39), and Wierzbicka (2006: 5, 299–301).

11. Vincent (1982: 658). Also see, inter alia, Doty (1993), Krishna (2001), Lauren (1988), Long and Schmidt, eds. (2005), Mazrui (1977), Oren (2003), and Vitalis (2000, 2005).

12. To signal to the reader their awareness of the ontological and other problems involved, scholars sometimes refer to race with quotation marks ("race") or an asterisk (race*). I trust the reader will steer clear of the pitfalls of essentialism and reification, and so I will sparingly use such signaling practices.

13. On the concept of racialization, see Murji and Solomos (2005). The term *anti-eliminativist constructivism* flattens all sorts of conceptual, ontological, and normative positions in the philosophy of race. For relevant discussions in the mid-2000s alone, see Alcoff (2006), Blum (2002), Mallon (2006), Sullivan (2006), and Taylor (2004).

14. Against ethnicity-oriented substitutionism in the study of race, see Alcoff (2006), Blum (2002), and Mills (1997). On race and pan-ethnicity, see Blum (2002). On intersectionality, see Weldon (2008).

15. Roberts (2006), van der Pijl (1998),Phillips (1999), Gamble (2003, 2007), and Belich (2009).

16. Vucetic (2010) offers only a partial discussion. For the latest call to bring the normative back to IR theory, see Reus-Smit and Snidal (2008).

17. In constructivist IR, structures refer to the intersubjective meanings that make up the context of social life, while agents refer to entities that act in that context. For a constructivist perspective on the complex relationship between the levels-of-analysis problem and the agent-structure problem, see Wendt (1999).

18. On critical realism, as understood and used in IR theory, see Wendt (1999) and Wight (2006). Race theory used in this book can also be regarded as critical realist (Alcoff 2006). For the relevant discussion of causation, see, inter alia, Kurki (2008) and Wendt (2003). Cf. Jackson (2010).

19. In this view, states are (like) persons who need ontological security: Without intersubjective identities, there can be no certainty in the world and therefore no "international relations" as we know it. See, inter alia, Hopf (2002), Mitzen (2006), and Wendt (1999, 2004).

20. After more than a century of debate, consensus holds that nationalism is a modern phenomenon and that most nations claim a bounded territory for themselves. Nearly all theorists, from primordialists who believe that nations have ancient ethnic, racial, linguistic, or religious foundations to instrumentalists who see nations as objects of elite manipulation, imply that nations always arise in relation to at least one other nation or human group. For this literature, see Delanty and Kumar (2006).

21. Rather than inductive, this approach is closer to what Charles Pierce termed abduction (Quieroz and Merrell 2005). For relevant discussions in IR, see, inter alia, Hansen (2006), Hopf (2002), Jackson (2006), and Wæver (2002, 2005).

22. For sympathetic critiques, see Barnett (1999) and Hemmer and Katzenstein (2002). Cf. Bially Mattern (2002), Hopf (2002), Weldes (1999), and Wendt (1999).

23. Note that not all IR theories incorporating talk are constructivist and that not all constructivists theorize talk. I cannot review these distinctions here, but see

Crawford (2002), Bially Mattern (2005), Kornprobst (2008), Krebs and Jackson (2007), Krebs and Lobasz (2007), Mitzen (2005), Müller (2004), and Risse (2000).

24. Talk and audiences influence politics in every social system, liberal and illiberal alike. For empirically minded elaborations of this point from different IR perspectives, see, inter alia, Crawford (2002), Fearon (1998), Mitzen (2005), Risse (2000), and Weeks (2008).

25. For discussions, see Krebs (forthcoming), Johnston (2003), Wæver (2005), and Weldes (1999).

26. Framing theories began to develop with Erving Goffman in the 1970s, possibly even with Kenneth Boulding in 1950s, but have mushroomed since the 1980s, thanks to George Lakoff and others. The basic observation that whoever succeeds to frame the debate tends to win it goes back to Plato and Aristotle. For a critical overview of the framing literature, see Polletta and Ho (2006), but my outline borrows mostly from Benford and Snow (2000), Bially Mattern (2005), Chong and Druckman (2007), Crawford (2002), Entman (2003), Jackson (2006), Kornprobst (2008), Krebs and Jackson (2007), and Steinberg (1998).

27. In this type of frame analysis, actors' motives, preferences, sincerity, and intention (intentions *to*) are irrelevant. References to intentionality may be useful for exposition but hold no causal value (cf. Crawford 2002: 124–128 and Krebs and Jackson 2007: 21–24; more generally, see Foucault 1977 and Tully 1988).

28. This is a simplification, but see, respectively, Ted Hopf's (2002) "logic of habit" and Janice Bially Mattern's (2005) "representational force." I will return to both concepts later in the book.

29. Constructivists recognize, but rarely theorize on, the fact that all social environments are subject to endogenous and exogenous shocks. In this account, new events are an analytical device, meant to be recovered empirically. They themselves do not have an independent causal value. For discussions, see, inter alia, Baum and Groeling (2008), Burke (2005), Hansen (2006), Legro (2005) and, especially, Sewell (2005).

30. On what can be called the genealogization of contemporary history, see Clark (2004) and Berkhofer (1995). I discuss genealogy as a methodology in IR elsewhere (Vucetic, forthcoming).

31. See, for example, Duchesne (2007) and Mead (2007).

32. On case theory, see Eckstein (1975), George and Bennett (2005) and Gerring (2007). I was also guided by earlier attempts to methodologize the subject. Bially Mattern (2005: 16–20) explains why the Suez crisis as paradigmatic for the literatures on security communities and alliance management, while Haglund (2005: 76) assessed Canada as an "outlier" in the Anglosphere core.

33. For DA in IR, see Abdelal et al. (2009), Doty (1993), Hansen (2006), Weldes (1999), and, especially, Hopf (2002).

34. On this point, see Legro (2005) and Krebs (forthcoming).

35. On this method/methodology, see George and Bennett (2005: Ch. 10) and Gerring and Thomas (2007: Ch. 7).

36. Where my reading of history disagreed with the dominant readings supplied by professional historians, I placed a warning sign in the form of footnote. A mix of primary and secondary sources was necessary to ameliorate a selection bias, or bias *and* selectivity, which arises when analysis follows on historical facts hitherto interpreted by similar theoretical perspectives (Thies 2002: 358–366).

Chapter 2: Empire, Venezuela, and the "Great Rapprochement"

1. Rock (1989: 31).

2. For Bradford Perkins, who coined the term, referred to a *re*establishment of cordial relations, namely those that characterized the Anglo-American relationship at the turn of the nineteenth century (Perkins 1955, 1968, cf. Myers 2008). On the puzzling status of the "great rapprochement" in history, see Belich (2009: 479).

3. On these textbook historical observations, see, respectively, Knight (1999: 139–142) and Bridge and Bullen (2003: 6). I use the term *empire* loosely. Retrospective and partly interchangeable terms include *first-rate power, great power,* and *major power.*

4. Bourne (1967: 403).

5. The list of high-level declarations against war is too long to be reviewed here, but see, inter alia, Adams (2005: 12–13), Bourne (1967: 320–321), Campbell (1974: 183), Rock (1989: 29, 55, 59–62), Russett (1963: 4, 39), and Tilchin (1997: 19, 110). A content analysis of *New York Times* and London *Times* editorials between 1890 and 1913 shows remarkably high levels of intramural approval, compared to the "outside world" (Russett 1963: 140).

6. Dilke (1869, II: vii). The references for primary sources in this and subsequent chapters—archived government documents, books, newspapers, and newsmagazines corresponding to each historical period under study—are listed in the Appendix.

7. According to Bell (2007), the idea of Greater Britain at first—that is, since the 1870s—related to the union between Britain and its settler colonies and only later—in the 1890s—to a broader Anglo-American unity. On the basis of a simple content analysis of *The Times,* James Belich suggests that by the 1880s the term "Greater Britain had made its way into at least middle-class conceptual language" (Belich 2009: 457). My own keyword search through *New York Times* found only four discrete uses of the term before 1880 and seventy before 1900, including one mentioned in the epigraph to this chapter.

8. For example, Britain's economic, military, and diplomatic ties to Portugal, with claim of continuity that goes back to 1373, never led to the talk of an Anglo-Portuguese union.

9. See Rock (1989), Roussel (2004), and Thompson (1999).

10. I have in mind Layne (1994), Maoz (1997), Owen (1994, 1997), and Russett (1995), cf. Rock (1997).

11. Compare, for example, Owen (1997: 15, 589–590) to Weldes (1999: 1–4).

12. See, for example, Deutsch et al. (1957: 40–41, 66–67), Layne (1994: 27, fn. 71), and Russett (1963: 27, 128–129, 217). The most relevant historical interpretations are Anderson (1981), Horsman (1981), Kohn (2004), and Kramer (2002), but also see Campbell (1960), Campbell (1974), Drinnon (1984), Frantzen and Niles (1997), Gossett (1999 [1963]), Hunt (1987), Jacobson (1998), Knuth (1958), Mandler (2007), Naanami (1951) and Tulloch (1977).

13. Horsman (1981: 17–24). On the history of the idea of "Anglo-Saxon race," see Frantzen and Niles (1997), Kramer (2002), Mandler (2007), and Horsman (1981). The Anglo-Saxons gradually became known as "whites," with an occasional ethno-racial relapse such as that carried in the 1960s by the American term WASP or "Anglo-Protestantism" (Huntington 2004). On the relationship between the "Anglo culture group" and the "imagined community of white men" before the 1930s, see Belich (2009: 58–65) and Lake and Reynolds (2008, especially Parts 2 and 3). Cf. Synder (1984: 93–113).

14. Burk (2007: 529–542).

15. This is a simplified interpretation drawn from Burgess (1890), Carnegie (1894), Fiske (1885), Hosmer (1890)and Thomas (1894). John W. Burgess, the putative founding father of American political science, argued that the French, Scandinavians, and Lombards were Teutons but advocated only a dual German–American alliance (Anderson 1981: 42, cf. Higham 1988: 140–153). In Britain, "Teutomania" was even more pervasive, as Robert Mandler shows (2007: 86–105). Cf. Kennedy (1980: 386–409).

16. Compare with Bederman (1995: 23–31), Hall (2000), Mandler (2007: 72–105), and Roediger (2008). .

17. The figure and labels come from U.S. social scientist William Ripley, whose influential *Races of Europe* (1899) is discussed in Baum (2006: 144–151) and Hattam (2007: 24–31). On the contemporary variations in the sciences of race, including social Darwinism, Spencerism, Galtonism, Lamarckianism, and other strands, also see Hofstadter (1992 [1955]), Lorimer (1996), and Stein (1989). On races, ethnic groups and ethnicity, see Hattam (2007).

18. See, for example, Curzon (1894), Kidd (1894), Seeley (1900 [1883]), and Strong (1889, 1890, 1893) and Grant (1894).

19. For a sample of the American debate on immigration, compare Fisher (1893) and Holladay-Claghorn (1900). At what points in space and time these new immigrant groups—Irish, Italian, Jewish and others—became white is a matter of much historical debate, at least in U.S. history. For discussions, see Guglielmo (2003), Higham (1988), Ignatiev (1996), Jacobson (1998), Roediger (2008), and Saxton (1990). On the British case, see Curtis (1968), Swift and Gilley (1999), and Panayi (1994). As Duncan

Bell observes, the British elites were equally worried about emigration—how best to keep the much-dispersed racial stock together (Bell 2007: 46–55).

20. For the rise of Anglo-Saxonism in the 1890s, see Anderson (1981: 176), Floyd (2004), Horsman (1981: 302), Jacobson (1998: 76–77), and Gossett (1997 [1963]: 311).

21. These challenges were quite separate from subaltern antiracist voices. In the primary source archive created for this chapter very few texts even implicitly denied the idea of race and racial hierarchies. This reading accords with Robert Beisner, who notes that only one (Senator Hoar) of his "twelve anti-imperialists" actually argued for the irrelevance of race (1968: 219, 232; compare to Hansen 2003 and Meyers 2007: Ch. 8). Antiracist voices did indeed exist. They included old abolitionists, Christian as well as scientific socialists, pacifists, and liberal human rights activists including, to use U.S. examples, Jane Addams, Eugene Debs, John Dewey, Frederick Douglass, W. E. B. Du Bois or Ida B. Wells.

22. "Constructive imperialism" is retrospective, but it roughly corresponds to "new imperialism" in historiography (Green 1999: 347).A third position, mixing radicals, socialists, and "Little England" ideas against empire, was too weak to affect the dynamic of foreign policy debates in the period under study (cf. Claeys 2007, Krebs 1999, Owen 1999). For other interpretations of the debate, see, inter alia, Adams (2005), Bell (2007), Deudney (2001), Friedberg (1988), Gooch (1994), Kennedy (1981), Owen (1999) and Porter (2004).

23. These keywords are taken from the newspaper coverage of the Colonial Conference held in Ottawa in the summer of 1894. On sampling criteria, see Appendix.

24. There was some disagreement over whether the referent object of security and prosperity was Britain or the entire self-governing empire. For discussions, see Green (1999: 348–354) and Offer (1999: 704–707).

25. The alliance with Japan stood out as experimental, for here was a distant racial Other that nonetheless demonstrated considerable imperial fitness in the 1890s. The ambiguity was subsequently resolved in a position that held that Japan was a valuable proxy in the British and Western attempt to civilize Asia (Iikura 2004: 226, Tomes 1997: 252, cf. Holmes and Ion 1980).

26. On Balfour's racial ideas, see Tomes (1997). On Chamberlain's, see Mock (1981).

27. On these ideas, see Bell (2007: 254-9). Cf. Belich (2009) and Eddy and Schreuder (1988).

28. Turner (1894).

29. The slogans and the dichotomy will be familiar to students of American history. For a range of relevant accounts, see, inter alia, Hansen (2003), Hofstadter (1965), Kaplan (2002), LaFeber (1998 [1963]), May (1991), Mead (2002), Shoultz (1998), Tompkins (1970), and Williams (1972).

30. The nature of the hemispheric expansion was ambiguous. Senator Lodge believed in the "citadel" North America but argued that Hawaii was "essential to the

defence of that citadel" (cited in Kohn 2004: 16–17). Historiography deals with these ambiguities under the rubric "salt water fallacy" (Louis 1977: 570).

31. On Anglophobia, see Crapol (1973: 122–123). Racial supremacy did not automatically imply supremacist imperialism; on the contrary, it probably helped thwart American imperialism since 1870 (Love 2004: 106, cf. Beisner 1968, Jacobson 1998: 205–213, Hannigan 2002: 276–277, McCarthy 2009: 73).

32. Anglo-Saxonist self-awareness was also necessary lest aliens tried to assimilate in form but not in substance (Drage 1895).

33. Irish Americans were divided by religion, and their representatives never voted as a bloc, partly due to their low numbers in political institutions. In 1894, there were were fifteen self-declared Irishmen in the House and three in the Senate. See Jacobson (1998: 46–47), Moser (2007: 10), May (1991: 62–63), O'Day (2000: 174-176), Ward (1969: 47, 5, 68–69). Some Irish-American politicians promoted the Anglo-Saxon-Celtic unity against new immigrants (Belich 2009: 466, Horsman 1981: 93–94, 250–251, cf. Curtis 1968).

34. For key documents, see *FRUS* 1895: 1: 542–576. Olney's invocation of the Monroe Doctrine swiftly became known as the "Olney Doctrine" (*Literary Digest* 12, January 4, 1896, p. 272; also see Campbell 1974:177).

35. See the summaries in *Public Opinion*, December26, pp. 837–843, and *Nation*, November 14 and 12, December 21 and 26.

36. See *Times* (London), February 18 and 21, 1896, and *Nation*, February 27, 1896. Petitions and individual letters are discussed in FO 80/364 and 367, 96/200 and *FRUS* 1895 1: 75–76. Also see May (1991: 49–61).

37. For the changes in the U.S. press, compare the summaries in *Literary Digest* between October 1, 1895, pp. 664–665 and January 4, 1896, pp. 271–273, to Ibid., January 18, 1896, pp. 339–340, February 8,1896, pp. 426–427 and February 28, 1896, pp. 511–512. For representative views in the British press, see *Westminster Gazette*, December 18, 21, 23, 24, 1895, and *The Times* (London) December 18, 1895. For a contemporary review of the British press, see Bryce (1896). Compare with Allen (1969: 539–540, 568), Campbell (1974: 201), and Orde (1996: 14–15).

38. See *Times* (London) November 10, 1896, and *The Economist*, November 14, 1896.

39. Grenville (1964: 55), also see Bourne (1967: 319, 330), and Allen (1969: 531). These works provided a standard domestic process explanation of the crisis, which formed the empirical bedrock of the realist-liberal debate over the democratic peace. For an interpretation closer to mine, see Hilton and Ickringill (1996) and Kohn (2004).

40. *Literary Digest*, May 25, 1895, pp. 112–113, Ibid., January 11, 1896, p. 301. *Public Opinion* April 26, 1894, pp. 88–89, April 24 and May 2, 1895, p. 406. Cf. *FRUS* 1895: 1: 696–697.

41. See Orde (1996: 11). Chamberlain, for example, described the Anglo-American war as "horror" in December. Also, strategic thinkers at the time argued that the Western Hemisphere constituted an exceptional environment for the British Empire (Shaw 1895).

42. May (1991: 46–47).

43. That Venezuela I helped materialize the American empire for the British is evidenced by the increase in attention paid to the United States in parliamentary debates and the media (Gerlach 2001: 258; Rock 1989: 49).

44. Unnamed cabinet minister cited in Bourne (1970: 171). British policy shift can be traced in Foreign Office (FO) files 80/362, 364, 367.

45. These phrases were reported in the *Times* (London), January 16 and 28, 1896. Already in the 1850s, British authors argued that an Anglo-American war would be fratricidal (Crawford 1978: 209).

46. Quotations from Kohn (2004: 27) and Gerlach (2001: 223).

47. Quotations are from Shoultz (1998: 118-9. Also see Carnegie (1895).

48. May (1991: 57)

49. For debates regarding America's "liberal tradition," see Smith (1999). For a broader context, see Gerlach (2001), Butler (2007), and Quinault (2000). On the status of Venezuela I in liberal IR, see Owen (1997).

50. Campbell (1974: 183).

51. Quoted in Gerlach (2001: 214). A survey of the press found that 90 percent of newspaper editors in the United States supported the Anglo-American arbitration (Rock 1989: 27; also see Kohn 2004: 39–40). The arbitration movement was popular in Europe, too, save for Germany (May 1991: 35; Collin 1990: 104).

52. Edward Dicey, quoted in Orde (1996: 27–28). Also see Anderson (1981), Kohn (2004), Kramer (2002), and Seed (1958, 1968). Even Salisbury supported America's acquisition of the Philippines (Bourne 1967: 345).

53. Orde (1996: 198n47).

54. On the effect of these rumors, see Rock (1989: 28n23), Campbell (1974: 192) On Olney and Lodge, se Rock (1989: 28, 53). It took two decades for Lodge to call for a *formal* Anglo-American alliance, however (Moser 2007: 11).

55. Roosevelt to Arthur Lee, November 25, 1898 (Morison, Blum, and Chandler, 1951, Volume 2: 890). Also see Anderson (1981: 129).

56. Roosevelt to Lee, Dec 31, 1901 (Morison, Blum, and Chandler 1951, Volume 3: 214). Also see Roosevelt to Hay, July 1, 1902 (Ibid.: 214). For discussions, see Campbell (1974: 190–193). Orde (1996: 26–27), Tilchin (1997: 17).

57. It found that six in ten Americans were Anglo-Saxons, one-quarter were "Continental Teutons," and one-tenth were Celts (Belich 2009: 67).

58. Respectively, George Wharton Pepper, cited in Rystad (1991: 12) and Frederick William Chapman, cited in Kramer (2002: 1321, fn. 15), Martellone (1994: 88) and Hofstadter (1965: 164).

59. Hannigan (2002: 90) Cf. Hofstadter (1965), Kramer (2002) and Ninkovich (1986).

60. Quoted in Kramer (2002: 1331). Also see Jacobson (1999: 218). Turner, who favorably reviewed Roosevelt's book, in all likelihood agreed (Collin 1990: 51).

61. Hofstadter (1965: 169, also see 171).

62. For Aaron Friedberg, Britain's appeasement of America was a major "gamble" (1988: 298). The appeasement thesis can indeed be sweeping in scope, as in Paul Kennedy's famous argument that the British Empire maintained its preeminent position among great powers from 1865 onward chiefly by managing to appease some challengers in order to retain resources to deter others (Kennedy 1981, 1987, cf. Black 2008).

63. Rock (2000: 40). One East Coast newspaper thus saw British appeasement in January 1896: "No American has dreamed of attributing this to cowardice" (Ibid. 2000: 43).

64. See Allen (1969: 563) and Turk (1987: 3, 28).

65. For Roosevelt, civilization was always policy, but the "foremost civilizing power" was usually Britain, not America (Ninkovich 1986: 241, 234; Tilchin 1997: 19, 99). As it developed in the 1880s Germany, the discourse of *geopolitik* argued that the ultimate goal of the state is competition for the control of resources, territory, and populations.

66. See the chapters in Hilton and Ickringill (1999), Sears (1927), and Perez (1998).

67. Pitt (2000: 151, 153). For historical samples of French perspectives on the Anglosphere, see, inter alia, Demolins (1897), Herrison (1936), and Duchesne (2007).

68. It is important to note that pro-Boer Americans voiced their anti-British protest in the same way as some antiwar Liberals in Britain (Kramer 2002: 1340–1344). On the meanings of the war in the United States and elsewhere, see Anderson (1981), Gooch (2000), Kohn (2004), Koss, ed., (1973), Knee (1984), Krebs (1999), Mulanax (1994), Noer (1978), and Wilson (2001).

69. Cited in Mulanax (1994: 83).

70. Roosevelt to John Strachey, January 27, 1900, and to Cecil Spring Rice, July 3, 1901 (Morison et al. 1951, Vol. 3, pp. 9 and 109). Also relevant are the president's letters to A. D. White, December 18, 1901 and January 16, 1902 (Morison et al., 1951, Vol. 2, pp. 208, 218), to Arthur Hamilton Lee, January 30, 1900 (Ibid.: 1152), and Elihu Root, January 29, 1900 (Ibid.: 1151), to Frederick Selous, February 7, 1900 (Ibid., p. 1152), and to Anna Roosevelt Cowles, December 17, 1899 (Ibid., p. 1112–-1113).

71. On the framing and counterframing moves, see Allen (1969: 586, 592), Campbell (1974: 182), Noer (1978: 135–136), and Tilchin (1997: 9).

72. The writer Mark Twain and William Jennings Bryan were well aware of the double standard, as were many others (Kohn 2004, Kramer 2002). Anglophobic anti-imperialism was more discursively resonant before the United States took over Spain's colonial possessions in Asia (Montbard 1896).

73. Perkins (1968: 89). The policy was all the more remarkable considering that it constituted a major liability in the November 1900 elections.

74. *New York Times*, September 14, 1900.

75. At some point, Rhodes hoped his scholarships would help create a secret society of men who would recover the United States for the British empire (Schaeper and Schaeper 2004: 14).

76. Roosevelt to Hermann Speck von Sternburg, July 12 and October 11, 1901 (Morison, Blum and Chandler, 1951, Vol. 3: 115–116, 172). Nancy Mitchell finds that the British framed the crisis identically (1999: 86).

77. See Mitchell (1999: 34), Pletcher (1998: 391), and Ricard (1991: 66).

78. The nature of the ultimatum remains a historiographic controversy (Ricard 1991; Collin 1990: 98–99; Mitchell 1999: 65, 87, 98; Healy 1988: 103-4).

79. The poem was published in the London *Times*, December 22, 1902. Two years earlier, the same newspaper reported that German s identified themselves as Huns during the anti-Boxer intervention in China in 1900 (*OED*, 1989).

80. "White Man's Burden" addressed American men singularly, and Kipling even personally sent an advanced copy to Roosevelt (Collin 1990: 156).

81. Germans were the second largest immigrant group in the United States, but like the Irish they did not vote as a single bloc. In addition, some Germans identified as both Anglo-Saxons and Teutons (Jacobson 1998: 45, cf. Belich 2009: 62–65).

82. Compare, for example, *The Times* on December 10, 12, and 16 to December 22, 25 and 27. Liberal newspapers such as the *Guardian* and *Westminster Gazette* were critical of the government from the week one of the crisis. For detailed overviews of the press, see Guthrie (1983: 138–147), Holbo (1970), Kneer (1975: 37-60), Lee (1976: Ch. 4), and Mitchell (1999: Ch. 2).

83. Two *Guardian* editorials, on December9 and 12, carefully explained that the war is with Venezuela, not the United States; the Anglo-American peace was the "cardinal principle of foreign policy," while on December 5 *The Times* informed the reader, without interpreting anything, about move of Admiral Dewey's fleet to the area. Tellingly, the presence of the U.S. fleet was ignored in the rest of the media and the parliament. For the key parliamentary debate, see Hansard's IV (1908), p. 1224–1287.

84. Memorandum 144 (Lord Lansdowne, "Proposed Coercion of Venezuela") October 17, 1902, CAB 37, vol. 63, roll 18.On the broader political context, see Allen (1969: 606), Campbell (1970: 182) and Mitchell (1999: 96–97).

85. *The Times*, December 25. Going easy on the government, *The Times* or *The Morning Post* argued in the first week of December that there was no crisis as long

as Washington singled out Germany as its main problem in the Caribbean (Mitchell 1999: 122).

86. See, for example, Lansdowne to George Buchanan, December 7 and 11, 1902, FO 420/206 and Herbert to Lansdowne, December 18, 1902, and February 8, 1903 (cited in Kneer 1975: 40, 52).

87. His Liverpool speech, noted *The Times* on February 14, 1903, marked the completion of a significant shift in the way the British government in general and the Conservative Party in particular stood on the issue of the Western Hemisphere. Salisbury also concluded, in private, that the Monroe Doctrine should be seen as a "rule of policy" (Herwig 1986: 193–194; also see Gerlach 2001: 213–224).

88. The agreement between Berlin and London might have been "iron-clad," but the British people had the power to dissolve it. See *New York Times*, January 26, 1903. Also see *Nation* 75, December 18 and 25. On these framing moves, see Adams (2005: 61–62), Collin (1990: 101, 116), and Herwig (1986: 240).

89. The terms are from *Nation* 8, January25 and 29, *Harper's* January 27, and *New York Times*, January 29.

90. Quoted in Collin (1990: 111). On anti-German feelings on both sides of the Atlantic, see Herwig (1986: 202), Adams (2005: 55), Guthrie (1983: 205–209), Kneer (1975: 44), and Mitchell (1999: 105).

91. Both speeches are in Boyd (1970). For discussions, see Allen (1969: 567), Bourne (1970: 164–165, 456–457), Kohn (2004: 109–122), Rock (1989: 28), May (1991: 53) and Mock (1981).

92. Roosevelt thus came to see Venezuela II in terms of Kiaochow, not only the Monroe Doctrine (Collin 1990: 101).

93. Kennedy (1980: 292). For latest overviews of realism's balancing theories, see Schweller (2006) and Nexon (2009).

94. Kennedy (1984: 21). Also see Ibid. (1980: 389, 399).

95. Liberals, too, have observed that the meanings of race and liberalism mixed together, but only in passing (Owen 1997: 203n29). On the evolution of the meanings of German democracy in U.S. foreign policy thought, see Oren (2003).

96. See, especially, Roussel (2004), Shore (1998), and Warner (1960).

97. Compare, for example, Mulanax (1994: 208) and Campbell (1960: 4–5).

98. Most Canadians emphasized differences, as did foreign observers like Friedrich Engels and James Bryce (Lipset 1990: 6). For contemporary debates on annexation, see Smith (1891)and Douglas (1894). For historical assessments, see Hastings (2006), Kohn (2004) and Sarty (1996).

99. On the positive reception of his speech, see Kohn (2004: 148–149).

100. See, inter alia, Risse-Kappen (1995a) and Hopf (2002).

101. Indeed, neither are democracy and liberalism the same thing nor are all democracies the same across time and space. See, inter alia, Oren (2003), Widmeier (2005), Risse-Kappen (1995b), cf. Williams (2001).

102. German foreign office memos would indeed typically state that "the Monroe Doctrine has not become an international law, to which the European nations are tied. It remains largely a question of power for the United States of North America to gain general acceptance" (Kennedy 1980: 196; also see Ibid: 178–179, Mitchell 1999: 82; and Herwig 1986: 209–116). Tellingly, the "N" in the "USNA" was dropped after Venezuela II.

103. Sir Michael Herbert to Lansdowne, 25 February 1903, cited in Tilchin (1997: 60–61).

104. See Herwig (1986: 234–235), Kennedy (1984: 18–22), and Mitchell (1999: 105). On the changing status of Germany in the Anglo-American foreign policy discourse, see Hannigan (2002), Oren (2003), and Jackson (2006).

105. Belich (2009).

106. Citations are from Belich (2009: 127, 208, 68, 480, 473, respectively).

107. van der Pijl (1998). This is but an example drawn from a rich family of IR theories divided into "Amsterdam," "York," "market civilization," and other schools of thought. Compare, for example, to Cox (1996) and Hobson (2007). To be sure, scores of diplomatic historians and IR scholars have also recognized the close relationship between Anglo-American economic "complementarities" and the rapprochement (for example, Rock 2000: 45–46; Campbell 1974: 201–202).

108. Belich (2009: 120, 480).

109. van der Pijl (1998: Chapter 1).

110. On the "deeper" origins of the AASR, also see discussions in Adams (2005), Bell (2007), Belich (2009), Burton (1973), D. A. Campbell (2007), Myers (2008), and Tilchin (1997).

111. It is true that Churchill's call for unity came after Washington terminated lend-lease and nuclear cooperation a year earlier, much to the displeasure of London. But it is also true that the "Iron Curtain" was a collective affair, whereby British foreign minister Bevin and U.S. President Truman were each given a say in the drafting of the speech. The American public opinion might not have cared much about the AASR at the time, but the American president cared enough about it to let Churchill trot about English-speaking unity. See Gilbert (1988: 159–220) and Harbutt (1986: 152, 159–182, 182–208).

112. Deudney (2001: 189). Compare to Bell (2007: 260–272) and Belich (2009: 457–460).

113. "Very white men" was the term used by U.S. Rear Admiral Charles Stillman Sperry, the commander of the so-called "Great White Fleet," to greet his Australian hosts in 1908 (Reynolds and Lake 2008: 3).

114. Streit privately published 300 copies of the first book in 1938, with the help from the friends in the world federalist movement. Streit's books (1939, 1941, 1961), like some of Churchill's wartime speeches on the same subject, represented a much broader intellectual trend at the time (Szent-Miklósy 1965).

Today, there exists the Streit Council for a Union of Democracies in Washington, D.C., which "works toward better-organized and stable cooperation among the experienced democracies as the key for more effective US engagement in world affairs" (Streit Council, 2008).

115. The latter term comes from Ovendale (1985). For considerations of its longevity and effectiveness of the AASR relative to other alliances, see Burk (2007), Danchev (2006), Dumbrell (2006), Gamble and Kearns (2007), and Reynolds (2006).

116. Young (2003: 100).

117. NZ Army (2006). This time, there was no change in the acronym.

118. See, especially, Haglund (2004) and Heuser (2000).

119. Canada became a party in 1948, Australia and New Zealand in 1956. See Richelson (2008: 342–349) and Reynolds (2006: 320–321). More generally, see Keefe (2006) and Walsh (2009).

Chapter 3: ANZUS, Britain, and the "Pacific Pact"

1. ANZAC stands for the combination for Australian and New Zealand Army Corps who fought in World War I. The historian F. L. W. Wood introduced the term *ANZAC dilemma* in 1953 to describe Australian and NZ alliance politics (McIntyre 1995: 396–402; McKinnon 1993: 117; Waite 2006: 899). In this chapter, I will use the term *ANZAC* alongside the terms Australasia, Antipodes, and Tasman neighbors to invoke, when present, the various forms of identity and unity between Australia and New Zealand.

2. Historians have used declassified archival documents to suggest that "ANZUS motives" were more complex, but the extant historical revisions have generally been kind to the traditional explanations (McIntyre 1995: 346–347; cf. McLean 2006: 70; Umetsu 2004: 172).

3. Simply put, white and mostly English-speaking men did not trust their Asian allies, and vice versa. For discussions, see Acharya (2005), Capie (2003) and Hemmer and Katzenstein (2002). The terms *Asia* and the *Pacific Area* are not necessarily retrospective, but this chapter will use the more contemporary label *Asia-Pacific*.

4. McIntyre (1995: 400; also see Ibid.: Ch. 1, 172–174; Lowe 1999: 77-9, Meaney 2003: 409 O'Neill 1981: 200; Waite 2006: 903).

5. The British diplomats talked about their informal membership as the "silent partnership" (Williams 1987: 253). As David McIntyre later discovered, the very acronym ANZUS was in fact coined in the Foreign Office, in October 1950 (1995: 286–287;

cf. Lowe 1999: 78). On U.S.–U.K. relations over ANZUS, see McHenry and Rosecrance (1958: 328); cf. Meaney (2003) and Trotter (2007).

6. A NZ official quoted in McKinnon (1993: 122n42). Also see McIntyre (1995: 299, 310) and Waite (2006: 908).

7. See memos and press clippings in the National Archive of Australia (NAA), FO 371/101240-1. For primary sources, see Appendix. In 1954, Churchill's foreign secretary Eden reportedly welcomed SEATO not least because it "remove[d] the anomaly of our exclusion from ANZUS" (Williams 1987: 260; also see McIntyre 1995: 362–363, 383–384).

8. Belich (2009: 461).

9. See Pocock (2005) and Belich (2001, 2009). Recall that the official "White Australia" policy was only slowly taking over the unofficial "British Australia" policy or that the move to restore the word "British" on Australian passports in 1950 received huge public approval (*The Age*, February 20). Early public opinion polls suggested that most Australians preferred the term *British* Commonwealth, not Commonwealth as well as British, not Australian citizenship. See Australian Public Opinion Polls (APOP), nos. 47–49 (November–December 1947); 775–787 (July 1951); and 788–799 (August–September 1951). Available at the National Archives of Australia (NAA). For an index, see Beed et al. (1983).

10. A declaration made by eight "Commonwealth Prime Ministers" in April 1949 (Australia, Canada, Ceylon, India, New Zealand, South Africa, Pakistan, and the United Kingdom) begins with the term "British Commonwealth" but ends with the "Commonwealth of Nations," which heretofore became official. When it was coined in the 1880s, the term *British Commonwealth* referred to the white part of the British Empire (Belich 2009: 469–470).

11. See *Australian Quarterly* 22: 2 (June 1950), p. 32. New Caledonia, wrote one Australian editor, is "French island in an Anglo-Saxon Ocean," *The Age*, April 22, 1950. All subsequent dates refer to this year, unless indicated otherwise.

12. For example, Aotearoa, the indigenous and exotic name for New Zealand, had no equivalent in Australia (Reeves 1924/1950). On the historical status of Aryanism among the Maori and Pakeha, see Belich (2001: 210–234, Ibid.: 466). In line older Aryan ideas, the second-best Pakeha were the Dutch (*NZ Herald*, July 8). For comparative perspectives on Britishness in the Antipodes, see, inter alia, Meaney (2001), Ward (2001), Belich (2001, 2009), McKinnon (1993), and Rickard (1996).

13. Prime Minister Holland once offered New Zealand meat to Britain for free (McKinnon 1993: 114, 99–101). Also see Belich's discussion of the "protein bridge" (Belich 2001). On the differences among Australian, Canadian, and New Zealand nuclear policies and their relationships to the Anglo-American Atomic Energy Defence Agreement of 1958, see Reynolds (2003) and Dumbrell (2006).

14. Belich (2001: 319), McLean (2006: 72), and McKenzie (2006: 566).

15. "Where she goes, we go" is famous phrase uttered by New Zealand Prime Minister Michael Joseph Savage when he declared war on Germany on 3 September 1939. For discussions of the trope, see Belich (2001: 320), McKinnon (1993: 113), and Trotter (2007: 414). The phrase was meaningful in Australia, where the British declaration of war against Germany was interpreted as automatically committing all dominions, as well as in Canada, whose government famously "waited" a week before officially joining the war. Writing in *The Atlantic* in 1939, Stephen Leacock, Canadian satirist, captured what the much-vaunted sovereign status meant to Canadians then: "If you were to ask any Canadian, 'Do you have to go to war if England does?' he'd answer at once, 'Oh, no.' If you then said, 'Would you go to war if England does?' he'd answer, 'Oh, yes.' And if you asked, 'Why?' he would say, reflectively, 'Well, you see, we'd have to.'" (quoted in Nossal 1997:149).

16. On Evatt, see Day (1996). The middle power discourse arguably informed the drafting of Articles 23 and 44 of the U.N. charter. For its history in Australian and Canadian foreign policy, respectively, see Ungerer (2007) and Chapnick (2005a). On the concept itself, see Stairs (1998: 271–279).

17. For a statement on this new role, see Casey (1949) and Spender's address to the Australian-American association, March 20, 1950, *Current Notes on International Affairs* 21: 30 (March), 226–227. Also see Spender (1972).

18. The passage is from *Walkabout*, March 1, p. 12.

19. See *Meanjin* 9:1, Autumn, p. 47, and *Sydney Morning Herald*, January 9.

20. Nuclear weapons took away the safety of distance such that Soviet submarines, argued one military man in the *Canberra Time* (June 15), would soon be able to nuke Australia's capital cities. Communism was the top problem identified in the Australian Morgan-Gallup polls (APOP, numbers 690–699 [June–July 1950] and numbers 822–834 [December 1951–January 1952]).

21. In August, Australian communists were merely a concern; by October, with the outbreak of the war in Korea, they became "enemies" and "traitorous minority" (*Sydney Morning Herald*, August 4; *The Age*, October 21). In New Zealand, labor strikes were thought to be organized by "Commos" or "Communist wreckers," many of whom directly worked for the Soviets (*NZ Herald*, March 3).

22. Like new immigrants, these new states were potentially "good neighbors" (*Canberra Times*, July 15 and *Advertiser*, April 1). Rich in these ambiguities is Clune (1950).

23. Speech on May 30, 1950. Reprinted in *Current Notes* 21:5 (May), pp. 353–355.

24. Australian historiography, too, is quick to chalk up the Colombo plan as "Spender's Plan," but it is more likely British, whose diplomats were inspired by America's Marshall Plan for Europe. Compare J. B. Hunt's ANZUS memo in (British) National Archives (NA), FO, FE 36/37/2, November 12, 1952 , to Spender's address to Parliament on March 20, 1950, in *Current Notes* 20:3 (March), pp. 226–229. For the context, see Oakman (2004).

25. The *Bulletin* editorial of January 11 is quoted in Lowe (1999: 54–55). For *Sydney Morning Herald*, compare editions from January 16 and 22.

26. For *Sydney Morning Herald*, compare editions from January 16 and 22.

27. No sentence better captures the anti-Japanese feeling of the Australian elites than that from a memo from Spender to Menzies written in January 1951, which identified Japan as "the only country which represents an actual threat to Australian security in the foreseeable future." This was in the midst of the Korean War, of course (quoted in Meaney 2003: 404).

28. Quotations are from McIntyre (1995: 334, 297).

29. Quoted in Umetsu (2004: 180) .

30. Quoted in McIntyre (1995: 263). The New Zealand cabinet described such pact as "disastrous" (Trotter 2007: 420).

31. These memos are discussed in McIntyre (1995: 250, 255, 259. 267–268, 302).

32. Spender to Harrison, February 21, 1951, NAA, A6768, EATS 77/A, 1071.

33. Quotations are from McIntyre (1995: 333) and Lowe (1999: 81); cf. *DNZER* III, pp. 606–609, McKinnon (1993: 117n20), Cheeseman (1999: 278), McLean (2006: 68), and Meaney (2003: 400).

34. For discussions of various types of evidence, see Lowe (1999: 51, 56n60) and Meaney (2003: 406).

35. Williams (1987: 245, 248).

36. New Zealand Prime Minister Holland in *DNZER* III: 573–574, 582–584, 586.

37. On the role of British diplomacy at this stage, see the documents in NA DO35/2937 as well as McIntyre (1995: 327-31, 335) and McKinnon (1993: 121).

38. Lowe (1999: 81).

39. Quoted in Belich (2001: 319). On the contentious politics of China recognition from the perspective of Anglosphere countries, see Beecroft (1991).

40. For the decision, see *DNZER* III: 536–537; cf. Templeton (1994).

41. Quoted in McKenzie (2006: 567).

42. Quoted in Trotter (2007: 421).

43. Canberra contributed an air force contingent as well as military aid to colonial authorities in Malaya, but greater resources in the end went to the Middle East. The decision carried despite the fact that the memories of Singapore were refreshed by the tenth anniversary of Pearl Harbor. For discussions, see McIntyre (1995: 190) and Lowe (1999: 59–62, 2001: 193).

44. For blow-by-blow official histories of the war from ANZAC perspectives, see McGibbon (1993) and O'Neill (1981). On Korea in the context of East–West confrontation, see Stueck (1997).

45. Quote is from Meaney (2003: 402) and McIntyre (1995: 277).

46. For figures, see O'Neill (1981: 75–76).

47. Quoted in Lowe (1999: 67, cf. 114).

48. *Advertiser*, October 3.

49. Speech on June 26, 1950 (Menzies 1958: 3–20). Footnotes later inserted in the speech indicate that the prime minister regarded the outbreak of the war as consistent with the speech he made.

50. Respective quotations are from McLean (2006: 70) and McKinnon (1993: 112).

51. On the varying reception of these statements in the press, see Belich (2001: 319), McKinnon (1993: 112, 177, 120–125), McLean 2006: 77–78), and Trotter (2007: 420–421). Both governments were aware of the need to finesse ANZUS to their audiences. The alliance with America was the "richest prize," wrote New Zealand External Affairs Minister Doidge in private but then added: "In embarking on any forward step in this direction, we must be certain that we are not appearing to be turning away from Britain" (*DNZER* III, p. 545–546).

52. These calls were made in the aftermath of the visit of the U.S. "Great White Fleet" in 1908 and in 1937, following Japan's invasion of China, but the general idea probably goes back to the nineteenth century (cf. Horne 2007, Lake and Reynolds 2008).

53. On the racialized feedback from the United States, see Capie (2003).

54. Sinclair (1959: 304). For Wellington, double nationalism always required balancing act. Indeed, a seemingly sharp pro-American turn symbolized by the signing of the ANZUS treaty had to be matched by a number of pro-British moves, including a parliamentary motion recognizing Queen Elizabeth II as the "Queen of New Zealand," a category distinctive from her role elsewhere in the empire.

55. This argument was occasionally put forward by both Evatt and Menzies in the Australian debates (O'Neill 1981: 87; McIntyre 1995: 302; McLean 2006: 288).

56. Menzies to Holland, March 16, 1951, NAA A6768 EATS 77/3.

57. See *DNZER* III: 593–613.Spender's contribution to the making of ANZUS was undeniable, yet grossly exaggerated in Spender's own account (Spender 1969; cf. Lowe 1999, 2001; Martin 1999, McIntyre 1995, Umetsu 2004).

58. Quoted in Trotter (2007: 418).

59. McKenzie (2006: 559).

60. See, especially, Koremenos, Lipson, and Snidal (2004).

61. The comment could be apocryphal (McIntyre 1995: 21, Meaney 2001: 17, Ibid., 2003; 403).

62. See, for example, Maryanne Kelton's analysis of bargaining within an "Anglo cultural context" in Australia–U.S. relations (2008: 13).

63. See Shimazu (1998: Ch. 6).

64. For figures and discussion, see Mein Smith (2005: 223), Belich (2001: 438-440), and Hoadley (2000: 45–48)

65. Young (2003: 94). Compare to Hoadley (2000).

66. Ibid.

Chapter 4: Suez, Vietnam, and the "Great and Powerful Friends"

1. See MacMillan and McKenzie (2003) and Donaghy (1995).

2. It was with irony that Australia's Prime Minister Menzies used this phrase to describe Australia's alliances with Britain and the United States during the West New Guinea dispute in 1962 (Chauvel 1997). For perspectives on Australian and Canadian foreign policies that generally resonate with my narrative in this chapter, see Wesley and Warren (2000), Stairs (1982), and Ross (1984).

3. For example, the movie *Manchurian Candidate*, argued one magazine for men, is "fiction, but could be fact" and then proceeded to explain that prostitutes could be KGB agents (*Man*, February 1964, p. 6 [for primary sources, see Appendix]). Australia and Canadian Gallup polls suggest that communism and the Cold War were among top five national problems in the period covered in this chapter (APOP, Nos. 1070–1080, February–March 1955, and Nos. 1581–1591, February–March 1962; Schwartz 1967: Ch. 3 and Ch. 6; Bothwell 2007: 214). More generally, see Whitaker and Marcuse (1995) and Lowe (1999).

4. Paul Martin's speech to the House of Commons, May 22, 1964. On Canada's overwhelming Euro-Atlanticism at the time, see Bothwell (2009), Roussel (1998), Nossal (1997), and Haglund (2000).

5. Frank Underhill, quoted in Rutherford (2005: 198). As in Australia and New Zealand, Canadian history textbooks, historical novels, and special occasion media reports from the 1950s strongly implied that Canada "owed" both its statehood *and* its nationhood to Britain (Igartua 2006).

6. Hindsight suggests otherwise, but no look at primary sources can dismiss the contemporary belief in the Commonwealth. What historiography now calls the "fourth empire" was an all-Commonwealth attempt to reverse Britain's postwar decline, perhaps comparable to the "new imperialism" of the turn of the twentieth century (Darwin 2006, McKenzie 2006).

7. Alexander (1956: 145). For similar statements, see Greenwood (1955, esp. Ch. 5 and 9) and Stone (1955).

8. Edwards with Pemberton (1992: 168, 173). Also see Bridge (1998).

9. Menzies, cited in *Current Notes* 26: 2 (February 1955), p. 117,Also see *Sydney Morning Herald*, January 26 and 29.

10. Casey to U.S. Secretary Dulles, ANZUS meeting, July 30, 1954. Quoted in Pemberton (1987: 46). Cf. Edwards and Pemberton 1992: 127–138, Lee 2005: 432–433. Menzies said the same thing, but the word was "unthinkable" (Waite 2006: 909). For more on the proposed intervention, see *FRUS* 1952–1954 Vol. 13, 1181–1236. The intervention failed because congressional approval was contingent on British participation.

11. The metaphor was coined by the historian J. B. Brebner in 1945. On its uses, see Underhill (1964), Holmes (1979: Part III), Eldridge (1997), Haglund (2000), and

Spittal (2009). Alternative metaphors include the "bridge," "hinge," "interpreter," "honest broker," "linchpin," or, more recently, "go-between." Australia positioned itself similarly at the time (Casey in Millar 1972: 338; Donaghy 1995: 11).

12. Belich (2009: 466).

13. Ross (1954: xi).

14. Both terms are simplifications. For the necessary correctives and contextualizations, see Chapnick (2005b), Massolin (2001), Roussel (2004), and Stairs (1982).

15. The quotations is from Brown et al. (1950: 57, also see Ibid.: 127, 146, 165; cf. Trudel and Jain 1970). For a variety of anti-Americanisms in Canada over time and across its regions, see Bothwell (1992), Donaghy (2002, esp. Ch. 5), Granatastein (1996), Lipset (1990: Ch. 3–4), Massolin (2001), Rutherford (1990, esp. Ch 8), Sturgis (1997), and Wise and Brown (1967). For a useful taxonomy of anti-Americanisms in the world, see Katzenstein and Keohane (2006).

16. For statements of this doctrine, see Pearson (1970: 140–147) and Holmes (1979). On the differences between Canadian liberal internationalism and American "Wilsonianism," compare Keating (2002, 2006) to Doyle (1997) and Ikenberry (2004). On Canada's move from the Triangle to the Atlantic, see Haglund (2000: 46–49) and Roussel (1998).

17. Comparable international data suggest that only the Americans held a more favorable view of the United Nations at the time. For data and discussion, see Schwartz (1967: 77–79).

18. Like other Anglosphere allies, Britain kept Australia in the dark about its Suez policy from the planning stage to the decision to collude with Israel (Hudson 1989: 65–67; Martin 1999: 331, 347). On New Zealand, see Templeton (1994: 179–180). For other international reactions, see and Louis and Owen (1989).

19. On Menzies and his towering influence on the Australian foreign policy at the time, see discussions in Cain (1997), Hudson (1989), Lowe (1999), Martin (1999), and Bongiorno (2005).

20. External Affairs Minister Casey and Defense Minister Philip McBride abstained from the cabinet vote, expressing worries about rifts in the Western alliance and wider instabilities. See Cabinet conclusions on August 7, NAA A5462/118/2/4. Menzies's internal correspondence shows that pro-British policy was a foregone conclusion (NAA MS 4936, Series 1-16-Suez). In September, Casey wrote in his diary that the use of force would be make Britain "lose face," not least because "America and Russia are likely to be strongly against" but also because "Israel would want to horn in" (Millar 1972: 244–246).

21. See *Advertiser,* November 9, and *Argus,* November 2.

22. Quoted in Martin (1999: 347).

23. Bothwell (2007: 127–130) and O'Reilly (1997: 90–91).

24. In the English-language texts, Suez signified a disagreement between the United States and Britain; apart from glib references to the "Anglo-French" invasion, France was irrelevant (Igartua 2006: 124, 129). Also note that, prior to invasion, Pearson suspected a French-Israeli secret deal (Bothwell 2007: 126).

25. Quoted in Eayrs (1957: 107). Family metaphors varied across texts and contexts: Britain and France were mothers or stepmothers, while the United States was a cousin, a brother, or an uncle.

26. Canada's Conservatives indeed applauded the governments of New Zealand and Australia (O'Reilly 1997: 87*n*110).

27. With an exception of Finance Minister Walter Harris, the Canadian cabinet argued for the wait-and-see policy. In dealing with the British government, however, Canada's overarching concern was the Anglo-American "divergence," not the United Nations (St. Laurent to Eden, October 31, 1956, *DCER*, p. 187).

28. The frame resonated among the elites. Britain's own Foreign Office asked Ottawa to help and OK'd the peacekeeping proposal before the fateful U.N. vote (Telegram 1501, November 1, *DCER* 22: 191–192).

29. Canada's permanent representative to the United Nations noted that Britain did not want to solve the crisis but to humiliate the enemy (Telegram 755, September 25, *DCER* 22, 167–169).

30. Records of Cabinet discussions in November–December 1956 are in Library and Archives Canada (LAC), RG 2 Vol. 5775, Ser. A-5-a; Vol. 6109 and Vol. 5775, various files. For analysis of press reactions to this debate, see Igartua (2006: 124–129) and Bothwell (2007: 129).

31. Bothwell (1992: 144), Eayrs (1957: 103), Hilliker and Donaghy (2005: 31). Another Gallup poll, taken in October, indicated that a slight plurality of anglophone Canadians preferred British foreign policy over American foreign policy, though it was unclear from the wording whether the questions referred to Suez (Schwartz 1967: 64–65; 70; cf. Igaratua 2006: 118–119).

32. Adams (1988). Also see Eayrs (1957) and Igartua (2006: 119–124).

33. For this newspaper, American policy in Suez was "erratic" and confused (October 3, October 16), while Britain invaded to "make peace" (November 2). The letters to the editor overwhelmingly supported this line, accusing Ottawa for "kowtowing" to the United States and describing the Liberals as "sell-outs" and "American lapdogs" (November 9 and 20). Even when Pearson's peacekeeping proposal was met with near-universal welcome, the newspaper continued to deride it, calling their own Canadian peacekeepers "a typewriter army" and an "international farce" (November 20 and 21). A few of published letters positively treated the United Nations (November 5).

34. See Rooth (2005) and Muirhead (2007: Ch. 5).

35. Arnold Heeney, Speech to the Canadian Club, Hamilton, 29 April, 1964. In Arnold D. P. Heeney Papers, MG 30 E144, Vol. 10, LAC.

36. For Quebec-centered perspectives, see Létourneau (2004) and Rudin (1997).

37. A rare and limited survey of francophone Quebeckers found that roughly a quarter of respondents favored Quebec's separation from the rest of Canada at the time (Schwartz 1967: 49, n. 32).

38. *Maclean's*, February 8, p. 20.

39. *The Globe and Mail*, November 2, 1964.

40. Conway's essay "What Is Canada?" from *The Atlantic Monthly*, was cited even by government officials (for example, Martin 1967: 71). Compare Conway to Lipset (1964).

41. On the Australian and Canadian interpretations of Britain's turn to Europe, see, inter alia, Benvenuti and Ward (2005), Darwin (1988), Goldsworthy (2002), Muirhead (2007), and Ward (2001).

42. For example, in response to De Gaulle's veto to its application to the Common Market, London proposed the establishment of a joint Anglo-American nuclear force (Colman 2004). Had this proposal succeeded, the AASR and the Anglosphere would have probably become as institutionalized as NATO.

43. *The Australian*, July 15.

44. Hasluck (1964: 53) In selling the American alliance to their audiences, Australian authors would typically invoke the trope Coral Sea, which signified U.S.–Australian victory against Japan in World War II, against Gallipoli, Singapore, and Tobruk, Australia's wartime defeats associated with British incompetence.

45. *Man*, April 1964, pp. 40, 80.

46. Quoted in Martin (1999: 500).

47. See Edwards (2005: Chs. 7 and 8), Lee (2005), and Woodard (2004: Ch. 13).

48. Pearson's speech to the Canadian Club in Ottawa, February 10, 1965, *Statements & Speeches* 1965/6, LAC.

49. Martin's speech to Canadian and American Public Relations Societies, Montreal, November 9, 1964 (Martin 1967).

50. Schwartz (1967: 73–77).

51. On this point, see Holmes in *The Globe the Mail* 2 November, 1964, Pearson in *Maclean's* 2 May, 1964.In comparison to their Canadian counterparts, peacekeepers from other nations were merely "tourists" (*Le magazine Maclean*, 2 October, 1964, p. 5).

52. Quotations are from Holmes (1964: 106–107) and Ibid. (1971: 190–191).

53. Bothwell (2007: 215).

54. Britain and the United States assigned this role to Canada, who accepted it rather grudgingly (Bothwell 2000–2001).

55. For these two claims, see, inter alia, Bothwell (2000–2001), Edwards with Pemberton (1992: 335–340), Ross (1984: Ch. 1), Woodward (2004: Ch. 15).

56. Edwards with Pemberton (1992: 280).

57. McEwen to Wilson, January 19, 1965, quoted in Edwards with Pemberton (1992: 341).

58. It also supported the U.N.–French proposal for neutralization of Indochina and also envisaged support for Thailand if all of Indochina fell to communists. Cabinet document 493, October 22, 1964, CS file 1473, A4940/1, NAA. The hypothetical location for the military exercise in September 1964 was Thailand (Edwards with Pemberton 1992: 11).

59. Scherger became known to history as a "politician in uniform" (Edwards with Pemberton 1992: 375). Hasluck and Paltridge were Menzies appointments during the Cabinet reshuffle in April 1964.

60. The counterfactuals are developed by Woodard (2004: Ch. 16). On Casey, see Hudson (1989: 252–253). Barwick was asked to resign after he had upset both the Americans and the ALP opposition with his argument that ANZUS would apply should Indonesia escalate its conflict in Borneo (Edwards with Pemberton 1992: 281–282).

61. Consider the discussion in *Quadrant*, January–February 1965, p. 3. Hasluck specifically argued against this interpretation (Edwards with Pemberton 1992: 353–354).

62. Fifty-nine percent supported and 23 percent opposed the intervention in Borneo/Malaysia in May 1964; in February 1965, the relation was 65 percent to 26 percent (APOP nos. 1745–62, April–July 1964; nos. 1804–19, February–March 1965). Hawkish opinion against Indonesia also obtained in October and December, following the face-off with the Royal Navy in the Sunda Straits (Edwards with Pemberton 1992: 322). In comparison, the Vietnam intervention in May 1965 was supported by 52 percent and opposed by 37 percent of Australian respondents (*Advertiser*, May 15).

63. The opposition ALP failed to offer a unified alternative reading: Gough Whitlam endorsed American retaliation, while his colleague John Cairns suggested that Washington could have fabricated the incident. On the parliamentary debate and press reactions, see Edwards with Pemberton (1992: 307–314, 347–349).

64. *The Australian*, September 16; *Sydney Morning Herald*, September 14. On the government reaction, see Edwards with Pemberton (1992: 320–321).

65. Quoted in Edwards with Pemberton (1992: 375).

66. Quoted in Edwards with Pemberton (1992: 362). Recently, Woodard (2004) found evidence that Canberra committed combat troops to Vietnam on December 17, 1964. This is still unclear. Compare cabinet minutes of December 17, 1964, 659/FAD; and April 7, 1965, 859/FAD; and in CS file C4643, respectively, part I and II, A4940/1, NAA.

67. The parliamentary quotes are from Hansard, 29 April 1965, vol. 45, pp. 1060–1061, and 4 May, vol. 46, 1107–1121. The government's expressed rationale for intervention was consistent with internal government documents. Vietnam was Australia's long-term project of containing Asian communism and building the American alliance. Key sources are A1838 Department of External Affairs (DEA) files 3014/2 and 30140/10, and A4950 Cabinet discussions (CS), file C4643, NAA.

68. Quoted in *Australian*, April 6, 1965.

69. Menzies (1968b: 8).

70. Internal memo, quoted in Bothwell (2000–2001: 109).

71. On the international discourses on the war, see Logevall (1999) and Daum, Gardner, and Mausbach (2003).

72. For an eyewitness account, see Richie (1983: 79–80) and compare to Pearson (1975: Vol. 3 137–143). Historiography sees the incident as overblown. Pearson had publicly implied disagreement with U.S. policies earlier that year but was well aware that the Temple speech would constitute a risky "political act" (Bothwell 2007: 225–227; Donaghy 2002: 128–131; English 1992: 362–369; Thompson and Randall 2008: 219–220, Ross 1984: 262–263).

73. Acheson's views on Canada are discussed in Bothwell (2009).

74. Holmes (1971: 185).

75. For an overview of the literature, see Preston (2003: 74–76). For a month-to-month account of Canadian foreign policy in the period under study, see Eayrs (1983).

76. Canadian polls on the Vietnam War show an average 44:33 ratio in favor of American intervention until mid-1965. Thereafter the prowar opinion fell, but the balance between critics and supporters was more or less equal until 1968, possibly even 1970 (Azzi 1999: 135 Holmes 1971: 199; Bothwell 2007: 216, 230; Ross 1984: 450). Johnson was popular with a majority of Canadians and was probably more popular in April 1965 than in April 1964 (English 1992: 144, cf. *Maclean's*, January 23, 1965, p. 18).

77. See Donaghy (2002: 126–127), Logevall (1999: 156–163), Preston (2003: 96–99, 104), and Ross (1984: 275–280).

78. Ross (1984: 32–33, 267).

79. Gordon resigned from his post in 1965 but later established himself as a vocal critic of the American intervention in Vietnam and one of the leaders of the influential "new nationalist" movement in Canadian politics (Azzi 1999: Ch. 7). Canadian cabinet memos are not as clear on Vietnam as are those in Australia, but see Pearson Papers, MG 26 N 6, Vols. 9–10 and in Department of External Affairs (DEA), RG 25/10122/20-22-VIET.S, LAC.

80. Martin's memoirs tell a story of growing disillusionment with the United States (Martin 1985). Also see Reid (1985).

81. The gas in question turned out to be a tear gas, but this wasn't clarified before many Canadian commentators called the United States militarist and racist (Bothwell 2007: 224). The alternative media were even more critical. The newsmagazine *Canadian Dimension*, self-defined as "the product of the post-nuclear generation of leftish thinker," reported on the use of napalm and torture and argued as early as March 1965 that the United States had lost the war; see March–April 1965, p. 4.

82. Bothwell (2009: 20). In one of his speeches at the time, Holmes pointed out that moralism often led to hypocrisy. Canada would have not been so "noble" had it possessed limited land and resources, or "large communities of non-European peoples."

Speech to Hamilton Canadian Club, April 29, 1964, in LAC, Heeney Papers MG 30 E144, Vol. 10 (file not numbered).

83. Eayrs (1983: 242–450) and Bothwell (2000–2001: 110).

84. Bothwell (2007: 131, fn. 42).

85. Levant (1986: 174).

86. Cf. Bothwell (2000–2001: 110).

87. Pierre Trudeau, White Paper on Indian policy, 1968, cited in Weaver (1981: 55). The disproportional political power of the French-speaking province is also reflected in the geographic, religious, and linguistic identities of sixteen Canadian prime ministers between 1896 and 2006. In a crude and retrospective essentialization, half of them could be described as WASPs. In contrast, between 1789 to 2008, the White House was continually occupied by WASPs, save for the 1,000 days of John F. Kennedy, 1961–1963.

88. Pearson (1972, II: 296). It was through much debate in 1964 that the Canadian Red Ensign, the British merchant marine flag displaying a colonial heraldic shield for Canada, was changed to the current red and white flag with a single maple leaf. According to a 1964 Gallup poll, the new flag was supported by a majority of Quebeckers, but no more than a third of respondents elsewhere in Canada (Schwartz 1967: 106–109, cf. Johnson 2005, Igartua 2006: Ch. 4). Save for Quebec and Nunavut, all Canadian federal units have at least one English or British symbol in their flags. The province of Ontario adopted a modified version of the Red Ensign in 1965. In Australia, the national flag debate was sparked only by the 1988 bicentennial and has continued since.

89. See Haglund (2005) and, especially, Massie (2010).

90. O'Reilly (1997: 93).

91. For telling reflections, see Holmes (1971: 196–198).

92. See Kelton (2008), cf. Higgott and Nossal (1998).

93. Reportedly, so rich was the network of cross-border institutions in 2000s that neither government has been able to count them (cf. Roussel 2004).

94. In the aftermath of 9/11, the US and Canada agreed to allow troops from either country to cross their mutual border and serve under the command of the country that they enter, if either country is attacked by terrorists. For various discussions, see Sokolsky (2004), Haglund (2005) and Charbonneau and Cox (2008).

95. On this finding, there seems to be a near-consensus among the students of U.S.–Canadian relations. See, inter alia, Bothwell (2007, 2009), Legault et al. (2005), Massie and Roussel (2005), and Thompson and Randall (2008).

96. Not unlike the success of efforts to end slavery and slave trade in the nineteenth century, the campaign functions as a unifying, feel-good story in contemporary Anglosphere-talk. On the antiapartheid campaign from constructivist IR perspective, see Klotz (1995).

97. According to Stuart Hall, *multi-cultural* refers to demographic facts, while *multiculturalism* refers to "strategies and policies" (2000: 209). From this point of view, core Anglosphere societies were "multi-cultural" long before they were "multicultural."

98. For parts of this story, see Lake and Reynolds (2008).

99. Hattam (2007). Doubtless, students of racialization will continue to rework the conceptual distinctions between ethnicity and race. Theo Goldberg's "ethno-race" might prove to be the most descriptively accurate concept (Goldberg 2008; cf. McCarthy 2009).

Chapter 5: Empire, Iraq, and the "Coalition of the Willing"

1. Consider, for example, Canada's defense "strategy 2020" and Britain's defense white paper Cm 4446, both of which were drafted in 1999.

2. David Haglund finds that Ottawa and Paris had identical positions on the war and submits that "if Paris decreed the war to be justified, Ottawa would have snapped to attention" (2005: 180). Some Labour Party members reportedly asked Blair in private to join the Europeans (Stothard 2003: 207, 81–83).

3. See Jedwab (2003) and Goot (2007).

4. Quoted in *Globe and Mail*, March 29, 2003. Thanks to its prior deployments to the Gulf and various military exchange programs it had with the United States, Canada had more troops in the theatre of operations during the fighting most coalition member states (Maloney 2003, Haglund 2005, cf. Sokolsky 2004).

5. In addressing young Canadians, newcomers, and permanent residents, Citizenship and Immigration Canada (CIC) stressed the importance of individual rights and responsibilities, but also of compromise and diversity, including "Canadian values" of respect, freedom, belonging, and peace, among others (CIC 2003, also see Ibid., 2001, 2002).

6. See Smith (2002: 91) and Sinclair (2002: 437) For these sources, see Appendix.

7. Parekh et al. (2000: 38–39). For the historical context, see Mandler (2007: 229–242).

8. Kundani (2002a, 2002b).

9. See *The Globe and Mail*, March 20, 2002; Shields (2002: 75); Elton (2002: 204); and McMillan (2002: 493–494).

10. Blair (2002a). Cf. Parmar (2005).

11. Menno (2004).

12. Giddens (1998).

13. Gamble (2003). For the bridge metaphor, also see Hill (2005: 397, 391), Clarke (2007: 601–602), and Paterson (2007). That this metaphorization structured British foreign policy options was obvious to Blair's cabinet minister Robin Cook, when he concluded in his diary that a "bridge cannot make choices" (2003: 133).

14. The idea was Churchill's, but it was put in practice by Attlee and Bevin. For British Atlanticism in 2000s, see, especially, Dunne (2004), Danchev (2007), O'Meara and Lavallée (2006), Riddell (2003), and Williams (2004).

15. Reynolds (2006: 330).

16. On liberal internationalism in British foreign policy discourse at the time, see Dunne (2004), Hill (2005), Clarke (2007), and various contributions in Little and Wickham-Jones (2000).

17. On the doctrine, see Blair (2001, 2002a, 2002b). For a sample of responses, see Boyce (2003), Edmonds (2002), Leonard (2002), Rogers (2002), and Mepham and Eavis (2002).

18. Blair (2003a, cf. Ibid.: 1997, 1998, 2002a, 2003c) and Labour Party (2001: 38). On the contradictions, see Williams (2004).

19. See, for example, Blair (2002c). On the centrality of the United States (and the Commonwealth) in Blair's liberal internationalism, see Kampfner (2003: 16–17). Cf. Parmar (2005) and Hill (2005).

20. For much-discussed statements, see Cooper (2002) and Ferguson (2002). For Blair's own views on empire, see Parmar (2005).

21. Each label can be regarded as an update of slightly more retrospective catch-phrases and caricatures such as "helpful fixer," "honest broker," "mediator," "do-gooder," and "good international citizen."

22. *Maclean's*, February 24, 2003.

23. Axworthy spoke at Princeton University in April 1999. On the idea of human security as "security for all people, everywhere," see Axworthy (2001). Also see DFAIT (2000), ICISS (2001), McRae and Hubert (2001), Jockel and Sokolsky (2000–2001) and Nossal (1998–1999). For an *ex-post* analysis, see Keating (2006).

24. This critique was associated with a variety of positions. See, inter alia, Crosby (2005 [2003]), Cohen (2003), Sjolander et al. (2003). . Indicatively, relatively few Canadian critics questioning the idea of human security in the abstract.

25. For critical discussions, see Hart and Tomlin (2002), Clarkson (2002), and Byers (2002–2003).

26. This strand was associated with individuals like Allan Gotlieb, former ambassador to Washington, and Wendy Dobson of the C. D. Howe Institute. Compare Gotlieb (2003) and Goldfarb (2003) to Jackson (2003). For a review of this debate, see Barry (2007).

27. On Canada's policy of dithering, see Harvey (2005:193–215), Keating (2006), Massie and Roussel (2005), and Legault et al. (2005).

28. The day after Chrétien announced Canada's non-participation, a *Globe & Mail* reporter made the following observation: "The decision to deploy the Canadian Forces to Afghanistan has a couple of political benefits for Ottawa. Washington welcomed

it, and it also effectively swept aside the option of sending any significant number of Canadian troops on an Iraq mission" (March 18, 2002).

29. January 15, 2002. Also see *The Scotsman*, April 30, 2002.

30. *The Economist*, January 11, 2003. *Daily Telegraph* was more sympathetic to U.S. efforts. Because of superior facilities and treatment—forceful feeding, "clean and relatively comfortable" cages, free health care—Afghan captives in Guantanamo were unlikely to "starve themselves to death in the manner of the 1980s IRA prisoners" (March 10, 2002).

31. Ipsos-Reid poll, *The Globe and Mail*, May 7, 2002. For a comprehensive media analysis, see Yaniszewski (2007).

32. Preemptive strikes related to tactical or anticipatory self-defence, as in the idea of "first strike," while preventive strike relates to strategic gain. The distinction was blurry in most usages. As for morality, the document argued that the United States had a "special" task to defend liberty, justice and human dignity "everywhere" (NSS 2002: 3-4). On the NSS and its reception, see Peterson and Pollack (2003).

33. The term gained currency after the Iraq fiasco, but see Clarkson (2002).

34. See the pieces by Jonathan Freedland (September 18, 2002), Linda Colley (December 27, 2002), and Paul Kennedy (January 16, 2003). In March 2003, U.S. Secretary of State Donald Rumsfeld famously proclaimed that "we don't do empire." For the meanings of empire denial, see Cox (2005).

35. Blair's biographers see 9/11 to be the genesis of this link (Seldon 2004: 498; Stothard 2003: 69-70, 87-88; Kampfner 2004: 173; also see *Daily Telegraph*, October 17, 2002, 27).

36. See Danchev (2007) , Keohane (2005: 69, 74) and Naughtie (2004: 22).

37. For early public dismissals of the war in Iraq in Britain, see Kampfner (2003: 152-160). Compare to Marcel (2002).

38. Frum was then fired by Bush (Thompson and Randall 2008: 307).

39. Kampfner (2003: 168).

40. Blair apparently believed that the Gulf War–era resolutions against Hussein (that is, Resolution 687) could be used to justify war. Eventually, Lord Goldsmith, Britain's attorney general at the time, declared the invasion legitimate and (probably) legal (Kampfner 2004: 30).

41. Stothard (2003: 42).

42. Quoted in Seldon (2004: 574). On the idea of trading support for influence, see Blair (2003a, 2003e). It is known that Blair had a wish list on the Middle East, but it is unclear if he shared it with Bush and, if so, when, at the Crawford meeting or at the Camp David meeting in September 2002. The official sources significantly differ on this issue (Kampfner 2004: 167-168; Meyer 2005: 207-213, Woodward 2004: 119-120, 177-179; Seldon 2004: 578). Another open question is whether Blair could have had any influence in Washington, given the asymmetric nature of the AASR

(Meyer 2005: 27). For one, note that Israel and Saudi Arabia were informed of the exact timing of the U.S. attack on Baghdad, not Britain (Woodward 2004: 395–399; also see Steele 2009).

43. See Cook (2003: 102), Naughtie (2004: 129), Kennedy-Pipe and Vickers (2007: 217–218), Stothard (2003: 70). On Blair's hawkishness and pro-Americanism, as well as his dominance in the political process on Iraq, see, inter alia, Kampfner (2003: 161) and McLean and Patterson (2006: 362).

44. Quoted in *The Times*, January 14. Blair was confident on the second resolution despite the fact that Washington said it was not going to wait for it and the fact that only two U.N. Security Council votes, Bulgaria and Spain, were seen as "guaranteed" (Clarke 2007: 606; Kampfner 2003: 256; Cook 2003: 308–309, 314, 324; Stothard 2003: 218; Woodward 2004: 297, 337–338).

45. Doves were Robin Cook (Leader of the House of Commons), Clare Short (International Development), Margaret Beckett (Environment), Alastair Darling (Transport), Andrew Smith (Work and Pensions), and possibly Jack Straw (Foreign Affairs). See the reports in *The Times*, August 16 and September 2, and *The Guardian*, August 16, 2002. It was the norms of collective responsibility and "sofa government" that prevented a full-blown cabinet-level debate (Cook 2003: 212–214; also see Seldon 2004: 261 and O'Malley 2007). On the diffidence of Whitehall to challenge Downing Street and other intragovernmental politics that stymied the Iraq debate, see Steele (2009).

46. Keohane (2005: 68). Among senior Conservatives, dissent was heard from MPs John Gummer, Kenneth Clarke, Malcolm Rifkin, and Douglas Hurd (Ibid. 2005: 68).

47. Claire Short also resigned in protest against the war, though two months later. As Christopher Hill noted, no prime minister had accepted two cabinet-level resignations over foreign policy since 1914 (2005: 403).

48. Gamble (2003: 230).

49. Interview in *The Guardian*, March 1, 2003. Blair made the same point in a speech to his party in February (Riddell 2003: 1, Woodward 2004: 337). At the time of this writing, five inquiries have found that Blair acted on false intelligence, but not a single one concluded that the prime minister lied to the public. The "B-liar" debate will probably continue, philosophically as well as empirically (Bluth 2005; Cook 2003: 311; Hoggett 2005a, 2005b; Danchev 2007).

50. The quote is from Naughtie (2004: 79). Bush was reportedly concerned that the Blair government would fall over Iraq, so he suggested that British troops participate in "a second wave [as] peacekeepers or something." Blair declined, stating: "I absolutely believe in this too" (Kampfner 2004: 168, 203: Seldon 2004: 74: Woodward 2004: 338).

51. Kampfner (2004: 146). Also see Seldon (2004: 593), Naughtie (2004: 144), and Woodward (2004: 204-211).

52. Dunne (2004: 908). For a broader historical context, see Dumbrell (2006: 210-215).

53. Cook (2003: 320).

54. Dunne (2004: 895).

55. For a different interpretation, see Martin (2003: 418).

56. On the level of plagirization, see Bothwell (2009: 35*n*30). Much like Bush, Harper, who became the prime minister in 2006, idolized Churchill and his ideas on the English-speaking peoples (Spittal 2009).

57. Quoted in Legault et al. (2005: 155).

58. See, especially, Ignatieff (2003). Ignatieff later was elected as the leader of the Liberal Party of Canada.

59. Here my interpretation differs from that by Legault et al. (2005: 157–162). The details are sketchy, but McCallum did not change his position even after he learned that Canadian military representatives had been shut out from a U.S.–led NATO work group on the invasion of Iraq in February 2003. Author's confidential interview with a Department of Defense official, May 2005.

60. For roughly similar readings, see Michaud (2006) and Legault et al. (2005).

61. See, inter alia, Legault et al. (2005: 153) and Thompson and Randall (2008: 309).

62. Quoted in *The Globe and Mail*, January 30, 2003.

63. Quoted in *National Post*, February 15, 2003.

64. Graham wished the Americans "godspeed," but Chrétien said this: "Of course, I hope that the Americans will do as well as possible." Quotes from *National Post*, March, 25, 2003 and Thompson and Randall (2008: 310).

65. The effect of this election on the Iraq debates has been debated. Compare Sokolsky (2004, Lachapelle (2003), Legault et al. (2005), Harvey (2005), and Keating (2006). The decision makers' memoirs minimize the impact of the election (Chrétien 2007: Chs. 12–13; Goldberger 2006: Ch. 18).

66. On the pervasiveness of this framing, see Legault et al. (2005: 171–173). Paul Cellucci, the American ambassador to Ottawa, arguably played up Canadian fears.

67. Keohane and Nye (2001).

68. More accurately, Keohane and Nye contend that sensitivity and vulnerability shape international relations; the first refers to the openness to external economic pressures and the second to the ability to withstand costs associated with these pressures (2001; for the Canada–U.S. dyad, see Ibid., Ch. 7).

69. The cross-border trade in fact increased in the aftermath of Chrétien's Iraq decision on March 18 (Author's e-mail correspondence with Kim Richard Nossal, June 2005).

70. Compare Russett and Oneal (2001: Ch. 4) to Wendt (1999: 344–349).

71. For a critique of representational knowledge and a call for a Bourdieu-inspired practice turn in IR theory, see Adler (2005), Pouliot (2008). Also see, inter alia, Hopf (2002), Mitzen (2006), and Williams (2001).

72. Hopf (2002). For a call to keep the practice-habit distinction in IR theory, see Hopf (forthcoming). Race theory normally goes beyond discourse to theorize perception, practices, and habits. For example, on habit and the mind–body distinction in philosophy from a pragmatist/transactional perspective, see Sullivan (2006: Chs. 2–3). Also see Alcoff (2006: Chs. 7–8).

73. Holmes (1964: 107).

74. See, for example, the report in *The Globe and Mail*, April 8, 2003.

75. Bothwell (2007: 226), Thompson and Randall (2008: 217). Also see Holmes (1971: 185, 192).

76. Kissinger (1979: 383).

77. For a discussion, see Nossal (1997: 80). On the mutual invisibility of Americans and Anglophone Canadians, see Belich (2009: 61, 152).

78. An Ipsos-Reid poll published in the same newspaper on April 14, 2003, showed that most U.S. respondents were unaware of Canada's stance on the Iraq war.

79. Holmes himself noted that the collaboration between Australian and Canadian diplomats during the Cold War was "so habitual that it was taken for granted" (1979: 44).

80. Cited in Dumbrell (1996: 220). One could argue that Washington's effort to internationalize its war in Vietnam (the "more flags" program) failed mainly because Britain, as America's go-to ally, never got on board (Ellis 2004: 267; cf. Colman 2004: 145–149).

81. It was Clive Ponting who argued that an informal and secret deal was made in 1960s in which the United States agreed to prop up the (nondevalued) pound as long as Britain politically (for example, Vietnam) and strategically (that is, holding the "east of Suez" line) supported American foreign policy. For discussions, see Busch (2003: 196) and Colman (2004: 78–85). Cf. Danchev (2006), Dumbrell (1996), Logevall (1999), and Marsh and Baylis (2007).

82. Ricks (2006: 430–440).

83. Bennett (2004, 2007).

84. Conquest (2005: 221–232).

85. The newsmagazine urged Conquest to follow up on his Anglo association idea ("Bones of Contention," December 1, 2005).

86. Bell (2007: 272).

Chapter 6: The Anglosphere Identity and Its Limits

1. In this aspect, salutary is the work by Gheciu (2005) and Legro (2005), and Krebs (forthcoming).

2. This process has many angles. See, inter alia, Borstelmann (2002), Hyam (2007), and Klotz (1995).

3. These scholars are too numerous to cite. For a small sample from the second half of the 2000s, see Balibar (2007), Goldberg (2008), Lake and Reynolds (2008), McCarthy (2009), and Roediger (2008).

4. *Islamophobia* is an exceedingly unhappy term, but it can be said to refer to a general refusal to recognize claims to certain multicultural historical narratives as well as the fact that the majority of second- or third-generation immigrants tend to embrace the dominant discourses of state/national identity. On the Muslim Other in the Anglosphere, see, inter alia, Birt (2009), Jones (1993), and Mamdani (2004).

5. *The Economist*, November 13, 2009.

6. See Friedman (2009) and Wingfield and Feagin (2010). Compare to McCarthy (2009: 125–126) and Roediger (2008: 212–130).

7. On the changing racialized status of Latino and Chicano identity in the United States, see Alcoff (2006) and Hattam (2007).

8. See, especially, Goldberg (2008: 228–236). The logic of racialization suggests that ethnic groups can be reinscribed as racial (Ibid.; Baum 2006: Ch. 7).

9. Lake and Reynolds (2008: 352). McCarthy suggests that this line is almost exactly where it was when W. E. B. Du Bois first wrote about it a century ago (2009: 11; cf. Vincent 1982, Gilroy 2000, Borstelmann 2002). On the idea of "global apartheid," see Mazrui (1977).

10. Mearsheimer (2001: 141, 251).

11. Elman (2004: 563).

12. Ibid. (2004: 567).

13. Perkins (1955).

14. The Mortefontaine agreement that ended this conflict in 1800 also paved the way to the Louisiana purchase (De Conde 1966).

15. See, inter alia, Allen (1969: 577–584, 608), Bourne (1967: 343–344; 1970: 172), Burk (2007: 212–224). For a recent revisionist account of this piece of history, see D. A. Campbell (2007).

16. Bourne (1967).

17. See, in addition to Bourne (1967), Allen (1969), Campbell (1960), Campbell (1974), Friedberg (1988) and Rock (2003). For a critical review of balance-of-power explanations of the post-1812 peace in North America, see Roussel (2004).

18. Burk (2007: 265).

19. On the relationship between America's conquest of Mexico and Anglo-Saxonism, see Horsman (1981). In the aftermath of the war, U.S. federal courts ruled in favor of granting citizenship to conquered Mexicans, without granting them "white" status (Hattam 2007, Jacobson 1998, Roediger 2008)

20. Quoted in Schultz (1998: 70). For a thesis that transatlantic Anglo-Saxonism emerged in the 1950, see Crawford (1978, 1987). My keyword searches through the

digital newspaper databases of suggest that the term *Anglo-Saxon* rose in popularity only toward the end of the century.

21. Quoted in Prochaska (2006:165).

22. See, especially, Little (2007) and Thompson (2007).

23. Elman (2004: 568, fn. 5) and Schweller (2006: 2).

24. For recent discussions from the perspective of IR theory, see Steele (2005) and, once again, Little (2007) and Thompson (2007). For recent historical reinterpretations, see Blackett (2001), D. A. Campbell (2007) and Myers (2008).

25. Rock (2000: 43). Also see Azubuike (2005).

26. A *Washington Post* article from December 30, 2005, suggested that the aim of the Crimson Plan was to "bring these Molson-swigging, maple-mongering Zamboni drivers *to their knees!*" (italics in the original). The comic tone is a testament to the unthinkability of war in Northern America. My discussion draws on Preston (1977), Grenville (1979), Ross (2004), and Rudmin (1993).

27. See Ross (2004: 8–10, 95–96), Bourne (1967: 40), Grenville (1964: 389), and Kennedy (1979: 8–10).

28. See, especially, War Office: 35/55; 106/40; CAB 8/1. Bourne has suggested that some key British documents were lost (1967: 325, 330). Campbell notes that at this time Chamberlain sometimes intervened in the planning process to remove the United States from the list of potential enemies (1970: 175).

29. Ross (2004: 8–10).

30. Ibid.: 15.

31. By this I mean that a random English-speaking nation was found to be more likely to fight alongside the United States than a state where another language is in primary use. For this analysis and its limits, see Vucetic (2011).

32. In the 2000s, the term empire was back in fashion as was the debate on how to define it. See, inter alia, Cox (2005), Porter (2006), Barkawi and Laffey (2001), Ikenberry (2004), Lake (2009), and Nexon and Wright (2007).

33. On power in IR, see Barnett and Duval (2005).

34. Doyle (1997) and Russett and Oneal (2001). The proponents of the democratic peace often recognize Clarence Streit as one of the discoverers of the democracies peace.

35. See Doyle (1997: 284). For the reasons of space, I cannot discuss disagreements over how to interpret and apply Kant's thought within the liberal agenda in IR. Is interdependence primarily economic? Are international institutionalization and legalization as important as unit-level constitutionalism or individual human rights? Are electoral democracies a poor proxy for Kantian republics? For this discussion, see, inter alia, Ellis (2005), Jahn (2005), and MacMillan (2006).

36. Kant (1991 [1795]). The constructivists I have in mind are Risse-Kappen (1995b) and Williams (2001).

37. From a constructivist perspective, security communities can therefore manifest themselves not only as liberal zones of peace but also as zones of separate peace made up by authoritarian and illiberal state members (Acharya 2001).

38. See, especially, Owen (1997) and compare to Roussel (2004).

39. Fanis (2001: Ch. 4).

40. For an overview, see George and Bennett (2005: 45–54).

41. On learning and socialization in constructivist literature, see Adler and Barnett (1998: 37–45) and Wendt (1999: 326–335).

42. Russett and Oneal (2001: 49–52).

43. Barkawi and Laffey (2001: 2; also see 2006: 346–349), Gheciu (2005: Ch.6), MacMillan (2006: 58–67), and Williams (2001). This ontology is already implicit in realism and liberalism, given their intimate familiarity with binarizations such as democracies versus autocracies, great versus middle powers, revisionist versus status quo states, and so on.

44. Barkawi and Laffey (2001) and Henderson (2008). For liberalism-versus-empire perspective on the liberal peace, see Jahn (2005), MacMillan (2006), and, indeed, Doyle (1997).

45. Barkawi and Laffey (2006: 332). Also see Grovogui (2007: 235).

46. Jahn (2005: 180–185), MacMillan (2006: 54–58); cf. Ellis (2005).

47. On Kant's human hierarchy, see Mills (1997: 71; cf. McCarthy 2009: 50n27). Liberals must not forget that Kant's day job was to teach racist anthropology and geography, not liberal philosophy (Harvey 2000: 532, also see Eze 1995 and Elden and Mendieta, eds., 2011).

48. A textbook treatment of Kant's "political writings" underscores how the great philosopher denied the "superiority of any one race or people. His conviction of the historical nature of all events, whether past, present or future, prevented him from promoting this dangerous intellectual aberration" (Reiss 1991: 199–200, compare to Jahn 2005: 194, MacMillan 2006: 72).

49. Mills (2005: 169). Also see, inter alia, Bernasconi (2001, 2003), Ellis (2005), Eze (1995), Larrimore (1999, 2008), and McCarthy (2009).

50. Bernasconi (2003: 22; also see 2001), Ellis (2005), and Mills (2005).

51. Michael Williams has argued that membership in a Kantian community always carries moral superiority (Williams 2001).

52. See, especially, Mills (1997). Feminist critics have made a similar point about the public/private line.

53. Internal and external colonial regimes were typical in the era of classical liberalism; now, the status of inegalitarian ideas, institutions and practices within liberal polities is more ambiguous. For discussions, see Mehta (1999), Smith (1999), and Goldberg (2008).

54. Haglund (2004). Also see Heuser (2000).

55. Hitchens (2007). What is "natural" in this passage was unnatural for Hitchens in his earlier work on the subject (Hitchens 2004). Indeed, that young officer's ancestors might have also fought in the American Revolutionary War, the Maori Wars, or some other conflict that is to the Anglosphere what World War I and II are for the EU.

56. The document also added this: "We also need to be able to operate alongside our most technically advanced allies and in coalitions of the willing." See Ministry of Defence (2003: 8, 14).

57. Thanks go to Stephanie Carvin for drawing my attention to the latter.

58. Young (2003: 114).

59. Reported in *USA Today*, March 25, 2006. I thank Sandra Halperin for addressing me to this quote.

60. As I said in Chapter 5, this self-reinforcing connection was acknowledged even by the government experts in Washington, who concluded that the Iraq War was a net loss in security for the United States in the WOT. For this discussion, see Closs Stephens and Vaughan-Williams (2008) and Kennedy-Pipe and Vickers (2007).

61. Miliband (2009). On Demos's report, see Mandler (2007: 235).

62. Slaughter (2009).

63. Citations are from Daalder and Kagan (2007) and Ikenberry and Slaughter (2006), respectively. Italics are mine.

64. Blair (2006).

65. Clarke (2007: 599).

66. For the reasons of space, I cannot engage the enormous and sparsely connected literature on the power of English in the global society. On the Anglo cultural zone from a neo-Whorfian perspective, see Wierzbicka (2006). On "linguistic imperialism," see Mazrui (1975), Ives (2006), and Phillipson (2009). For a useful conceptualization of "language communities," see Laitin (2000).

67. On the centrality of India in contemporary Anglosphere-talk, see Hitchens (2007) and Windschuttle (2005).

68. Singh concurred but added that "both principles and pragmatism" counted in this partnership. See Obama and Singh (2009).

69. Vucetic (2010).

70. For a classic discussion of this case in IR theory, see Risse-Kappen (1995a). In Andrew Roberts's revisionist account, the spat had much to do with the contingencies of the U.S. presidential election in November 1956 (Roberts 2006: 434). On the British side, the proverbial lesson was learned, memorably captured by one of its politicians: "We must never get out of step with Americans—never" (Ibid.).

71. By (anthropomorphic) analogy, like the best of nuclear and extended families, mature security communities are characterized by their ability to resolve conflict as peacefully and as efficiently as possible. Also, U.S. sanctions against Britain over Suez must be juxtaposed against a long and continuous history of American economic sup-

port in the issues surrounding the convertibility of the pound, which began in 1947 when the holders of British currency sold truckloads of it (the currency crises occurred in 1951, 1955, 1956, 1964, 1965, 1966, 1967, 1972, and 1975). For this story, compare Roberts (2006) and Van der Pijl (1998). Also note that Suez has long been a paradigmatic case for theories of alliance politics. Studies from a variety of perspectives (misperceptions, two-level games, institutional context, transgovernmental politics, transnational networks, collective identity), have all observed the extraordinary resilience of the Anglo-American alliance. See, inter alia, Pressman (2008), Richardson (1996), Risse-Kappen (1995a), and Bially Mattern (2005).

72. Louis (1990: 152). Also see Risse-Kappen (1995a: 97) and Louis and Owen (1989).

73. Bially Mattern (2005).

74. Ibid: 10, 56, 98. For a more traditional alliance theory perspective on Anglo-American interactions in the "transitional" post World War II period, including Suez, see Pressman (2008).

75. Bothwell (2007: 227; also see 1992: 70–1), Donaghy (2002: 178), Granatastein and Hillmer (1991: 234), Thompson and Randall (2008: 236–241, 254–257). Once again, this is *not* to say that issue-linked bargaining never takes place in security communities (for example, Kelton 2008: Chs. 6–8).

76. In the original formulation by Karl Deutsch, pluralistic security communities are peace and cooperation communities among states; when states integrate to the point of formal unification, security communities become amalgamated (Deutsch et al. 1957; Adler and Barnett 1998: 30). On the civil wars in the Anglosphere, see Phillips (1999).

77. See, for example, the work on NATO by Risse-Kappen (1995a) and Gheciu (2005).

78. Mitzen (2005).

79. See the reports in *The Guardian* and *The Washington Post* on March 25, 2009.

80. Wendt (1999: 36).

81. Pierson (2004).

82. Stephenson (1995). For a discussion, see Vucetic (2010).

83. Wendt (1999: 299, 306).

84. See discussions in Wendt (1999: Ch. 5; 2004); cf. Wight (2006: Ch. 5).

85. Collective agents can be more or less institutionalized, which affects their authority to coerce members into cooperation. The EU is more institutionalized than the "coalitions of the willing" or international campaigns to ban or promote certain practices (for example, R2P, land mines). On different forms of agency in world politics, see Wendt (1999, 2003).

86. The empire's corporate agency was cut short by the success of the American Revolution. The French diplomatic recognition of the United States induced the British

parliament to relinquish the right to tax settler colonies for revenue, thus forever differentiating Canada from Kent. Cf. Bell (2007).

87. Roberts (2006: 1). The American empire discourse of the 2000s typically emphasized the analogies with Rome, not, say, Ming or Soviet empires. Belich concludes that the Anglo-world has more in common with the Greek, Arab, and Mongol cultural zones than with Rome (2009: 559).

88. On the world state from the perspective of one U.S. official, see Talbott (1992). On the world state from the point of view of IR theory, see Wendt (2004).

Appendix: Note on Primary Sources

1. Angenot (1989).

2. For a discussion, see Belich (2009: 148–152).

3. I used a true random number generator for each publication period—1–30 for daily newspapers, 1–4 for weekly or quarterly periodicals—and then accessed data accordingly.

4. Mott (1957: 131–134, 225–230).

5. As a rule of thumb, priority was given to the documents in Cabinet Office (CAB), Foreign Office (FO), and Colonial Office (CO) concerning Venezuela in 1894–1896 and 1902–1903 and among these to typed letters, memos and minutes, that is, the equivalent of those published in *FRUS*. When appropriate, analyzed were handwritten texts, such as comments left by senior officials, on the back, margins, and various printed attachments.

6. I excluded Canadian editions of American magazines like *Time* and *Reader's Digest*.

7. These are listed in the main bibliography (Cohen 2003, Clarkson 2002, Keating 2002, McRae and Hubert 2001, Michaud and Nossal 2002, Hillmer and Molot 2002, Sjolander, Smith and Stienstra 2003).

8. In 2009, the British government vetoed attempts by freedom-of-information campaigners to obtain records of cabinet proceedings from the run-up to the war. On the limits of the current evidence, see Danchev (2007) and Steele (2009).

9. For Blair's speeches in the study period, I followed the leads by McLean and Patterson (2006), Dyson (2006), and Saraceni (2003). In the Canadian context, Michaud (2006) was useful.

REFERENCES

BIBLIOGRAPHY OF PRIMARY SOURCES BY CHAPTER

Chapter 2: America and Britain, 1894 and 1900

Fiction and Nonfiction

Adams, Brooks. *America's Economic Supremacy*. New York: Macmillan, 1900/1947.

Adams, George Herbert. *Why Americans Dislike England*. Philadelphia: Franklin, 1896.

Baker, Marcus. *The Anglo-Venezuelan Boundary Dispute*. Washington, DC: Self-published, 1900.

Boutwell, George S. *The Venezuelan Question and the Monroe Doctrine*. Washington, DC: Gibson, 1896.

Bryce, James. *The American Commonwealth*, 2 vols. New York: McMillan, 1895 (facsimile reprint, Indianapolis: Liberty Fund, 1995).

Carnegie, Andrew, *Triumphant Democracy, or Fifty Years' March of the Republic*. London: H & Sons, 1894; revised edition.

Curzon, George Nathaniel. *Problems of the Far East*. New York: Longmans Green & Co., 1894.

Danyers, Geoffrey. *Blood Is Thicker than Water. A Political Dream. On the Desirability of a Commercial and Naval Union between Great Britain and the United States of America*. London: Tower Publishing Company, 1894.

Demolins, Edmond. *Anglo-Saxon Superiority: To What It Is Due* (translated by Louis Bert-Lavigne, *A quoi tient la superiorité des Anglo-Saxons*). New York: R. F. Fenno & Co., 1897.

Dicey, Albert Venn. *A Leap in the Dark: A Criticism of the Principles of Home Rule as Illustrated by the Bill of 1893*. London: John Murray, 1893.

Dilke, Charles W. *Greater Britain: a Record of Travel in English-speaking Countries during 1866 and 1867, Volume II*. London, Macmillan, 1869.

Fisher, Sydney G. "Alien Degradation of American Character," *Forum* (January 1893), 608–615.

Giddins, Franklin Henry. *Democracy and Empire, with Studies of Their Psychological, Economic and Moral Foundations*. New York: Thompson, 1900.

Grant, Ulysses S. (Ulysses Simpson). *Personal Memoirs of U.S. Grant, 1822–1885*. New York: AMS Press, 1972. (Facsimile reprint of 1st edition: Vol. 1, New York: C. L. Webster, 1894)

Holladay-Claghorn, Kate. "Our Immigrants and Ourselves," *The Atlantic* (October 1900), 535–548.

Hosmer, James. *A Short History of Anglo-Saxon freedom. The Polity of the English-speaking Race. Outlined in Its Inception, Development, Diffusion, and Present Condition*. New York: Charles Scribner's Sons, 1890.

Kidd, Benjamin. *Social Evolution*. New York: Rosset and Dunlap, 1894; facsimile reprint, 1906.

Kipling, Rudyard. *From Sea to Sea and Other Sketches*. London: Macmillan, 1900.

Lalor, John J. *Cyclopædia of Political Science, Political Economy, and the Political History of the United States by the Best American and European Writers*. New York: Maynard, Merrill, and Co., 1899.

Mahan, A. T. *The Influence of Sea Power upon History 1660–1783*. Boston: Little, Brown, 1890.

Mahan, A. T. *Lessons of the War with Spain and Other Articles*. London: Samson Low, 1900.

Montbard, Georges. *The Case of John Bull in Egypt, the Transvaal, Venezuela and Elsewhere*. London: Hutchinson, 1896.

Nye, Edgar Wilson. *Bill Nye's History of the United States*. Illustrated by F. Opper. Philadelphia and London: Lippincott Co. and Chatto & Windus, 1894.

Roosevelt, Theodore. *The Strenuous Life: Essays and Addresses*. New York: Century Co., 1900.

Roosevelt, Theodore. *The Winning of the West*, 6 vols. New York: G. P. Putnam's Sons, 1889–1896.

Seeley, John. *The Expansion of England: Two Courses of Lectures*. London: Macmillan, 1909 (reprint 1883).

Smith, Edward. *England and America after Independence*. London: Constable, 1900.

Smith, Goldwin, *Canada and the Canadian Question*. Toronto: Macmillan and Co., 1891.

Stead, William T. *The Americanization of the World, or, The Trend of the Twentieth Century*. London, 1900. (Facsimile reprint, Garland Publishing, 1972)

Stoddard. William Osborne, ed. *The Table Talk of Abraham Lincoln*. New York: F. A. Stokes Co.,1894.

Strong, Josiah. *The New Era, or The Coming Kingdom.* London: Hodder and Stroughton, 1893.

Strong, Josiah. *The US and the Future of Anglo-Saxon Race.* London: Saxon & Co, 1889.

Strong, Josiah. *Expansion under New World Conditions.* New York: Baker and Taylor Co., 1900.

Thomas, Allen Clapp. *A History of the United States.* Boston: D. C. Heath & Co., 1894.

Turner, Frederick Jackson. "The Significance of the Frontier in American History." In J. M. Faragher, ed., *Reading Frederick Jackson Turner,* 31–60. New Haven, CT: Yale University Press. (Reprinted from American Historical Association. Annual Report Edition for the Year 1893, 1894)

Unpublished Government Records

British Documents: CAB 37/40/54, FO 80/362–474, FO 420/157, FO 881/6710–6745; WO 106/40, B1/5–17 (Venezuela I); CAB 37/63/143–169, FO 80/458–475; FO 199/141–162; FO 420/206, 446–486; FO 800/114; CO 295/400–415 (Venezuela II); WO 35/55; 106/40; CAB 8/1 (general).

Foreign Relations of the United States (FRUS), Government Printing Office, Washington, DC, 1895: 488–504; 65–678; 1896: 23–31; 78–89; 234–245; 1902: 419–420, 439–441, 461–462, 477–479, 601–602; 1903: 1–5, 426–428, 439–441, 461–469, 473–474, 601–602, 791–792, 793–800, 804–805.

Published Private and Government Records

Boyd Charles W., ed. *Mr. Chamberlain's Speeches.* London: Constable and Co., 1914; New York: Kraus Reprint Co., 1970.

British Documents on Foreign Affairs. "Expansion and Rapprochement," by Kenneth Bourne, ed., Vol. 10 in Part I, Series C, North America, 1845–1914, in Kenneth Bourne and Cameron Watt, eds., Frederick, MD: University Publications of America, 1987.

British Documents on Foreign Affairs. "Venezuela, 1897–1908," by George Phillip, ed., Vol. 6 in Part I, Series D, Latin America, 1845–1914, in Kenneth Bourne and Cameron Watt, eds. Frederick, Md.: University Publications of America, 1987.

Cleveland, Grover. *Presidential Problems.* New York: The Century Co., 1904.

Hay, John. *Addresses of John Hay.* New York: The Century Co., 1906.

Hagedorn, Hermann, ed. *The Works of Theodore Roosevelt,* 20 vols, New York: Scribner, 1926.

Hansard (The Official Report/British Parliamentary Debates) Fourth series, v. 1/199 (1892–1908). London: Reuter's Telegram Co., 1908.

Johnson, Donald Bruce, and Kirk H. Porter (compilers). *National Party Programs, 1840–1972,* 2 vols. Urbana: University of Illinois Press, 1973.

Long, John. *After Dinner and Other Speeches.* Cambridge, MA: The Riverside Press, 1895.

Chapter 3: Australia and New Zealand, 1950–1951

Fiction and Nonfiction

Clune, Frank. *Ashes of Hiroshima: A Post-War Trip to Japan and China.* Sydney: Angus and Robertson, 1950.

Grattan, C. Hartley, ed. *Australia.* Berkeley: University of California Press, 1947.

Hardy, Frank. *Power without Glory.* Melbourne: Realist Printing and Publishing Co., 1950.

Levi, Werner. *American-Australian Relations.* Minneapolis: University of Minnesota Press, 1947.

Miller. Harold. *New Zealand.* London: Hutchinson, 1950.

Reeves, William Pember. *The Long White Cloud: "Ao Tea Roa."* London: George Allen & Unwin, 1950. (Reprint of original 1924 publication).

Rich, Colin. *Teko-Teko in Waitomo, Being an Unusual Adventure in the Underworld and the Glow-Worm River Cavern of Waitomo—A Familiar Haunt of the Maori Teko Teko.* Rotorua: Richlake, 1949.

Shute, Nevil. *A Town Like Alice.* Melbourne: Heinemann, 1950.

Tierney, John (aka Brian James). *The Advancement of Spencer Button.* Sydney: Angus & Robertson, 1950.

Unpublished Government Records

National Archives of Australia (series A462 Prime Minister, A1838 External Affairs, A3094 Pacific Pact, A4311 Canberra Conference, A5460 Pacific Pact, A5461 ANZUS).

National Archives, Kew, London (series DO 35 Commonwealth Relations, including FE 36 Far Eas; FO 371, Foreign Office, PREM 11 Prime Minister)

Published Private and Government Records

Holdich, Roger, Vivianne Johnson, and Pamela Andre, eds. *Documents on Australian Foreign Policy: The ANZUS Treaty, 1951.* Canberra: Department of Foreign Affairs and Trade, 2001.

Kay, Robin, ed. *Documents on New Zealand External Relations, vol. III: The ANZUS Pact and the Treaty of Peace with Japan.* Wellington: New Zealand Government Printer, 1985.

McGibbon, Ian, ed. *Unofficial Channels: Letters between Alister McIntosh and Foss Shanahan, George Laking and Frank Corner 1946–1966.* Wellington: University of Victoria Press, 1999.

New Zealand Foreign Policy Statements and Documents. Wellington: New Zealand Government Printer, 1972.

U.S. Department of State. *Foreign Relations of the United States, 1950,* Volume 6: East Asia and the Pacific. Washington, DC: U.S. Government Printing Office, 1976, 1–188.

U.S. Department of State. *Foreign Relations of the United States, 1951, Volume 6: East Asia and Pacific, Part I.* Washington, DC: U.S. Government Printing Office, 1978, 132–265.

Chapter 4: Australia and Canada, 1955 & 1964–5

Fiction and Nonfiction

Alexander, Fred. "Problems of Australian Foreign Policy July–December 1955." *Australian Journal of Politics and History* 1: 2 (May 1956), 145–154.

Berton, Pierre. *The Golden Trail: The Story of the Klondike Rush.* Illustrated by Duncan Macpherson. Toronto: MacMillan (Great Stories of Canada), 1954.

Brown, George W., Eleanor Harman, and Marsh Jeanneret. *The Story of Canada.* Toronto: Copp Clark, 1950.

Conway, John. "What Is Canada?" *Atlantic Monthly* (November 1964), 100–105.

Creighton, Donald. *John A. Macdonald, The Old Chieftain,* vol. 2. Toronto: Macmillan, 1955.

Hasluck, Alexandra. *Portrait with Background: A Life of Georgiana Molloy.* Melbourne, Victoria: Oxford University Press, 1955.

Horne, Donald. *The Lucky Country: Australia in the 1960s.* Ringwood, Victoria: Penguin, 1964.

Johnston, George H. *My Brother Jack.* Sydney: Collins, 1988 [1964].

Laurence, Margaret. *The Stone Angel.* Toronto: McClelland & Stewart, 1988 [1964].

MacLennan, Hugh. *Two Solitudes.* Toronto: Macmillan, 1978 [1945].

McDougall, W. D., and T. G. Finn. *Canada in the Western World.* Toronto: Gage, 1955.

McInnis, Edgar. *North America and the Modern World.* Toronto: J. M. Dent, 1954.

McNaught, Kenneth W., and Ramsay Cook. *Canada and the United States: A Modern Study.* Toronto: Clarke & Irwin, 1963.

Morton, W. L. *The Kingdom of Canada: A General History from Earliest Times.* Toronto: McClelland and Stewart, 1963.

O'Grady, John (aka Nino Culotta). *They're a Weird Mob.* Sydney: Ure Smith, 1964 (paperback edition).

Saywell, John, ed. *Canadian Annual Review for 1964.* Toronto: University of Toronto Press, 1965.

Stone, Julius. "Problems of Australian Foreign Policy, January–June 1955." *Australian Journal of Politics and History* 1: 1 (December 1955), 7–14.

Underhill, Frank H. *The Image of Confederation.* Toronto: Canadian. Broadcasting Corporation, 1964.

Whalley, George, ed. *Writing in Canada: Proceedings.* Introduction by F. R. Scott. Toronto: Macmillan, 1956.

Unpublished Government Records
Australia: National Archives of Australia (NAA) and National Library of Australia (NLA)
Australian Public Opinion Polls/Australian Morgan Gallup, NLA.
Department of External Affairs CRS A1838 (multiple numbers series), NAA.
Department of Prime Minister and Cabinet CRS A4940 (C series), NAA.
Menzies Papers, MS 4936, various volumes, NLA.
Canada: Library and Archives Canada (LAC)
Canadian Institute for Public Opinion (CIPO)/Canadian Gallup, Inc. LAC and Carleton University Library.
Heeney (A. D. P.) Papers, Vols. 9–11, multiple files. LAC.
Pearson (Lester B.) Papers, MG 26, N 1–2, Vols. 9–10, 37–41, multiple files. LAC.
Privy Council Office/Cabinet Conclusions, RG 2 Ser. A-5-a, Vol. 5775 (1956) and Volume 6265, 6271 (1964–1965)
Department of External Affairs, RG 25 Vol. 10122, files 20–22 (VIET.S), LAC.

Published Private and Government Records
Australia: Commonwealth Parliamentary Debates (Hansard), House of Representatives, 1955–1956, 1964–1965. Canberra: Commonwealth Government Printer.
Blanchette, Arthur, ed. *Canadian Foreign Policy 1955–1965: Selected Speeches.* Toronto and Ottawa: McClelland and Stewart and Institute of Canadian Studies, Carleton University, 1977.
Canada. Parliament. House of Commons Debates (Hansard), 1955–1956, 1964–1965. Ottawa: Queen's Printer and Controller of Stationery.
Current Notes on International Affairs. Canberra: Department of Foreign Affairs, 1955–1956, 1964–1965.
Documents on Canadian External Relations (DCER), Volume 22 (1956–1957, Part I and II), ed. by Greg Donaghy. Ottawa: Department of Foreign Affairs and International Trade, 2001.
Hasluck, Paul. "Australia and Southeast Asia." *Foreign Affairs* 43:1 (October 1964), 51–63.
Menzies, Robert. *Afternoon light; Some Memories of Men and Events.* New York, Coward-McCann, 1968a.
Menzies, Robert. *American-Australian Relations: What Are They, and Why?* Tucson: University of Arizona, 1968b.
Menzies, Robert. *Speech Is of Time; Selected Speeches and Writings.* London: Cassell, 1958.

Pearson, Lester B. *The Crisis in the Middle East, October–December 1956.* Ottawa: Queen's Printer and Controller of Stationery, 1957.

Chapter 5: Britain and Canada, 2002–2003

Fiction and Nonfiction

Alexis, Andre, Derek McCormack, and Diane Schoemperlen, eds. *The Journey Prize Anthology: Short Fiction from the Best of Canada's New Writers.* Toronto: McClelland & Stewart Ltd., 2002.

Bailey, Jacqui, and Christopher Maynard. *The Story of London: From Roman River to Capital City.* London: A & C Black (Children's Books), 2000.

Cruxton, J. Bradley and W. Douglas Wilson, *Flashback Canada, Fourth Edition.* Toronto: Oxford University Press, 2000.

Elton, Ben. *High Society.* London: Bantam Press, 2002.

Ferguson, Will, and Ian Ferguson. *How to Be a Canadian.* Vancouver, BC: Douglas & MacIntyre, 2001.

Fielding, John, and Rosemary Evans. *Canada: Our Century, Our Story.* Scarborough, Ontario: Nelson Thomas Learning, 2000.

Hacker, Carlotta. *The Kids' Book of Canadian History.* Illustrated by John Mantha. Toronto: Kids Can Press, 2002.

Kundani, Arun. "The Death of Multiculturalism," Comment for the Institute of Race Relations, London, April 1, 2002a. Retrieved on January 3, 2007, from: www.irr .org.uk/2002/april/ak000001.html.

Kundnani, Arun. "Home Office Research Heralds 'Managed Migration' Policy." Comment for the Institute of Race Relations, London, December 11, 2002b. Retrieved on January 3, 2007, from: www.irr.org.uk/2002/december/ak000004.html.

Leonard, Mark, and Phoebe Griffith, eds. *Reclaiming Britishness.* London: Foreign Policy Centre Report (September 2002).

MacMillan, Margaret. *Paris 1919: Six Months That Changed the World.* New York: Random House, 2002.

Moore, Michael. *Stupid White Men . . . and Other Sorry Excuses for the State of the Nation!* New York: HarperCollins, 2002.

Newman, Garfield. *Canada: A Nation Unfolding, Ontario Edition.* Toronto: McGraw-Hill Ryerson, 2000.

Parkin, Andrew, and Matthew Mendelsohn. "A New Canada: An Identity Shaped by Diversity." Montreal: Centre for Research and Information on Canada, Paper 11, October 2003.

Pearson, Allison. *I Don't Know How She Does It: A Comedy about Failure, a Tragedy about Success.* London: Chatto & Windus, 2002.

Shields. Carol. Unless. New York: Fourth Estate, 2003.

Sinclair, Iain. *London Orbital: A Walk around the M25*. London: Granta, 2002.

Smith, Zadie. *The Autograph Man: A Novel*. New York: Random House, 2002.

Walsh, Ben. *Modern World History*. National Curriculum/General Certificate of Secondary Education History in Focus Series. London: John Murray, 2001.

Published Private and Government Records

Blair, Tony. "The Principles of a Modern British Foreign Policy." Speech at the Lord Mayor's Banquet, London. November 10, 1997.

Blair, Tony. "Britain's Role in the EU and the Transatlantic Alliance." Speech at the Associated Press, London. December 15, 1998.

Blair, Tony. "Doctrine of International Community." Speech to the Economic Club of Chicago, April 22, 1999.

Blair, Tony. Speech to the Labour Party Conference, Brighton, UK, October 2, 2001.

Blair, Tony. Speech to the Partnership Summit, Banglore. January 5, 2002a.

Blair, Tony. Speech at the George Bush Senior Presidential Library, April 7, 2002b.

Blair, Tony. Speech to the Trades Union Congress, Blackpool, September 10, 2002c.

Blair, Tony. House of Commons. September 24, 2002d.

Blair, Tony. Press Conference: PM Tony Blair and President George Bush. November 21, 2002e.

Blair, Tony. Speech at Foreign Office Conference. January 7, 2003a.

Blair, Tony. Transcript of Blair's Iraq interview, BBC *Newsnight*. February 6, 2003b.

Blair, Tony. PM Answers Questions at MTV Forum. March 6, 2003c.

Blair, Tony, Press Conference: PM Blair and Portuguese PM Barroso, March 11, 2003d.

Blair, Tony. Prime Minister's Address to the Nation. March 20, 2003e.

Blair, Tony. Foreword to Iraq's Weapons of Mass Destruction: The Assessment of the British Government. London: Stationary Office, 2003f.

Blunkett, David. *The Blunkett Tapes: My Life in the Bear Pit*. London: Bloomsbury, 2006.

Campbell, Alastair. *The Blair Years: Extracts from The Alastair Campbell Diaries*. London: Hutchinson, 2007.

Chrétien, Jean. *My Years as Prime Minister*. Toronto: Knopf Canada, 2007.

Cook, Robin. *The Point of Departure*. London: Simon and Schuster, 2003.

Department of Foreign Affairs and International Trade (DFAIT) Canada, "Freedom from Fear: Canada's Foreign Policy for Human Security," 2000. Retrieved on February 2, from: www.dfait-maeci.gc.ca/foreignp/humansecurity/HumanSecurity Booklet-e.asp

Goldenberg, Eddie. *The Way It Works: Inside Ottawa*. Toronto: McClelland and Stewart, 2006.

Short, Clare. *An Honourable Deception? New Labour, Iraq and the Misuse of Power*. London: Free Press, 2005.

U.K. Ministry of Defence. "Delivering Security in a Changing World." Defence White
Paper Cm 6041-I (Presented to Parliament in December 2003). Retrieved on April 7,
2007, from: www.mod.uk/NR/rdonlyres/051AF365-0A97-4550-99C0-4D87D7C95
DED/0/cm6041I_whitepaper2003.pdf.

BIBLIOGRAPHY

Abdelal, Rawi, Yoshiko M. Herrera, Alastair Iaian Johnston, and Rose McDermott (eds.), *Measuring Identity: A Guide for Social Science Research*. Cambridge, UK: Cambridge University Press, 2009.

Acharya, Amitav. *Constructing a Security Community in Southeast Asia: ASEAN and the Problem of Regional Order*. London: Routledge, 2001.

Acharya, Amitav. "'Why Is There No NATO in Asia?' The Normative Origins of Asian Multilateralism," Weatherhead Center for International Affairs, No. 05-05, Harvard University, July 2005, Ms.

Adams, Iestyn. *Brothers across the Ocean: British Foreign Policy and the Origins of the Anglo-American Special Relationship, 1900–1905*. London: I. B. Tauris, 2005.

Adams, Patricia Helen. "Canada and the Suez Crisis 1956: The Evolution of Policy and Public Debate." MA thesis, Acadia University, Wolfville, Nova Scotia, 1988.

Adler, Emanuel. *Communitarian International Relations: The Epistemic Foundations of International Relations*. New York: Routledge, 2005.

Adler, Emanuel, and Michael Barnett. "A Framework for the Study of Security Communities," in Emanuel Adler and Michael Barnett, eds., *Security Communities*, 29–66. New York: Cambridge University Press, 1998.

Alcoff, Linda Martín. *Visible Identities: Race, Gender and the Self*. Oxford, UK: Oxford University Press, 2006.

Allen, H. C. *Great Britain and the United States; a history of Anglo-American Relations, 1783–1952*. Hamden, CT: Archon Books, 1969.

Anderson, Stuart. *Race and Rapprochement: Anglo-Saxonism and Anglo-American Relations, 1895–1904*. Cranbury, NJ,: Associated University Presses, 1981.

Angenot, Marc. *1899: un état du discours social*. Montreal/Longueuil: Éditions du Préambule, 1989.

Axworthy, Lloyd. "Introduction." In Rob McRae and Don Hubert, eds., *Human Security and the New Diplomacy: Protecting People, Promoting Peace*, 3–13. Montreal: McGill-Queen's University Press: 2001.

Azubuike, Samuel. "To Appease or to Concede? Contrasting Two Modes of Accommodation in International Conflict." *International Relations* 20.1 (2006): 49–68.

Azzi, Stephen. *Walter Gordon and the Rise of Canadian Nationalism*. Montreal: McGill-Queen's University Press, 1999.

Balibar, Étienne. "Le Retour de la Race." *Mouvements* 50 (2007), 162–171.

Barkawi, Tarak, and Mark Laffey. "Introduction." In Tarak Barkawi and Mark Laffey, eds., *Democracy, Liberalism, and War: Rethinking the Democratic Peace*, 1–24. Boulder, CO: Lynne Rienner, 2001.

Barkawi, Tarak, and Mark Laffey. "The Postcolonial Moment in Security Studies." *Review of International Studies*, 32. 2 (2006), 329–352.

Barnett, Michael. "Culture, Strategy and Foreign Policy Change: Israel's Road to Oslo." *European Journal of International Relations* 5.1 (1999): 5–36.

Barnett, Michael. *Dialogues in Arab Politics: Negotiations in Regional Order*. New York: Columbia University Press, 1998.

Barnett, Michael, and Raymond Duvall. "Power in International Politics," *International Organization* 59 (1, 2005): 39–75.

Barry, Donald. "Managing Canada–US Relations in the Post-9/11 Era: Do We Need a Big Idea?" In Duane Bratt and Christopher J. Kukucha, eds., *Readings in Canadian Foreign Policy*, 113–138. Toronto: Oxford University Press, 2007 [2003].

Baum, Bruce. *The Rise and Fall of the Caucasian Race: a Political History of Racial Identity*. New York: New York University Press, 2006.

Baum, Matthew, and Tim Groeling, "Crossing the Water's Edge: Elite Rhetoric, Media Coverage and the Rally-Round-the-Flag Phenomenon, 1979–2003," *Journal of Politics* 70 (October 2008), 1065–1085.

Bederman, Gail. *Manliness and Civilization: A Cultural History of Gender and Race in the United States 1880–1917*. Chicago: University of Chicago, 1995.

Beisner, Robert L. *Twelve against Empire: The Anti-Imperialists, 1898–1900*. New York: McGraw-Hill, 1968.

Beecroft, Stephen. "Canadian Policy Towards China, 1949–1957: The Recognition Problem." In Paul Evans and Bernie Michael Frolich, eds., *Reluctant Adversaries: Canada and the People's Republic of China, 1949–1970*, 43–72. Toronto: University of Toronto Press, 1991.

Beed, Terrence W., Murray Goot, Hodgson Stephen, and Ridley Peggy. *Australian Opinion Polls, 1941–1990: An Index*. Melbourne: Thorpe, D. W., and the National Center for Australian Studies, 1993.

Bell, Duncan. *The Idea of Greater Britain: Empire and the Future of World Order, 1860–1900*. Princeton, NJ: Princeton University Press, 2007.

Belich, James. *Paradise Reforged: A History of the New Zealanders from the 1880s to the Year 2000.* Honolulu: University of Hawaii Press, 2001.

Belich, James. *Replenishing the Earth: The Settler Revolution and the Rise of the Anglo-World, 1783–1939.* Oxford, UK: Oxford University Press, 2009.

Bellocchio, Luca. *Anglosfera. Forma e forza del nuovo Pan-Anglismo.* Milan: Il Nuovo Melangolo, 2006.

Benford, Robert D., and David A. Snow. "Framing Processes and Social Movements: An Overview and Assessment." *Annual Review of Sociology.* 26 (2000): 611–639.

Bennett, James C. *Anglosphere: The Future of the English-Speaking Nations in the Internet Era.* Lanham, MD: Rowman & Littlefield Publishers, 2004.

Bennett, James C. *The Third Anglosphere Century: The English-Speaking World in an Era of Transition.* Washington, DC: Heritage Foundation, 2007.

Benvenuti, Andrea, and Stuart Ward. "Britain, Europe and the 'Other Quiet Revolution' in Canada." In Philip Buckner, ed., *Canada and the End of Empire,* 165–182. Vancouver: University of British Columbia Press, 2005.

Berkhofer, Robert. *Beyond the Great Story: History as Text and Discourse.* Cambridge, MA: Harvard University Press, 1995.

Bernasconi, Robert. "Who Invented the Concept of Race? Kant's Role in the Enlightenment Construction of Race." In Bernasconi, ed., *Race,* 11–36. Malden, MA: Blackwell, 2001.

Bernasconi, Robert. "'Will the Real Kant Please Stand Up? The Challenge of Enlightenment Racism to the Study of the History of Philosophy." *Radical Philosophy* 117 (2003): 13–22.

Bially Mattern, J. (2005). *Ordering International Politics: Identity, Crisis, and Representational Force.* New York: Routledge.

Birt, Yahya. "Islamophobia in the Construction of British Muslim Identity Politics." In Peter E. Hopkins and Richard Gale, eds. *Muslims in Britain: Race, Place and Identities,* 210–227. Edinburgh: Edinburgh University Press, 2009.

Black, Jeremy. *Great Powers and the Quest for Hegemony: The World Order since 1500.* London: Routledge, 2008.

Blackett, R. J. M. *Divided Hearts: Britain and the American Civil War.* Baton Rouge: Louisiana State University Press, 2001.

Blum, Lawrence. *I'm not a Racist, but . . . The Moral Quandary of Race.* Ithaca, NY: Cornell University Press, 2002.

Bluth, Christopher. "The British Road to War: Blair, Bush and the Decision to Invade Iraq." *International Affairs* 80.5 (2004): 871–892.

Bluth, Christopher. "'Iraq: Blair's Mission Impossible': A Rejoinder to Paul Hoggett." *The British Journal of Politics and International Relations* 7.4 (2005): 598–560.

Bongiorno, Frank. "The Price of Nostalgia: Menzies, the 'Liberal' Tradition and Australian Foreign Policy." *Australian Journal of Politics and History* 51.3 (2005): 400–417.

Borstelmann, Tim. *The Cold War and the Color Line: American Race Relations in the Global Arena.* Cambridge, MA: Harvard University Press, 2002.

Bothwell, Robert. *Canada and the United States: The Politics of Partnership.* New York: Twayne, 1992.

Bothwell, Robert. "The Further Shore: Canada and Vietnam." *International Journal* 56.1 (2000–2001): 89–114.

Bothwell, Robert. *Alliance and Illusion: Canada and the World, 1945–1984.* Vancouver: University of British Columbia Press, 2007.

Bothwell, Robert, "Foreign Affairs a Hundred Years On," in Robert Bothwell and Jean Daudelin, eds., *Canada among Nations 2008: 100 Years of Canadian External Relations,* 19–40.Montreal: McGill-Queen's, 2009

Bourne, Kenneth. *Britain and the Balance of Power in North America, 1815–1908.* Berkeley: University of California Press, 1967.

Bourne, Kenneth. The Foreign Policy of Victorian England, 1830–1902. Oxford, UK: Clarendon Press, 1970.

Boyce, Michael. "Achieving Effect: Annual Chief of Defense Staff Lecture." *RUSI Journal* 148 (1), February 2003, 31–37.

Bridge, Carl. "Australia and the Vietnam War." In Peter Lowe, ed., *The Vietnam War,* 181–195. Ed. Basingstoke, UK: Macmillan, 1998.

Bridge, F. R., and Roger Bullen. *The Great Powers and the European States System 1814–1914,* 2nd ed. New York: Longman, 2005.

Browning, Christopher S., and Ben Tonra, "Beyond the West and Towards the Anglosphere?" in Christopher S. Browning and Marko Lehti (eds.), *The Struggle for the West: A Divided and Contested Legacy.* London: Routledge, 2009, 292–329.

Bryce, James. "British Feeling on the Venezuelan Question," *North American Review* 142 (February 1896), 145–153.

Brysk, Alison, Craig Parsons, and Wayne Sandholtz. "After Empire: National Identity and Post-Colonial Families of Nations." *European Journal of International Relations* 8.2 (2002): 267–305.

Burgess, John W. *Political Science and Comparative Constitutional Law.* New York: Ginn and Company, 1890.

Burk, Kathleen. *Old World, New World: The Story of Britain and America.* London: Little, Brown, 2007.

Burke, Peter. "Performing History: The Importance of Occasions." *Rethinking History* 9.1 (2005), 35–52.

Burton, David. "Theodore Roosevelt and the 'Special Relationship' with Britain." *History Today* 23.8 (1973): 527–535.

Busch, Peter. *All the Way with JFK? Britain, the US, and the Vietnam War.* Oxford, UK: Oxford University Press, 2003.

Butler, Leslie. *Critical Americans: Victorian Intellectuals and Transatlantic Liberal Reform*. Chapel Hill: University of North Carolina Press, 2007.

Byers, Michael. "Canadian Armed Forces under United States Command," *International Journal* 89:1 (Winter 2002–2003), 89–114.

Campbell, Alexander. *Great Britain and the United States, 1895–1903*. London: Longmans, 1960.

Campbell, Charles S. *From Revolution to Rapprochement: The United States and Great Britain, 1783–1900*. New York: Wiley, 1974.

Campbell, Duncan Andrew. *Unlikely Allies: Britain, America and the Victorian Origins of the Special Relationship*. New York: Continuum, 2007.

Cain, Frank, ed. *Menzies in War and Peace*. Canberra: Allen and Unwin, in association with the Australian Defence Studies Centre, 1997.

Capie, David. Power, Identity and Multilateralism: Rethinking Institutional Dynamics in the Pacific 1945–2000. PhD Dissertation, Department of Political Science, York University, Toronto, Canada, 2003.

Carnegie, Andrew. "The Venezuelan Question." *North American Review* 162, 471, February 1895, 129–144.

Carr, E. H. *The Twenty Years' Crisis: Introduction to the Study of International Relations, 1919–1939*. London: Palgrave, 1939/2006.

Casey, Richard G. *Double or Quit*. Melbourne: Cassell, 1949.

Chapnick, Adam. *The Middle Power Project: Canada and the Founding of the United Nations*. Vancouver: University of British Columbia Press, 2005a.

Chapnick, Adam. "Peace, Order and Good Government: The 'Conservative' Tradition in Canadian Foreign Policy." *International Journal* 60:3 (2005b): 635–650.

Chauvel, Richard. "Up the Creek without a Paddle: Australia, West New Guinea, and the 'Great and Powerful Friends.'" In F. Cain, ed., *Menzies in War and Peace*, 55–71. Sydney: Allen & Unwin with the Australian Defence Centre, 1997.

Cheeseman, Graeme. "Australia: The White Experience of Fear and Dependence." In Ken Booth and Russell Trood, eds., *Strategic Cultures in the Asia-Pacific Region*, 273–298. London: Macmillan, 1999.

Chong, Dennis, and James N. Druckman. "Framing Public Opinion in Competitive Democracies," *American Political Science Review* 101 (2007), 637–655.

Churchill, Winston. *History of the English Speaking Peoples*. London: Cassell, 2002 [1956–1958].

Citizenship and Immigration Canada (CIC). *A Look at Canada*. Ottawa: Minister of Public Works and Government Services, 2001.

Citizenship and Immigration Canada (CIC). *A Newcomer's Introduction to Canada*. Ottawa: Minister of Public Works and Government Services, 2002.

Citizenship and Immigration Canada (CIC). *My Commitment to Canada: An Active Exploration of Democratic Citizenship. A Project of TEACH Magazine and Citizenship and Immigration Canada*. Ottawa: Minister of Public Works and Government Services, 2003.

Claeys, Gregory. "The 'Left' and the Critique of Empire c. 1865–1900: Three Roots of Humanitarian Foreign Policy." In Duncan Bell, ed., *Victorian Visions of Global Order: Empire and International Relations in Nineteenth-Century Political Thought*, 239–266. Cambridge, UK: Cambridge University Press, 2007.

Clark, Elizabeth A. *History, Theory, Text: Historians and the Linguistic Turn*. Cambridge, MA: Harvard University Press, 2004.

Clarke, Michael. "Foreign Policy." In Anthony Seldon, ed., *Blair's Britain, 1997–2007*, 593–614. Cambridge, UK: Cambridge University Press, 2007.

Clarkson, Stephen. Globalization, Neoconservatism, and the Canadian State. Toronto: University of Toronto Press, 2002.

Closs Stephens, Angharad, and Nick Vaughan-Williams, eds. *Terrorism and the Politics of Response: London in a Time of Terror*. New York: Routledge, 2008.

Cohen, Andrew. *While Canada Slept. How We Lost Our Place in the World*. Toronto: McClelland and Stewart, 2003.

Cohen, Robin. *Global Diasporas: An Introduction*. Seattle: University of Washington Press, 2008.

Collin, Richard H. *Theodore Roosevelt's Caribbean: The Panama Canal, the Monroe Doctrine, and the Latin American Context*. Baton Rouge: Louisiana State University Press, 1990.

Colman, Jonathan. *A Special Relationship? Harold Wilson, Lyndon B. Johnson and Anglo-American Relations "At the Summit," 1964–1968*. Manchester: Manchester University Press, 2004.

Conquest, Robert. *Dragons of Expectation: Reality and Delusion in the Course of History*. New York: Norton, 2005.

Cooper, Robert. "The Post-Modern State." In Mark Leonard, ed., *Re-Ordering the World: The Long-Term Implications of September 11*, 11–21. London: Foreign Policy Centre, September 2002. (First appeared in *The Observer*, April 7, 2002.)

Cox, Michael. "Empire by Denial: The Strange Case of the United States." *International Affairs* 81:1 (2005), 15–30.

Cox, Robert W., with Timothy J. Sinclair. *Approaches to World Order*. Cambridge, UK: Cambridge University Press, 1996.

Crapol, Edward P. *America for Americans: Economic Nationalism and Anglophobia in the Late Nineteenth Century*. Westport, Conn.: Praeger: 1973.

Crawford, Martin. "British Travellers and the Anglo-American Relationship in the 1850s," *Journal of American Studies* 12:2 (1978), 203–219.

Crawford, Martin. *The Anglo-American Crisis of the Mid-Nineteenth Century: The Times and America, 1850–1862*. Athens: The University of Georgia Press, 1987.

Crawford, Neta. *Argument and Change in World Politics: Ethics, Decolonization, and Humanitarian Intervention*. Cambridge, UK: Cambridge University Press, 2002.

Crosby, Ann Denholm. "Myths of Canada's Human Security Pursuits: Tales of Tool Boxes, Toy Chests, and Tickle Trunks." In Duane Bratt and Christopher J. Kukucha, eds., *Readings in Canadian Foreign Policy*, 265–284. Toronto: Oxford University Press, 2007 [2003].

Curtis, L. P. Jr. *Anglo-Saxons and Celts: A Study of Anti-Irish Prejudice in Victorian England*. Bridgeport, CT: University of Bridgeport, 1968.

Daalder, Ivo, and Robert Kagan. "The Next Intervention." *Washington Post,* August 6, 2007. Retrieved on January 2, 2008, from: www.washingtonpost.com/wp-dyn/content/article/2007/08/05/AR2007080501056.html on 2 January 2008.

Danchev. Alex. *On Specialness: Essays in Anglo-American Relations*. London: Macmillan Press, 1998.

Danchev. Alex. "The Cold War 'Special Relationship' Revisited." *Diplomacy and Statecraft* 17.3 (2006): 579–595.

Danchev, Alex. "Tony Blair's Vietnam: The Iraq War and the 'Special Relationship' in Historical Perspective," *Review of International Studies* 33:2 (2007): 189–203.

Darwin, John. *Britain and Decolonization: The Retreat from Empire in the Post-War World. The Making of the 20th Century*. New York: St. Martin's Press, 1988.

Darwin, John. "Was There a Fourth British Empire?" In Martin Lynn, ed., *The British Empire in the 1950s: Retreat or Revival?*, 16–31. Basingstoke, UK: Palgrave Macmillan, 2006.

Daum, Andreas, Lloyd C. Gardner, and Wilfried Mausbach, eds. *America, the Vietnam War, and the World: Comparative and International Perspectives*. New York: Cambridge University Press/German Historical Institute, 2003.

Day, David. "Dr H. V. Evatt and the Search for a Sub-Empire in the Southwest Pacific." In David Day and H. V. Evatt, eds., *Brave New World: Australian Foreign Policy, 1941–1949*, 47–61. Brisbane: University of Queensland Press, 1996.

De Conde, Alexander. *The Quasi-War: the Politics and Diplomacy of the Undeclared War with France 1797–1801*. New York: Scribner's, 1966.

Delanty, Gerard, and Krishnan Kumar. "Introduction." *The SAGE Handbook of Nations and Nationalisms*, 1–5. London: Sage Publications, 2006.

Deudney, Daniel. "Greater Britain or Greater Synthesis: Seeley, Mackinder, and Wells on Britain in the Global Industrial Era." *Review of International Studies* 27 (2001): 187–208.

Deutsch, W. Karl, et al. *Political Community and the North Atlantic Area: International Organization in the Light of Historical Experience*. Princeton, NJ: Princeton University Press, 1957.

Donaghy, Greg. *Parallel Paths: Canada-Australian Relations since the 1890s.* Ottawa: Department of Foreign Affairs and International Trade, 1995. Retrieved on June 11, 2006, from: http://geo.international.gc.ca/asia/australia/relations/ppaths-en.asp.

Donaghy. Greg. *Tolerant Allies: Canada and the United States, 1963–1968.* Montreal: McGill-Queen's University Press, 2002.

Doty, Roxanne Lynn. "Foreign Policy as Social Construction: A Post-Positivist Analysis of US Counterinsurgency Policy in the Philippines." *International Studies Quarterly* 37.2 (1993): 297–320.

Doyle, Michael W. *Ways of War and Peace.* New York: W. W. Norton, 1997.

Douglas, James. *Canadian Independence, Annexation and British Imperial Federation.* New York: G. P. Putnam's Sons, 1894.

Drage, Geoffrey. "Alien immigration." *Fortnightly Review* 57 (January 1895), 40–53.

Drinnon, Richard. *Facing West: The Metaphysics of Indian-Hating and Empire-Building.* Minneapolis: University of Minnesota Press, 1980.

Duchesne, Jean. *Petite histoire d'Anglo-Saxonnie : Tout ce dont vous avez besoin pour en savoir plus sur les Anglais et les Américains qu'eux-mêmes.* Paris: Presses de la Renaissance, 2007.

Dumbrell, John. "The Johnson Administration and the British Labour Government: Vietnam, the Pound and East of Suez." *Journal of American Studies* 30.2 (1996): 211–231.

Dumbrell, John. *A Special Relationship: Anglo-American Relations from the Cold War and After.* London: Macmillan, 2006.

Dunne, Timothy. "'When the Shooting Starts': Atlanticism in British Security Strategy." *International Affairs* 80.5, (2004): 893–909.

Dyson, Stephen B. "Personality and Foreign Policy: Tony Blair's Iraq Decision." *Foreign Policy Analysis* 2.3 (2006): 289–306.

Eayrs, James. "Canadian Policy and Opinion during the Suez Crisis." *International Journal,* 12.2 (1957), 97–108.

Eayrs, James. *In Defense of Canada, Volume 5—Indochina: Roots of Complicity.* Toronto: University of Toronto Press, 1983.

Eckstein, Harry. "Case Studies and Theory in Political Science," in F. I. Greenstein and N. W. Polsby, eds., *Handbook of Political Science. Political Science: Scope and Theory (Vol. 7),* 94–137. Reading, MA: Addison-Wesley, 1975.

Eddy, John, and Deryck Schreuder, eds. *The Rise of Colonial Nationalism: Australia, New Zealand, Canada, and South Africa First Assert Rheir Nationalities, 1880–1914.* Boston: Allen & Unwin, 1988.

Edmonds, Martin, ed. "Future Conditional: War & Conflict after Next." The Centre for Defence and International Security Studies, Lancaster University Bailrigg Paper 31. December 22, 2002.

Edwards, Peter. *Arthur Tange: Last of the Mandarins*. Crows Nest, NSW: Allen & Unwin, 2005.

Edwards, Peter, with Gregory Pemberton. *Crisis and Commitments: The Politics And Diplomacy of Australia's Involvement in Southeast Asian Conflicts, 1948–1965*. North Sydney: Allen & Unwin, 1992.

Elden, Stuart, and Eduardo Mendieta, eds. *Reading Kant's Geography*. Albany: SUNY Press, 2011.

Eldridge, C. C. "Introduction: The North Atlantic Triangle Revisited," In C. C. Eldridge, ed., *Kith and Kin: Canada, Britain and the United States from the Revolution to the Cold War*, xi–xxii. Cardiff, UK: University of Wales Press, 1997.

Ellis, Elisabeth. *Kant's Politics: Provisional Theory for an Uncertain World*. New Haven, CT: Yale University Press, 2005.

Ellis, Sylvia. *Britain, America, and the Vietnam War*. Westport, Conn.: Praeger, 2004.

Elman, Colin. "Extending Offensive Realism: The Louisiana Purchase and America's Rise to Regional Hegemony," *American Political Science Review* 98:4 (November 2004): 563–576.

English, John. *The Worldly Years: The Life of Lester Pearson. Volume II: 1949–1972*. New York: Alfred A. Knopf, 1992.

Entman, Robert. *Projections of Power: Framing News, Public Opinion, and U.S. Foreign Policy*. Chicago: University of Chicago Press, 2003.

Eze, Emmanuel Chukwudi. "The Colour of Reason: The Idea of 'Race' in Kant's Anthropology." In Katherine M. Faull, ed., *Anthropology and the German Enlightenment: Perspectives on Humanity*, 200–241. Lewisburg, PA: Bucknell University Press, 1995.

Fanis, Maria. *Hegemonic Peaces: Is The Liberal Peace Really Liberal, or Merely Hegemonic?* PhD Dissertation, Political Science, University of Michigan, September 2001.

Fearon, James D. "Deliberation as Discussion," in Jon Elster, ed., *Deliberative Democracy*, 44–68. Cambridge, UK: Cambridge University Press, 1998, 44–68.

Ferguson, Niall. *Empire: The Rise and Demise of the British World Order and the Lessons for Global Power*. London: Basic Books: 2002.

Fiske, John. American Political Ideas Viewed from the Standpoint of Universal History (The Town-Meeting, The Federal Union, "Manifest Destiny"). New York: Harper & Brothers, 1885.

Floyd, Richard. "449 and All That: Nineteenth- and Twentieth-century Interpretations of the 'Anglo-Saxons Invasion' of Britain." In Helen Brocklehurst and Robert Philips, eds., *History, Nationhood and the Question of Britain*, 184–196. London: Palgrave.

Frantzen, Allen, and John Niles. "Introduction." In Allen Frantzen and John Niles, eds., *Anglo-Saxonism and the Construction of Social Identity*, 1–14. Gainesville: University Press of Florida, 1997.

Friedberg, Aaron L. *The Weary Titan: Britain and the Experience of Relative Decline, 1895–1905*. Princeton, NJ: Princeton University Press, 1988.

Friedman, Max Paul. "Simulacrobama: The Mediated Election of 2008." *Journal of American Studies* 43:2 (2009), 341–356.

Foucault, Michel. "What Is an Author?," translated by Donald F. Bouchard and Sherry Simon, in *Language, Counter-Memory, Practice*, 124–127. Ithaca, NY: Cornell University Press, 1977.

Gamble, Andrew. *Between Europe and America*. Basingstoke, UK: Palgrave-Macmillan, 2003.

Gamble, Andrew. "From Anglo-America to the Anglosphere: Empire, Hegemony, and the Special Relationship," BISA US Foreign Policy Working Group Annual Conference, University of Manchester, September 20–21, 2007.

Gamble, Andrew, and Ian Kearns. "Recasting the Special Relationship." In David Held and David Mepham, eds., *Progressive Foreign Policy*, 142–161. Cambridge, UK: Polity, 2007.

George, Alexander, and Andrew Bennett. *Case Studies and Theory Development in the Social Sciences*. Cambridge, MA: MIT Press, 2005.

Gerlach, Murney. *British Liberalism and the United States: Political and Social Thought in the Late Victorian Age*. London: Palgrave, 2001.

Gerring, John. *Case Study Research: Principles and Practices*. Cambridge, UK: Cambridge University Press, 2007.

Gerring, John, with Craig Thomas. "Internal Valdity: Process Tracing." In John Gerring, *Case Study Research: Principles and Practices*, 172–186. Cambridge, UK: Cambridge University Press, 2007.

Gheciu, Alexandra. *NATO in the "New Europe": The Politics of International Socialization after the Cold War*. Stanford, CA: Stanford University Press, 2005.

Giddens, Anthony. *The Third Way*. Cambridge, UK: Polity Press, 1998.

Gilbert, Martin. *Winston Churchill Never Despair 1945–1965*. London: Houghton Mifflin, 1988.

Gilbert, Martin. *Churchill and America*. New York: Free Press, 2005.

Gilroy, Paul. *Against Race: Imagining Political Culture beyond the Color Line*. Cambridge, MA: Belknap Press of Harvard University Press, 2000.

Gong, Gerrit W. *The Standard of "Civilization" in International Society*. Oxford, UK: Oxford University Press, 1984.

Goldberg, David Theo. *The Threat of Race: Reflections of Racial Neoliberalism*. London: Wiley-Blackwell, 2008.

Goldfarb, Danielle. "Beyond Labels: Comparing Proposals for Closer Canada–US Economic Relations," *C. D. Howe Institute Backgrounder*, 76 (October 2003). Retrieved on January 6, 2005, from: www.cdhowe.org/pdf/backgrounder_76.pdf.

Goldsworthy David. *Losing the Blanket: Australia and the End of Britain's Empire.* Carlton, Victoria: Melbourne University Press, 2002.

Gooch, John. "The Weary Titan, Strategy and Policy in Great Britain, 1890–1918." In Ed. W. Murray, MacGregor Knox, and Alvin Bernstein, eds., *The Making of Strategy: Rulers, States, and War*, 278–386. Cambridge, UK, and New York: Cambridge University Press, 1994.

Gooch, John, ed. *The Boer War: Direction, Experience, and Image.* Portland, OR: Frank Cass, 2000. Goot, Murray. "Questions of Deception: Contested Understandings of the Polls on WMD, Political Leaders and Governments in Australia, Britain and the United States." *Australian Journal of International Affairs* 61.1 (2007): 41–64.

Gossett, Thomas F. *Race: The History of an Idea in America.* New York: Oxford University Press, 1997 [1963].

Gossett, Thomas F. "Imperialism and the Anglo-Saxon." In Michael L. Krenn, ed., *The Impact of Race on U. S. Foreign Policy: a Reader*, 49–89. New York: Garland, 1999.

Gotlieb, Allan E. "A North American Community of Law." Speech to the Borderlines Conference at the Woodrow Wilson International Center for Scholars,Washington, DC, February 27, 2003. Retrieved on January 6, 2005, from: www.borderlines.ca/washington/speech_allangotlieb.html.

Granatastein, Jack L. *Yankee Go Home? Canadians and anti-Americanism.* Toronto: HarperCollins, 1996.

Granatastein, Jack L., and Norman Hillmer. *For Better or For Worse: Canada and the United States to the 1990s.* Toronto: Copp Clark Pitman, 1991.

Green, E. H. H. "The Political Economy of Empire, 1880–1914." In Andrew Porter and Alaine Low, eds., *The Oxford History of the British Empire, Vol III: The Nineteenth Century*, 346–370. Oxford, UK: Oxford University Press, 1999.

Greenwood, Gordon, ed. *Australia: A Social and Political History.* Sydney: Angus and Robertson, 1955.

Grenville, J. A. S. *Lord Salisbury and Foreign Policy.* London: Allen & Unwin, 1964.

Grenville, John A. S. "Diplomacy and War Plans in the United States 1890–1917." In Paul Kennedy, ed., *The War plans of the Great Powers, 1880–1914*, 23–38. Boston: Allen & Unwin, 1979.

Grovogui, Siba N. "Postcolonialism." In Tim Dunne, Milja Kurki, and Steve Smith, eds., *International Relations Theories Discipline and Diversity*, 229–246. Oxford, UK: Oxford University Press, 2007.

Guglielmo, Thomas A. *White on Arrival: Italians, Race, Color, and Power in Chicago, 1890–1945.* Oxford, UK: Oxford University Press, 2003.

Guthrie, Wayne Lee, "The Anglo-German Intervention in Venezuela, 1902–3," Ph.D. Dissertation, University of California, San Diego, 1983.

Guzzini, Stefano, and Anna Leander, eds. *Constructivism and International Relations: Alexander Wendt and his Critics.* London: Routledge, 2007.

Haglund, David G. *The North Atlantic Triangle Revisited: Canadian Grand Strategy at Century's End.* Toronto: Irwin/CIIA, 2000.

Haglund, David G. "The Case of the Missing Democratic Alliance: France, the 'Anglo-Saxons' and NATO's Deep Origins." *Contemporary Security Policy* 25.3 (2004): 1–27.

Haglund, David. "Relating to the Anglosphere: Canada, 'Culture,' and the Question of Military Intervention." *Journal of Transatlantic Studies* 3.2 (2005): 179–198.

Haglund, David. "Canada and the Anglosphere: In, Out, or Indifferent?" *Policy Options* 26.2 (2006): 72–6.

Hall, Stuart. "Conclusion: The Multicultural Question." In Barnor Hesse, ed., *Un/settled Multiculturalisms: Diasporas, Entanglements, Un/settled Multiculturalisms: Diasporas, Entanglements, "Transruptions,"* 209–241. London: Routledge, 2000.

Hannigan, Robert E. *The New World Power: American Foreign Policy, 1898–1917.* Philadelphia: University of Pennsylvania Press, 2002.

Hansen, Jonathan M. *The Lost Promise of Patriotism: Debating American Identity, 1890–1920.* Chicago: University of Chicago Press, 2003.

Hansen, Lene. *Security as Practice: Discourse Analysis and the Bosnian War.* London: Routledge, 2006.

Harbutt, Fraser J. *The Iron Curtain: Churchill, America, and the Origins of the Cold War.* Oxford, UK: Oxford University Press, 1986.

Hart, Michael, and Brian Tomlin. "Inside the Perimeter: The US Policy Agenda and Its Implications for Canada." In Bruce Doern, ed., *How Ottawa Spends, 2002–3*, 48–68. Toronto: Oxford University Press, 2002.

Harvey, David. "Cosmopolitanism and the Banality of Geographic Evils," *Public Culture* 12:2 (2000), 529–564.

Harvey, Frank P. *Smoke and Mirrors: Globalized Terrorism and the Illusion of Multilateral Security.* Toronto: University of Toronto Press, 2005.

Hastings, Paula. "'Our Glorious Anglo-Saxon Race Shall Ever Fill Earth's Highest Place': The Anglo-Saxon and the Construction of Identity in the Late-Nineteenth Century Canada." In Phillip Buckner and R. Douglas Francis, eds., *Canada and the British World: Culture, Migration, and Identity*, 92–110. Vancouver: UBC Press, 2006.

Hattam, Victoria. *In the Shadow of Race: Jews, Latinos, and Immigrant Politics in the United States.* Chicago: University of Chicago Press, 2007.

Healy, David. *Drive to hegemony: the United States in the Caribbean, 1898–1917.* Madison: University of Wisconsin Press, 1988.

Hemmer, Christopher, and Peter J. Katzenstein, "Why Is There No NATO in Asia? Collective Identity, Regionalism, and the Origins of Multilateralism." *International Organization* 56.3 (2002): 575–607.

Henderson, Errol. "Disturbing the Peace: African Warfare, Political Inversion and the Universality of the Democratic Peace Thesis." *British Journal of Political Science* 39: 1 (2008), 25–58.

Herrison, Charles. *Les Nations Anglo-Saxonnes et la Paix.* Paris: Presses de la cite, 1936.

Herwig, Holger H. *Germany's Vision of Empire in Venezuela, 1871–1914.* Princeton, NJ: Princeton University Press, 1986.

Heuser, D. Beatrice G. "Alliances Bedeviled by History: Franks, Germanics and Anglo-Saxons in the Cold War." In Luciano Tosi, ed., *Europe, its Borders and the Others,* 313–349. Naples: Edizione Scientifiche Italiane, 2000..

Higgott, Richard A., and Kim Richard Nossal. "Australia and the Search for a Security Community in the 1990s." In Emanuel Adler and Michael Barnett, eds., *Security Communities,* 265–294. Cambridge, UK: Cambridge University Press: 1998.

Higham, John. *Strangers in the Land: Patterns of American Nativism, 1860–1925,* rev. ed. New Brunswick, NJ: Rutgers University Press, 1988.

Hill, Christopher. "Putting the World to Rights: The Foreign Policy Mission of Tony Blair." In Anthony Seldon, ed., *The Blair Effect, 2001–5,* 384–409. Cambridge, UK: Cambridge University Press, 2005.

Hilliker, John, and Greg Donaghy. "Canadian Relations with the United Kingdom at the End of Empire, 1956–73." In Philip Buckner, ed., *Canada and the End of Empire,* 25–46. Vancouver: University of British Columbia Press, 2005.

Hillmer, Norman, and Maureen Appel Molot, eds. *A Fading Power: Canada among Nations.* Don Mills, Ontario: Oxford University Press, 2002.

Hilton, Sylvia L., and Steve J. S. Ickringill. "Cleveland and the Anglo-Venezuelan Dispute in 1895: A Prelude to McKinley's Intervention in the Spanish-Cuban War." In Juan Pablo Fusi and Antonio Niño, eds., *Antes del 'desastre': Orígenes y antecedentes de la crisis del 98,* 337–358. Madrid: Universidad Complutense, 1996.

Hilton, Sylvia L., and Steve J. S. Ickringill, eds., *European Perceptions of the Spanish-American War of 1898.* Bern: Lang, 1999.

Hitchens, Christopher. *Blood, Class, and Nostalgia: The Enduring Anglo-American Relationship.* London: Nation Books, 2004.

Hitchens, Christopher. "An Anglosphere Future." *City Journal,* Autumn 2007. Retrieved on February 7, 2008, from: www.city-journal.org/html/17_4_anglosphere.html.

Hoadley, Stephen, *New Zealand United States Relations: Friends No Longer Allies.* Wellington: New Zealand Institute of International Affairs, 2000.

Hobson, John. "Civilizing the Global Economy: Racism and the Continuity of Anglo-Saxon Imperialism." In Brett Bowden and Leonard Seabrooke, eds., *Global Standards of Market Civilizations,* 60–76. London: Routledge, 2007.

Hofstadter, Richard, "Cuba, the Philippines, and Manifest Destiny," *The Paranoid Style in American Politics and Other Essays,* 145–187. Chicago: University of Chicago

Press, 1965Hofstadter, Richard. *Social Darwinism in American Thought.* Philadelphia: University of Pennsylvania Press, 1992 [1955].

Hoggett, Paul. "Iraq: Blair's Mission Impossible." *British Journal of Politics and International Relations* 7–4 (2005a): 418–428.

Hoggett, Paul. "A Reply to Christoph Bluth." *British Journal of Politics and International Relations* 7.4 (2005b): 603–604.

Holbo, Paul. "Perilous Obscurity: Public Diplomacy and the Press in the Venezuelan Crisis, 1902–3." *Historian* 32 (1970): 428–448.

Holmes, Colin, and A. H. Ion. "Bushido and the Samurai: Images in British Public Opinion, 1894–1914." *Modern Asian Studies* 14.2 (1980): 309–329.

Holmes, John. "The Diplomacy of a Middle Power." *The Atlantic Monthly* 214: 5 (1964), 106–110.

Holmes, John. "Canada and the Vietnam War." In J. L. Grantastein and R. D. Cuff, eds., *War and Society in North America*, 184–199. Toronto: Nelson, 1971.

Holmes, John W. *The Shaping of Peace: Canada and the Search for World Order 1943–1957,* Vol 1. Toronto: University of Toronto Press, 1979.

Hopf, Ted. *The Social Construction and International Politics: Identities and Foreign Policies, Moscow 1955 and 1999.* Ithaca, NY: Cornell University Press, 2002.

Hopf, Ted, "The Logic of Habit in International Relations." *European Journal of International Relations,* forthcoming.

Horne, Gerald. *The White Pacific: U.S. Imperialism and Black Slavery in the South Seas after the Civil War.* Honolulu: University of Hawai'i Press, 2007.

Horsman, Reginald. *Race and Manifest Destiny: The Origins of American Racial Anglo-Saxonism.* Cambridge, MA: Harvard University Press, 1981.

Hudson, W. J. *Blind Loyalty: Australia and the Suez Crisis, 1956.* Melbourne: Melbourne University Press, 1989.

"Hun, n." *The Oxford English Dictionary.* 2nd ed. OED Online. Oxford, UK: Oxford University Press, 1989. Retrieved on June 12, 2007, from: http://dictionary.oed.com/

Hunt, Michael H. *Ideology and U.S. Foreign Policy.* New Haven, CT: Yale University Press, 1987.

Huntington, Samuel P. *Who Are We? The Challenges to America's National Identity.* New York: Simon & Schuster, 2004.

Hyam, Ronald. *Britain's Declining Empire: The Road to Decolonisation, 1918–1968.* Cambridge, UK: Cambridge University Press, 2007.

ICISS. "The Responsibility to Protect: Report of the International Commission on Intervention & State Sovereignty." Ottawa: IDRC, December 2001.

Igartua, José E. *The Other Quiet Revolution: National Identities in English Canada, 1945–71.* Vancouver: UBC Press, 2006.

Ignatieff, Michael. "Canada in the Age of Terror—Multilateralism Meets a Moment of Truth." *Policy Options* 24.2 (2003): 14–18.

Ignatiev, Noel. *How the Irish Became White*. New York: Routledge, 1996.

Ikenberry, G. John, and Anne-Marie Slaughter (co-directors). *Forging a World of Liberty under Law: U.S. National Security in The 21st Century*. Princeton Project on National Security, 2006. Retrieved on September 4, 2008, from: www.princeton .edu/~ppns/report/FinalReport.pdf .

Ikenberry, John. "Liberalism and Empire: Logics of Order in the American Unipolar Age." *Review of International Studies* 30 (2004): 609–630.

Iikura, Akira. "The Anglo-Japanese Alliance and the Question of Race." In Phillips Payson O'Brien, ed., *The Anglo-Japanese Alliance, 1902–1922*, 222–235. London: Routledge, 2004.

Ives, Peter. "'Global English': Linguistic Imperialism or Practical Lingua Franca?" *Studies in Language & Capitalism* 1.1 (2006): 121–141.

Jackson, Andrew. "Why the 'Big Idea' is a Bad Idea," *Policy Options* 24: 4 (2003): 26–28.

Jackson, Patrick Thaddeus. *Civilizing the Enemy: German Reconstruction and the Invention of the West*. Ann Arbor: University of Michigan Press, 2006.

Jackson, Patrick Thaddeus. *The Conduct of Inquiry: An Introduction to the Philosophy of Science and its Implications for International Relations Research*. London: Routledge, 2010.

Jacobson, Matthew F. *Whiteness of a Different Color: European Immigrants and the Alchemy of Race*. Cambridge, MA: Harvard University Press, 1999.

Jahn, Beate. "Kant, Mill, and Illiberal Legacies in International Affairs." *International Organization* 59.1 (2005), 177–207.

Jedwab, Jack. "Canadian Opinion on the Possible Invasion of Iraq—Between Old and New Europe." Association of Canadian Studies, 2003. Retrieved on January 3, 2007, from: www.acs-aec.ca/oldsite/Polls/Poll16.pdf.

Jenkins, Roy. *Churchill: a Biography*. New York: Plume, 2002.

Jockel, Joe, and Joel Sokolsky. "Lloyd Axworthy's Legacy: Human Security and Rescue of Canadian Defense Policy," *International Journal* 56:1 (2000–2001), 1–18.

Jones, Mary Lucille. "Muslim Impact on Early Australian Life." In Mary Lucille Jones, ed., *An Australian Pilgrimage: Muslims in Australia from the Seventeenth Century to the Present*, 31–48. Melbourne: Victoria Press/Museum of Victoria, Melbourne, 1993.

Johnson, Gregory. "The Last Gasp of Empire: The 1964 Flag Debate Revisited." In Philip Buckner, ed., *Canada and the End of Empire*, 232–251. Vancouver: UBC Press, 2005.

Johnston, Alastair Iain. "Socialization in International Institutions: The ASEAN Way and International Relations Theory." In Michael Mastanduno and G. John Ikenberry, eds., *The Emerging International Relations of the Asia-Pacific Region*, 107–162. New York: Columbia University Press, 2003.

Kampfner, J. *Blair's Wars*. London: Free Press, 2003.

Kant, Immanuel. "Perpetual Peace (1795)." In Hans Siegbert Reiss, ed., *Kant's Political Writings,* second edition, 93–130. Translated by Hugh Barr Nisbet. Cambridge, UK: Cambridge University Press, 1991.

Kaplan, Amy. *The Anarchy of Empire in the Making of U.S. Culture.* Cambridge, MA: Harvard University Press, 2002.

Katzenstein, Peter, and Robert Keohane, eds. *Anti-Americanisms in World Politics.* Ithaca, NY: Cornell University Press, 2006.

Keating, Tom. *Canada and World Order: The Multilateralist Tradition in Canadian Foreign Policy.* Don Mills, Ontario: Oxford University Press, 2002.

Keating, Tom. "A Passive Internationalist: Jean Chrétien and Canadian Foreign Policy." In Lois Harder and Steve Patten, eds., *The Chrétien Legacy: Politics and Public Policy in Canada,* 124–141. Montreal and Ithaca, NY: McGill-Queen's University Press and the Centre for Constitutional Studies, 2006.

Keefe, Patrick Radden. *Chatter: Uncovering the Echelon Surveillance Network and the Secret World of Global Eavesdropping.* London: Random House, 2006.

Kelton, Maryanne, *"More than an Ally"? Contemporary Australia–US Relations.* Aldershot, UK: Ashgate, 2008.

Kennedy, Paul. *The Rise and Fall of the Great Powers: Economic Change and Military Conflict from 1500 to 2000.* New York: Random House, 1987.

Kennedy, Paul M. "Introduction." In P. Kennedy, ed., *The War Plans of the Great Powers, 1880–1914,* 1–22. Boston: Allen & Unwin, 1979.

Kennedy, Paul M. *The Rise of the Anglo-German Antagonism, 1860–1914.* Boston: Allen & Unwin, 1980.

Kennedy, Paul M. *The Realities behind Diplomacy: Background Influences on British External Policy, 1865–1980.* Boston: Allen & Unwin, 1981.

Kennedy, Paul M. "British and German Reactions to the Rise of American Power." In R. J. Bullen, Pogge von Strandmann, and A. B. Polonsky, eds., *Ideas into Politics: Aspects of European Politics 1880–1950,* 15–24. London: Croom Helm Ltd., 1984.

Kennedy-Pipe, Caroline, and Rhiannon Vickers. "'Blowback' for Britain?: Blair, Bush, and the War in Iraq." *Review of International Studies* 33.2 (2007): 205–221.

Keohane, Dan. "The United Kingdom." In Alex Danchev and John MacMillan, eds., *The Iraq War and Democratic Politics,* 59–76. London: Routledge, 2005.

Keohane, Robert, and Joseph Nye. *Power and Interdependence,* 3rd ed. New York: Longman, [1977] 2001.

Kissinger, Henry. *The White House Years.* Boston: Little Brown, 1979.

Klotz, Audie. *Norms in International Relations: The Struggle against Apartheid.* Ithaca, NY: Cornell University Press, 1995.

Knee, Stuart E. "Anglo-American Understanding and the Boer War." *Australian Journal of Politics and History* 30.2 (1984): 196–208.

Kneer, Warren. *Great Britain and the Carribbean, 1901–1913: A Study in Anglo-American Relations*. East Lansing: Michigan State University Press, 1975.

Knight, Alan. "Latin America" In Andrew Porter and Alaine Low, eds., *The Oxford History of the British Empire, Vol III: The Nineteenth Century*, 122–145. Oxford, UK: Oxford University Press, 1999.

Knuth, Helen E. "The Climax of American Anglo-Saxonism, 1898–1905," PhD dissertation, Northwestern University, 1958.

Kohn, Edward P. *This Kindred People: Canadian-American Relations and the Anglo-Saxon Idea, 1895–1903*. Montréal McGill-Queen's University Press, 2004.

Koremenos, Barbara, Charles Lipson, and Duncan Snidal, eds. *Rational Design of International Institutions*. Cambridge, UK: Cambridge University Press, 2004.

Kornprobst, Markus. *Irredentism in European Politics: Argumentation, Compromise and Norms*. Cambridge, UK: Cambridge University Press, 2008.

Koss, Steven, ed. *Pro-Boers: Anatomy of an Anti-War Movement*. Chicago: University of Chicago Press, 1973.

Kramer, Paul A. "Empires, Exceptions, and Anglo-Saxons: Race and Rule between the British and United States Empires, 1880–1910." *Journal of American History* 88 (2002): 1315–1353.

Krebs, Paula. *Gender, Race, and the Writing of Empire: Public Discourse and the Boer War*. Cambridge and New York: Cambridge University Press, 1999.

Krebs, Ronald R., and Jennifer K. Lobasz. "Fixing the Meaning of 9/11: Hegemony, Coercion, and the Road to War in Iraq." *Security Studies* 16.3 (2007): 409–451.

Krebs, Ronald. *Rhetoric and the Making of U.S. National Security. Book ms., forthcoming*.

Krebs, Ronald R., and Patrick Thaddeus Jackson. "Twisting Tongues and Twisting Arms: The Power of Political Rhetoric." *European Journal of International Relations*, 13.1 (2007): 35–66.

Krishna, Sankaran. "Race, Amnesia and the Education of International Relations," *Alternatives* 26:4 (2001), 401–424.

Kurki, Milja. *Causation in International Relations: Reclaiming Causal Analysis*. Cambridge, UK: Cambridge University Press, 2008.

Labour Party. Ambitions for Britain: Labour's Manifesto 2001, May 16, 2001. Retrieved on July 23, 2005, from: www.pixunlimited.co.uk/pdf/news/election/labourmanifesto1.pdf.

Lachapelle, Guy. "Pourquoi le gouvernement canadien a-t-il refusé de participer à la guerre en Irak?" *Revue française de science politique* 53: 6 (2003), 911–927.

LaFeber, Walter. *The New Empire: An Interpretation of American Expansion, 1860–1898*. Ithaca, NY: Cornell University Press, 1998 [1963].

Lake, David. *Hierarchy in International Relations*. Ithaca, NY: Cornell University Press, 2009.

Lake, Marilyn, and Henry Reynolds. *Drawing the Global Colour Line: White Men's Countries and the International Challenge of Racial Equality.* Cambridge, UK: Cambridge University Press, 2008.

Laitin, David. "What Is a Language Community?" *American Journal of Political Science* 44.1 (2000), 142–155.

Larrimore, Mark. "Sublime Waste: Kant on the Destiny of the 'Races.'" In Catherine Wilson, ed., *Civilization and Oppression*, 99–125. Calgary, Alberta: University of Calgary Press, 1999.

Larrimore, Mark. "Antinomies of Race: Diversity and Destiny in Kant." *Patterns of Prejudice* 42 (2008): 341–363.

Lauren, Paul Gordon. *Power and Prejudice: The Politics and Diplomacy of Racial Discrimination.* Boulder, CO: Westview, 1988.

Layne, Christopher. "Kant or Cant: The Myth of the Democratic Peace." *International Security* 19.2 (1994): 5–49.

Lee, David. "The Liberals and Vietnam." *Australian Journal of Politics and History* 51: 3 (2005), 429–439.

Legault, André, Marilou Grégoire-Blais, and Frédéric Bastien. "Les dernières années de l'ère Chrétien: Une gouverne divisée et incertaine à propos de l'Irak." In André Donneur, ed., *Le Canada, Les États-Unis et le Monde: La marge de manœuvre canadienne*, 151–188. Saint-Nicolas, Quebec: Les Presses de L'Université Laval, 2005

Legro, J. W. *Rethinking the World: Great Power Strategies and International Order.* Ithaca, NY: Cornell University Press, 2005.

Leonard, Mark, ed. "Re-Ordering the World: The Long-Term Implications of September 11th." London: Foreign Policy Centre Report, March 2002.

Létourneau, Jocelyn. *A History for the Future: Rewriting Memory and Identity in Quebec.* Phyllis Aronoff and Howard Scott, trans. Montreal: McGill-Queen's University Press, 2004.

Levant, Victor. *Quiet Complicity: Canadian Involvement in the Vietnam War.* Toronto: Between the Lines, 1986.

Lipset, Seymour Martin. "Canada and the United States." *Canadian Review of Sociology and Anthropology* 1.6, 1964, 173–185.

Lipset, Seymour M. *Continental Divide: The Values of the United States and Canada.* New York and London: Routledge, 1990.

Little, Richard. "British Neutrality versus Offshore Balancing in the American Civil War: The English School Strikes Back," *Security Studies* 16:1 (January 2007), 68–95.

Little, Richard, and Mark Wickham-Jones, eds. *New Labour's Foreign Policy: A New Moral Crusade?* Manchester, UK: Manchester University Press, 2000.

Logevall. Fredrik. *Choosing War: The Lost Chance for Peace and Escalation of War in Vietnam.* Berkeley: University of California Press, 1999.

Long, David, and Brian Schmidt, eds. *Imperialism and Internationalism in the Discipline of International Relations.* Albany: SUNY Press, 2005.

Lorimer, Douglas A. "Race, Science, and Culture: Historical Continuities and Discontinuities, 1850–1914," In Shearer West, ed., *The Victorians and Race,* 12–33. Aldershot, UK: Ashgate, 1996.

Louis, Wm. Roger. *Imperialism at Bay: The United States and the Decolonization of the British Empire 1941–45.* Oxford, UK: Clarendon Press, 1977.

Louis, Wm. Roger. "Dulles, Suez, and the British." In R. Immerman, ed., *John Foster Dulles and the Diplomacy of the Cold War,* 133–158. Princeton, NJ: Princeton University Press, 1990.

Louis, Wm. Roger, and Roger Owen, eds. *Suez 1956: The Crisis and Its Consequences.* New York: Oxford University Press, 1989.

Love, Eric Tyrone Lowery. *Race over Empire: Racism and U.S. Imperialism, 1865–1900.* Chapel Hill: University of North Carolina Press, 2004.

Lowe, David. *Menzies and the "Great World Struggle": Australia's Cold War 1948–1954.* Sydney: University of New South Wales Press, 1999.

Lowe, David, "Percy Spender's Quest." *Australian Journal of International Affairs* 55. 2 (2001): 187–198.

MacMillan, John. "Kant and the Democratic Peace." In Beate Jahn, ed., *Classical Theory in International Relations,* 52–73. Cambridge, UK: Cambridge University Press, 2006.

MacMillan, Margaret, and Francine McKenzie, eds. *Parties Long Estranged: Australia and Canada in the Twentieth Century.* Vancouver: British Columbia University, 2003.

Mallon, Ron. "Race: Normative, Not Metaphysical or Semantic." *Ethics* 116: 3 (2006), 525–551.

Maloney, Sean M. "Are We Really Just Peacekeepers? The Perception Versus the Reality of Canadian Military Involvement in the Iraq War," *IRPP Working Paper Series* No. 2003–02. Retrieved on January 21, 2004, from: www.irpp.org/wp/archive/wp2003-02.pdf.

Mamdani, Mahmood. *Good Muslim, Bad Muslim.* New York: Pantheon, 2004.

Mandler, Peter. *The English National Character: The History of an Idea from Edmund Burke to Tony Blair.* New Haven, CT: Yale University Press, 2007.

Maoz, Zeev. "The Controversy over the Democratic Peace: Rearguard Action or Cracks in the Wall?" *International Security* 22.1 (1997), 162–198.

Marcel, Valerie. *The Future of Oil in Iraq: Scenarios and Implications.* London: Chatham House Reports, December 2002.

Marsh, Steve, and John Baylis. "The Anglo-American 'Special Relationship': The Lazarus of International Relations." *Diplomacy & Statecraft* 17.1 (2006): 173–211.

Martellone, Anna Maria. "In the Name of Anglo-Saxondom, for Empire and for Democracy: The Anglo-American Discourse, 1880–1920." In David Adams and Cornelius van Minnen, eds., *Reflections on American Exceptionalism*, 83–96. Straffordshire, UK: Keele University Press, 1994.

Martin, Allan William. *Robert Menzies: A Life. Volume II*. Melbourne: Melbourne University Press, 1999.

Martin, Lawrence. *Iron Man: the Defiant Reign of Jean Chrétien: Volume II*. Toronto: Viking, 2003.

Martin, Paul. *A Very Public Life, vol. 2, So Many Worlds*. Toronto: Deneau, 1985.

Martin, Paul. *Martin Speaks for Canada: A Selection of Speeches on Foreign Policy, 1964–67*. Montreal: McClelland and Stewart, 1967.

Massie, Justin. *The North Atlantic Quadrangle: France's Role in Canadian Strategic Culture*. PhD dissertation, Department of Political Studies, Queen's University, Kingston, Ontario, 2010.

Massie, Justin, and Stéphane Roussel. "Le dilemme canadien face à l'Irak ou l'art d'étirer l'élastique sans le rompre." In Alex Macleod and David Morin, eds., *Diplomaties en guerre. Sept États face à la crise irakienne*, 69–87. Montreal: Athéna,

Massolin, Philip. *Canadian Intellectuals, the Tory Tradition and the Challenge of Modernity, 1939–1970*. Toronto: University of Toronto Press, 2001.

May, Ernest R. *Imperial Democracy: The Emergence of America as a Great Power*. Chicago: Imprint Publications, 1991 (1961 reprint, with new introduction).

Mayers, David. *Dissenting Voices in America's Rise to Power*. Cambridge, UK: Cambridge University Press, 2007.

Mazrui, Ali. "Afro-Saxons." *Society* 12.2 (1975), 15–21.

Mazrui, Ali. *Africa's International Relations: The Diplomacy of Dependency and Change*. Boulder, CO: Westview Press, 1977.

McCarthy, Thomas. *Race, Empire, and the Idea of Human Development*. New York: Cambridge University Press, 2009.

McGibbon, Ian. *New Zealand and the Korean War: Volume 1: Politics and Diplomacy*. Oxford, UK: Oxford University Press, 1993.

McHenry, Dean E., and Richard N. Rosecrance. "The 'Exclusion' of the United Kingdom from the Anzus Pact." *International Organization* 12: 3 (1958): 320–329.

McIntyre, W. David. *Background to the ANZUS Pact: Policy-Making, Strategy, and Diplomacy, 1945–55*. New York: St. Martin's Press, 1995.

McKenzie, Francine. "In the National Interest: Dominions' Support for Britain and the Commonwealth after the Second World War." *Journal of Imperial and Commonwealth History* 34.4 (2006): 553–576.

McKinnon, Malcolm. *Independence and Foreign Policy: New Zealand in the World since 1935*. Auckland: Auckland University Press, 1993.

McLean, Craig, and Allan Patterson. "A Precautionary Approach to Foreign Policy? A Preliminary Analysis of Tony Blair's Speeches on Iraq." *British Journal of Politics and International Relations* 8–3 (2006): 351–367.

McLean, David. "From British Colony to American Satellite? Australia and the USA during the Cold War." *Australian Journal of Politics and History* 52(1, 2006): 64–79.

McRae, Rob, and Don Hubert, eds. *Human Security and the New Diplomacy: Protecting People, Promoting Peace.* Montreal: McGill-Queens University Press, 2001.

Mead, Walter Russell. *Special Providence: American Foreign Policy and How It Changed the World.* London: Routledge, 2002.

Mead, Walter Russell. *God and Gold: Britain, America, and the Making of the Modern World.* New York: Alfred A. Knopf, 2007.

Meaney, Neville. "Britishness and Australian Identity: The Problem of Nationalism in Australian History and Historiography." *Australian Historical Studies* 32. 116 (2001): 76–90.

Meaney, Neville. "Look Back in Fear: Percy Spender, the Japanese Peace Treaty and the ANZUS Pact." *Japan Forum* 15.3 (2003): 399–410.

Mearsheimer, John J. *The Tragedy of Great Power Politics.* New York: Norton, 2001.

Mehta, Uday Singh. *Liberalism and Empire: A Study in Nineteenth-Century British Liberal Thought.* Chicago: Chicago University Press, 1999.

Mein Smith, Philippa. *A Concise History of New Zealand.* Australia: Cambridge University Press, 2005.

Menzies, Robert Gordon. *Speech Is of Time. Selected Speeches and Writings.* London: Cassell & Company, 1958.

Mepham, David, and Paul Eavis. "The Missing Link in Labour's Foreign Policy: The Case for Tighter Controls over UK Arms Exports." London: Institute for Public Policy Research/Saferworld Report, November 21, 2002.

Meyer, Christopher. *DC Confidential: The Controversial Memoirs of Britain's Ambassador to the US at the Time of 9/11 and the Iraq War.* London: Weidenfeld & Nicholson, 2005.

Michaud, Nelson. "Cheerleading behind the US Bench? Values and Autonomy in Canadian Foreign Policy." Paper presented at the 47th Annual International Studies Association (ISA) Convention, San Diego, CA, March 22–25, 2006.

Michaud, Nelson, and Kim Richard Nossal. *Diplomatic Departures: The Conservative Era in Canadian Foreign Policy, 1984–93.* Vancouver: University of British Colombia Press, 2001.

Miliband, David. Keynote speech, Fabian Society's "Change the World" Conference, London, January 19, 2009. Retrieved on January 30, 2009, from: www.fabiansociety.org.uk/events/speeches/david-miliband-nyc-speech-text/pdf.

Millar, T. B., ed. *Australian Foreign Minister: The Diaries of R. G. Casey, 1951–60.* London: Collins, 1972.

Mills, Charles Wade. *The Racial Contract.* Ithaca, NY: Cornell University Press, 1997.

Mills, Charles W. "Kant's Untermenschen." In Andrew Valls, ed., *Race and Racism in Modern Philosophy,* 169–193. Ithaca, NY: Cornell University Press, 2005.

Mitchell, Nancy. *The Danger of Dreams: German and American Imperialism in Latin America.* Chapel Hill: University of North Carolina Press, 1999.

Mitzen, Jennifer. "Reading Habermas in Anarchy: Multilateral Diplomacy and Global Public Spheres." *American Political Science Review* 99.3 (2005): 401–417.

Mitzen, Jennifer. "Ontological Security in World Politics: State Identity and the Security Dilemma." *European Journal of International Relations* 12.3 (2006): 341–370.

Mock, Wolfgang. "The Function of 'Race.' Imperialist Ideologies: the Example of Joseph Chamberlain." In Paul Kennedy and Anthony Nicholls, eds., *Nationalist and Racialist Movements in Britain and Germany before 1914,* 190–203. London: Macmillan, 1981.

Monbiot, George. "The New Chauvinism." *The Guardian.* August 9, 2005. Retrieved on August 28, 2005, from: www.monbiot.com/archives/2005/08/09/the-new-chauvinism/

Morison, Elting E., John Blum, and Alfred Chandler Jr., eds. *The Letters of Theodore Roosevelt,* Vols. 1–3. Cambridge, MA: HarvardUniversity Press, 1950–1954.

Moser, John E. "Anti-Americanism and Anglophobia." In Brendon O'Connor, ed., *Anti-Americanism: History, Causes, and Themes, Vol. 3: Comparative Perspectives,* 1–17. Westport, CT.: Greenwood, 2007.

Mott, Frank Luther. *A History of American Magazines, vol. IV: 1885–1905.* Cambridge, MA: Harvard University Press, 1957.

Muirhead, Bruce. *Dancing around the Elephant: Creating a Prosperous Canada in an Era of American Dominance, 1957–1973.* Toronto: University of Toronto Press, 2007.

Mulanax, Richard B. *The Boer War in American Politics and Diplomacy.* Lanham, MD: University Press of America, 1994.

Müller, Harald. "Arguing, Bargaining and All That: Communicative Action, Rationalist Theory and the Logic of Appropriateness in International Relations." *European Journal of International Relations* 10.3 (2004): 395–435.

Murji, Karim, and John Solomos. "Introduction: Racialization in Theory and Practice." In Karim Murji and John Solomos, eds., *Racialization: Studies in Theory and Practice,* 1–27. Oxford, UK: Oxford University Press, 2005.

Muthyala, John. "Twilight of the Gods: Britain, America, and the Inheritance of Empire." *American Quarterly* 57.4 (2005): 1253–1261.

Myers, Phillip E. *Caution and Cooperation: The American Civil War in British-American Relations.* Kent, OH: Kent State University Press, 2008.

Naanami, Israel T. "The 'Anglo-Saxon Idea' and British Public Opinion." *Canadian Historical Review* 32:1 (1951): 43–60.

Naughtie, James. *The Accidental American: Tony Blair and the Presidency.* New York: Perseus Books, 2004.

New Zealand Army. "Our Rightful Place," *Army News* 368, 28 November 2006. Retrieved on January 12, 2008, from: www.army.mil.nz/at-a-glance/news/army-news/archived-issues/2006/368/orp.htm.

Nexon, Daniel. "The Balance of Power in the Balance," *World Politics* 61.2 (2009), 330–359.

Nexon, Daniel, and Thomas Wright. "What's at Stake in the American Empire Debate." *American Political Science Review* 101.2 (2007): 253–271.

Ninkovich, Frank. "Theodore Roosevelt: Civilization as Ideology." *Diplomatic History,* 10 (1986): 221–245.

Noer, Thomas J. *Briton, Boer, and Yankee: The United States and South Africa, 1870–1914.* Kent, OH: Kent University State, 1978.

Nossal Kim Richard. "Pinchpenny Diplomacy: The Decline of 'Good International Citizenship' in Canadian Foreign Policy," *International Journal* 54:1 (1998–1999), 88–105.

Nossal, Richard Kim. *The Politics of Canadian Foreign Policy.* Toronto: Prentice-Hall, 1997.

Oakman, Daniel. *Facing Asia: A History of the Colombo Plan.* Canberra: Pandanus, 2004.

Obama, Barack, and Manmohan Singh. Remarks by President Obama and Prime Minister Singh during Arrival Ceremony. Washington, DC: The White House, Office of the Press Secretary Release, November 24, 2009.

O'Day, Alan. "Irish Nationalism and Anglo-American Relations in the Later Nineteenth and Early Twentieth Centuries." In Fred M. Leventhal and Roland Quinault, eds., *Anglo-American Attitudes: From Revolution to Partnership,* 161–194. Aldershot, UK: Asghate , 2000.

Offer, Avner. "Costs and Benefits, Prosperity and Security, 1870–1914." In Andrew Porter and Alaine Low, eds., *The Oxford History of the British Empire, Vol III: The Nineteenth Century,* 690–711. Oxford, UK: Oxford University Press, 1999.

O'Malley, Eoin. "Setting Choices, Controlling Outcomes: the Operation of Prime Ministerial Influence and the UK's Decision to Invade Iraq." *British Journal of Politics and International Relations* 9.1 (2007): 1–19.

O'Meara, Dan, and Chantal Lavallée. "Construire des ponts ou s'asseoir sur la clôture? La politique étrangère britannique depuis l'invasion d'Irak." In Alex Macleod and David Morin, eds., *Diplomaties en guerre: Sept États face à la crise irakienne,* 37–68. Montréal: Athéna éditions, 2006.

O'Neill, Robert. *Australia in the Korean War 1950–53. Volume 1: Strategy and Diplomacy.* Canberra: Australian War Memorial and Australian Government Publishing Service, 1981.

O'Reilly, Marc J. "Following Ike? Explaining Canadian–US Co-operation during the 1956 Suez Crisis." *Journal of Commonwealth & Comparative Politics* 35.3 (1997): 75–107.

Orde, Anne. *The Eclipse of Great Britain: the United States and British Imperial Decline, 1895–1956*. New York: St. Martin's Press, 1996.

Oren, Ido. *Our Enemies and US: America's Rivalries and the Making of Political Science*. Ithaca, NY: Cornell University Press. 2003.

Ó Tuathail, Gearóid. "Dissident IR and the Identity Politics Narrative: A Sympathetically Skeptical Perspective." *Political Geography* 15.6/7 (1996): 647–653.

Ovendale, Ritchie. *The English-Speaking Alliance: Britain, the United States, the Dominions and the Cold War 1945–1951*. London: Allen & Unwin, 1985.

Owen, John M. "Give Democratic Peace a Chance? How Liberalism Produces Democratic Peace." *International Security* 19.4 (1994), 87–125.

Owen, John M. *Liberal Peace, Liberal War: American Politics and International Security*. Ithaca, NY: Cornell University Press, 1997.

Owen, Nicholas. "Critics of Empire in Britain." In Judith Brown and William Roger Louis, eds., *The Oxford History of the British Empire. Vol IV: The Twentieth Century*, 47–63. Oxford, UK: Oxford University Press, 1999.

Panayi, Panikos. *Immigration, Ethnicity and Racism in Britain, 1815–1945*. Manchester, UK: Manchester University Press, 1994.

Parekh, Bhikhu, et al. *The Future of Multi-Ethnic Britain*. London: Profile Books, 2000.

Parmar, Inderjeet. "'I'm Proud of the British Empire': Why Tony Blair Backs George W. Bush." *The Political Quarterly* 76.2 (2005): 218–231.

Paterson, William E. "The United Kingdom between Mars and Venus: Bridge or Bermuda Triangle?" *Perspectives on European Politics & Society* 8.1 (2007): 1–12.

Pearson, Lester B. *Mike: The memoirs of the Right Honourable Lester B. Pearson, Vols I and II (1948–1968)*. Edited by John A. Munro and Alex I. Inglis. Toronto: University of Toronto Press, 1972 and 1975.

Pemberton, Gregory. *All the Way: Australia's Road to Vietnam*. Boston: Allen & Unwin, 1987.

Perez, Louis A. Jr. *The War of 1898: The United States and Cuba in History and Historiography*. Chapel Hill: University of North Carolina Press, 1998.

Perkins, Bradford. *The First Rapprochement: England and the United States, 1795–1805*. Philadelphia: University of Pennsylvania Press, 1955.

Perkins, Bradford. *The Great Rapprochement: England and the United States, 1895–1914*. New York: Basic Books, 1968.

Peterson, J., and M. Pollack, eds. *Europe, America, Bush*. London and New York: Routledge, 2003.

Phillips, Kevin. *The Cousins' Wars: Religion, Politics, and the Triumph of Anglo-America*. New York: Basic Books, 1999.

Phillipson, Robert. *Linguistic Imperialism Continued*. London: Routledge, 2009.

Pierson, Paul. *Politics in Time: History, Institutions, and Social Analysis*. Princeton, NJ: Princeton University Press, 2004.

Pitt, Alan. "A Changing Anglo-Saxon Myth: Its Development and Function in French Political Thought, 1860–1914." *French History* 14 (2000): 150–173.

Pletcher, David M. *The Diplomacy of Trade and Investment: American Economic Expansion in the Hemisphere, 1865–1900.* Columbia: University of Missouri Press, 1998.

Pocock, J. G. A. *The Discovery of Islands: Essays in British History.* Cambridge, UK: Cambridge University Press, 2005.

Polletta, Francesca, and M. Kai Ho. "Frames and Their Consequences," in Robert E. Goodin and Charles Tilly, eds., *Oxford Handbook of Contextual Political Analysis* 187–209. Oxford, UK: Oxford University Press, 2006.

Porter, Bernard. *The Absent-Minded Imperialists: Empire, Society, and Culture in Britain.* Oxford, UK: Oxford University Press, 2004.

Porter, Bernard. *Empire and Superempire: Britain, America and the World.* New Haven and London: Yale University Press, 2006.

Pouliot, Vincent. "The Logic of Practicality: A Theory of Practice of Security Communities." *International Organization* 62: 2 (2008), 257–288.

Pressman, Jeremy. *Warring Friends: Alliance Restraint in International Politics.* Ithaca, NY: Cornell University Press, 2008.

Preston, Andrew. "Balancing War and Peace: Canadian Foreign Policy and the Vietnam War, 1961–1965." *Diplomatic History* 27.1 (2003): 73–111.

Preston, Richard. *The Defence of the Undefended Border: Planning for War in North America, 1867–1939.* Durham, NC: Duke University Press, 1977.

Prochaska Frank. "Book Review of Ian Radforth's *Royal Spectacle: The 1860 Visit of the Prince of Wales to Canada and the United States.* University of Toronto Press, 2004." *Victorian Studies* 48.1 (2005) 164–165.

Quieroz, João, and Merrell, Floyd. "Abduction: Between Subjectivity and Objectivity." *Semiotica,* 153: 1 (2005), 1–7.

Quinault, Roland. "Anglo-American Attitudes to Democracy from Lincoln to Churchill." In Fred M. Leventhal and Roland Quinault, eds., *Anglo-American Attitudes: From R goevolution to Partnership,* 124–141. Aldershot, UK: Ashgate, 2000.

Reid, Escott. *Radical Mandarin: The Memoirs of Escott Reid.* Toronto: University of Toronto Press, 1989.

Reiss, Hans Siegbert, ed. *Kant's Political Writings,* second edition, 93–130. Translated by Hugh Barr Nisbet. Cambridge, UK: Cambridge University Press, 1991.

Reus-Smit, Chris, and Duncan Snidal, "Between Utopia and Reality: The Practical Discourses of International Relations," in C. Reus-Smit and D. Snidal, eds., *The Oxford Handbook of International Relations,* 3–37. Oxford, UK: Oxford University Press, 2008.

Reynolds, David. *From World War to Cold War: Churchill, Roosevelt, and the International History of the 1940s.* New York: Oxford University Press, 2006.

Reynolds, Wayne. "In the Wake of Canada: Australia's Middle Power Diplomacy and the Attempt to Join the Atomic Special Relationship, 1943–1957." In Margaret MacMillan and Francine McKenzie, eds., *Parties Long Estranged: Australia and Canada in the Twentieth Century*, 151–182. Vancouver: British Columbia University, 2003.

Ricard, Serge. "The Anglo-German Intervention in Venezuela and Theodore Roosevelt's Ultimatum to the Kaiser: Taking a Fresh Look at an Old Enigma." In S. Ricard and H. Christol, *Anglo-Saxonism in U.S. Foreign Policy: The Diplomacy of Imperialism, 1899–1919*, 65–78. Aix-en-Provence: Publications de l'Universite de Provence, 1991.

Richardson, Louise. *When Allies Differ: Anglo-American Relations during the Suez and Falklands Crises*. New York: St. Martin's Press, 1996.

Richelson, Jeffrey T. *The US Intelligence Community*. Boulder, CO: Westview Press, 2008.

Rickard, John. *Australia: A Cultural History*. London: Longman, 1996.

Ricks, Thomas E. *The American Military Adventure in Iraq*. New York: Penguin Press, 2006.

Riddell, Peter. *Hug Them Close: Blair, Clinton, Bush, and the 'Special Relationship.'* London: Methuen Publishing, 2003.

Risse, Thomas. "Let's Argue! Communicative Action in International Relations." *International Organization* 54, no. 1 (2000), 1–39.

Risse-Kappen, Thomas. *Cooperation among Democracies. The European Influence on US Foreign Policy*. Princeton, NJ: Princeton University Press, 1995a.

Risse-Kappen, Thomas. "Democratic Peace—Warlike Democracies? A Social Constructivist Interpretation of the Liberal Argument." *European Journal of International Relations* 1.3 (1995b), 491–517.

Ritchie, Charles. *Storm Signals: More Undiplomatic Diaries, 1962–1971*. Toronto: Macmillan of Canada, 1983.

Roberts, Andrew. *A History of the English-Speaking Peoples since 1900*. London: Weidenfeld & Nicolson, 2006.

Rock, Stephen R. *Why Peace Breaks Out: Great Power Rapprochement in Historical Perspective*. Chapel Hill and London: University of North Carolina Press, 1989.

Rock, Stephen R. "Anglo–U.S. Relations, 1845–1930: Did Shared Liberal Values and Democratic Institutions Keep the Peace?" In Miriam Fendius Elman, ed., *Paths to Peace: Is Democracy the Answer?* 101–149. Cambridge, MA: MIT Press, 1997.

Rock, Stephen. *Appeasement in International Politics*. Lexington: University Press of Kentucky, 2000.

Roediger, David. *How Race Survived U.S. History: From Settlement and Slavery to the Obama Phenomenon*. New York: Verso, 2008.

Rogers, Paul. "Iraq: Consequences of a War." London: Oxford Research Group Briefing Paper No. 6. October 2002.

Rooth, Tim. "Britain, Europe and Diefenbaker's Trade Diversion Proposals, 1957–58." In Philip Buckner, ed., *Canada and the End of Empire*, 117–132. Vancouver: University of British Columbia Press, 2005.

Ross, Douglas. *In the Interests of Peace: Canada and Vietnam, 1954–1973*. Toronto: University of Toronto Press, 1984.

Ross, Malcolm, ed. *Our Sense of Identity: A Book of Canadian Essays*. Toronto: Ryerson Press, 1954.

Ross, Steven T. *American War Plans, 1890–1939*. London: Routledge: 2004.

Roussel, Stéphane. "L'instant kantien: La contribution canadienne à la création de la Communauté nord-atlantique, 1946–1951." In Greg Donaghy, ed., *Canada and the Early Cold War, 1943–1957*, 119–158. Ottawa: Department of Foreign Affairs and International Trade, 1998.

Roussel, Stéphane. *The North American Democratic Peace: Absence of War and Security Institution-Building in Canada–US Relations, 1867–1958*. Montreal/: McGill-Queen's University Press, 2004.

Roussel, Stéphane, and Justin Massie. "Le dilemme canadien face à la guerre en Irak, ou l'art d'étirer l'élastique sans le rompre," In Alex MacLeod and David Morin, eds., *Diplomaties en guerre. Sept États face à la crise irakienne*, 69–87. Outremont, Québec: Athéna Éditions, 2005.

Rudin, Ronald. *Making History in Twentieth-Century Quebec*. Toronto: University of Toronto Press, 1997.

Rudmin, Floyd. *Bordering on Aggression*. Hull, PQ: Voyageur Press, 1993.

Russett, Bruce. "The Democratic Peace: And Yet It Moves." *International Security* 19.4 (1995): 164–175.

Russett, Bruce M. *Community and Contention. Britain and America in the Twentieth Century*. Cambridge, MA: MIT Press, 1963.

Russett, Bruce, and John Oneal. *Triangular Peace: Democracy, Interdependence, and International Organizations*. New York: W. W. Norton, 2001.

Rutherford, Paul. *When Television Was Young: Primetime Canada, 1952–1967*. Toronto: University of Toronto Press, 1990.

Rutherford, Paul. "The Persistence of Britain: The Culture Project in Postwar Canada." In Philip Buckner, ed., *Canada and the End of Empire*, 195–205. Vancouver: UBC Press, 2005.

Rystad, Goran. "The Constitution and the Flag: Aspects of American Expansionism at the Turn of the Century." In S. Ricard and H. Christol, ed., *Anglo-Saxonism in U.S. Foreign Policy Anglo-Saxonism in U.S. Foreign Policy: The Diplomacy of Imperialism, 1899–1919*, 10–23. Aix-en-Provence: Publications de l'Université de Provence, 1991.

Saraceni, Mario. "The Strange Case of Dr Blair and Mr Bush: Counting Their Words to Solve a Mystery." *English Today* (July 19, 2003), 1–13.

Sarty, Roger. "Canada and the Great Rapprochement, 1902–1914." In B. J. C. McKercher and Lawrence Aronsen, eds., *The North Atlantic Triangle in a Changing World: Anglo-American-Canadian Relations, 1902–1956*, 12–47. Toronto: University of Toronto Press, 1996.

Saxton, Alexander. *The Rise and Fall of the White Republic. Class Politics and Mass Culture In Nineteenth-century America.* New York: Verso, 1990.

Schaeper, Thomas J., and Kathleen Schaeper. *Rhodes Scholars, Oxford, and the Creation of an American Elite.* New York: Berghahn Books, 2004.

Schoultz, Lars. *Beneath the United States: A History of U.S. Policy toward Latin America.* Cambridge, MA: Harvard University Press, 1998.

Schwartz, Mildred A. *Public Opinion and Canadian Identity.* Berkeley: University of California Press, 1967.

Schweller, Randy L. *Unanswered Threats: Political Constraints on the Balance of Power.* Princeton, NJ: Princeton University Press, 2006.

Sears, Louis Martin. "French Opinion of the Spanish-Amerian War." *Hispanic American Historical Review* 7 (1927), 25–44.

Seed, Geoffrey. "British Reactions to American Imperialism Reflected in Journals of Opinion, 1898–1900." *Political Science Quarterly* 73 (1958), 254–272.

Seed, Geoffrey. "British Views of American Policy in the Philippines Reflected in Journals of Opinion, 1898–1907," *Journal of American Studies* 2 (1968), 48–64.

Seldon, Anthony. *Blair.* London: The Free Press, 2004.

Sewell, William H. *Logics of History: Social Theory and Social Transformation.* Chicago: University of Chicago Press, 2005.

Shaw, Timothy. *Commonwealth: Inter- and Non-State Contributions to Global Governance.* London: Routledge, 2007.

Shimazu Naoko. *Japan, Race and Equality: The Racial Equality Proposal of 1919.* London: Routledge, 1998.

Shore, Sean. "No Borders Make Good Neighbors: The Development of the US–Canadian Security Community, 1871–1914." In Adler Emanuel and Michael Barnett, eds., *Security Communities*, 333–367. Cambridge, UK: Cambridge University Press: 1998.

Schoultz, Lars. *Beneath the United States: A History of U.S. Policy toward Latin America.* Cambridge, MA: Harvard University Press, 1998.

Sinclair, Keith. *A History of New Zealand.* London: Penguin, 1959.

Sjolander, Claire Turenne, Heather A. Smith, and Debra Stienstra, eds. *Feminist Perspectives on Canadian Foreign Policy.* Don Mills, Ontario: Oxford University Press, 2003.

Slaughter, Anne-Marie. "America's Edge." *Foreign Affairs* 88: 1 (2009), 94–113.

Smith, Rogers. "Liberalism and Racism: The Problem of Analyzing Traditions." In David Ericson and Louisa Bertch Green, eds., *The Liberal Tradition in America*, 9–27. New York: Routledge, 1999.

Snyder, Louis L. *Macro-Nationalisms: A History of the Pan-Movements*. London: Greenwood Press (Global Perspectives in History and Politics), 1984.

Sokolsky, Joel J. "Realism Canadian Style: National Security Policy and the Chrétien Legacy," *Policy Matters* 5:2 (2004), 8–38.

Spender, Sir Percy. *Exercises in Diplomacy: The ANZUS Treaty and the Colombo Plan*. Sydney: Sydney University Press, 1969.

Spiering, Menno, "British Euroscepticism." In Robert Harmsen and Menno Spiering, eds., *Euroscepticism: Party Politics, National Identity and European Integration*, 127–150. Amsterdam: Editions Rodopi, 2004.

Spittal, Cara. "The Transatlantic Romance of the North Atlantic Triangle." In Robert Bothwell and Jean Daudelin, eds., *Canada among Nations 2008: 100 Years of Canadian External Relations*, 317–342. Montreal: McGill-Queen's, 2009.

Stairs, Denis. "The Political Culture of Canadian Foreign Policy." *Canadian Journal of Political Science* 15.4 (1982): 667–690.

Stairs, Denis. "Realists at Work: Canadian Policy Makers and the Politics of Transition from Hot War to Cold War." In Greg Donaghy, ed., *Canada and the Early Cold War, 1943–1957/Canada et la guerre froide, 1943–1957*, 96–116. Ottawa: Deptarment of Foreign Affairs and International Trade, 1998.

Steele, Brent. "Ontological Security and the Power of Self-Identity: British Neutrality and the American Civil War." *Review of International Studies* 31.3 (2005): 519–540.

Steele, Jonathan. *Defeat: Why They Lost Iraq*. London: I. B. Tauris, 2009.

Stein, Judith. "Defining the race, 1890–1930." In Werner Sollors, ed., *The Invention of Ethnicity*, 77–104. New York: Oxford University Press, 1989.

Steinberg, Marc W. "Tilting the Frame: Considerations on Collective Action Framing from a Discursive Turn." *Theory and Society* 27.6 (1998): 845–872.

Stephenson, Neal. *The Diamond Age*. New York: Bantam Spectra, 1995.

Stothard, Peter. *Thirty Days: Tony Blair and the Test of History*. New York: Harper Collins, 2003.

Streit, Clarence. *Union Now: A Proposal for a Federal Union of the Democracies of the North Atlantic*. New York: Harper & Brothers, 1939.

Streit, Clarence, *Union Now with Britain*. New York: Harpers & Brothers, 1941.

Streit, Clarence, *Freedom's Frontier: Atlantic Union Now*. New York: Harper & Brothers, 1961.

Streit Council for a Union of Democracies, "Mission Statement," Retrieved on April 2, 2008, from: http://streitcouncil.org/index.php?page=mission.

Stueck, William. *The Korean War*. Princeton, NJ: Princeton University Press, 1997.

Sturgis, James. "Learning about Oneself: The Making of Canadian Nationalism, 1867–1914." In C. C. Eldridge, ed., *Kith and Kin: Canada, Britain, and the United States from the Revolution to the Cold War.* Cardiff: University of Wales Press, 1997, 95–118.

Sullivan, Shannon. *Revealing Whiteness: The Unconscious Habits of Racial Privilege.* Bloomington: Indiana University Press, 2006.

Swift, Roger and Sheridan Gilley. eds., *The Irish Victorian Britain: The Local Dimension.* Dublin: The Four Courts, 1999.

Szent-Miklósy, István. *The Atlantic Union Movement: Its Significance in World Politics.* New York: Fountainhead Publishers, 1965.

Talbott, Strobe. "America Abroad: The Birth of a Global Nation" *Time,* July 20, 1992. Retrieved on July 12, 2005 from: www.time.com/time/magazine/article/0,9171,976015,00.html.

Taylor, Paul. *Race: A Philosophical Introduction.,* Malden, MA: Blackwell, 2004.

Templeton, Malcolm. *Ties of Blood and Empire: New Zealand's Involvement in Middle East Defence and the Suez Crisis 1947–57.* Auckland: Auckland University Press, 1994.

Thompson, John Herd, and Stephen J. Randall. *Canada and the United States: Ambivalent Allies.* Montreal: McGill-Queen's University Press, 2008

Thompson, Peter. "The Case of the Missing Hegemon: British Nonintervention in the American Civil War," *Security Studies* 16:1 (January 2007), 96–132.

Thompson, William R. "The Evolution of a Great Power Rivalry: The Anglo-American Case," In William R. Thompson, ed., *Great Power Rivalries,* 201–221. Columbia: University of South Carolina Press, 1999.

Thies, Cameron G. "A Pragmatic Guide to Qualitative Historical Analysis in the Study of International Relations." *International Studies Perspectives* 3: 3 (2002): 351–372.

Tilchin, William. *Theodore Roosevelt and the British Empire: A Study in Presidential Statecraft.* New York: St. Martin's Press, 1997.

Tocqueville, Alexis de. *Democracy in America,* Vol. 1. New York: Vintage Books, 1990 [1835].

Tomes, Jason. *Balfour and Foreign Policy: The International Thought of a Conservative Statesman.* New York: Cambridge University Press, 1997.

Tompkins, E. Berkeley. *Anti-Imperialism in the United States: The Great Debate, 1890–1920.* Philadelphia: University of Pennsylvania Press. 1970.

Trotter, Ann. "San Francisco Treaty Making and its Implications for New Zealand." *Japan Forum,* 15:3 (2007), 411–423.

Trudel, Marcel, and Genevieve Jain. *Canadian history textbooks; a Comparative Study.* Ottawa: Queen's Printer for Canada, 1970.

Tulloch, Hugh. "Changing British Attitudes towards the United States in the 1880s." *Historical Journal* 20: 4 (1977): 825–840.

Tully, James. *Meaning and Context: Quentin Skinner and His Critics*. Princeton, NJ: Princeton University Press, 1988.

Turk, Richard W. *The Ambiguous Relationship: Theodore Roosevelt and Alfred Thayer Mahan*. New York: Greenwood Press, 1987.

Umetsu, Hiroyuki. "The Birth of ANZUS: America's Attempt to Create a Defense Linkage Between Northeast Asia and the Southwest Pacific," *International Relations of the Asia-Pacific* 4:1 (2004), 171–196.

Underhill, Frank. *The Image of Confederation*. Toronto: The Canadian Broadcasting Corporation (Massey Lectures), 1964.

Ungerer, Carl, "The 'Middle Power' Concept in Australian Foreign Policy." *Australian Journal of Politics & History* 53: 4 (2007), 538–551.

van der Pijl, Kees. *Transnational Classes and International Relations*. London and New York: Routledge, 1998.

Vincent, R. J. "Race in International Relations." *International Affairs* 4.1 (1982): 658–670.

Vitalis, Robert. "The Graceful and Generous Liberal Gesture: Making Racism Invisible in American International Relations." *Millennium* 29.2 (2000), 331–356.

Vitalis, Robert. "Birth of a Discipline," in Brian Schmidt and David Long, eds., *Imperialism and Internationalism in the Discipline of International Relations*, 159–182. Albany: State University of New York Press, 2005.

Vucetic, Srdjan. "Anglobal Governance?" *Cambridge Review of International Affairs*, 23: 3 (2010), 455–474.

Vucetic, Srdjan. "Bound to Follow? The Anglosphere and U.S.-led 'Coalitions of the Willing,' 1950–2001." *European Journal of International Relations* (2011).

Vucetic, Srdjan. "Genealogy as a Research Tool in International Relations." *Review of International Studies*, forthcoming

Wæver, Ole. "European Integration and Security: Analysing French and German Discourses on State, Nation, and Europe." In David Howarth and Jacob Torfing, eds., *Discourse Theory in European Politics: Identity, Policy, and Governance*, 33–67. New York: Palgrave Macmillan, 2005.

Wæver, Ole. "Identity, Communities and Foreign Policy," In Lene Hansen and Ole Wæver, eds., *European Integration and National Identity*, 20–50. London: Routledge, 2002.

Waite, James. "Contesting 'the Right of Decision': New Zealand, the Commonwealth, and the New Look." *Diplomatic History* 30.5 (2006): 893–917.

Walsh, James I. *The International Politics of Intelligence Sharing*. New York: Columbia University Press, 2009.

Ward, Alan J. *Ireland and Anglo-American Relations 1899–1921*. London: Frank Cass, 1969.

Ward, Stuart. *Australia and the British Embrace: The Demise of the Imperial Ideal.* Carlton: Melbourne University Press, 2001.

Warner, Donald Frederic. *The Idea of Continental Union: Agitation for the Annexation of Canada to the United States 1849–1893.* Frankfort: University of Kentucky Press, 1960.

Weaver, Sally. *Making Canadian Indian Policy: The Hidden Agenda 1968–70.* Toronto: University of Toronto Press, 1981.

Weeks, Jessica L. "Autocratic Audience Costs: Regime Type and Signaling Resolve," *International Organization* 62:1 (2008), 35–64.

Weldes, Jutta. *Constructing National Interests: The United States and the Cuban Missile Crisis.* Minneapolis: University of Minnesota Press, 1999.

Weldon, Laurel S. "Intersectionality," in Gary Goertz and Amy Mazur, eds., *Politics, Gender and Concepts: Theory and Methodology,* 193–218. Cambridge, UK: Cambridge University Press, 2008.

Wesley, Michael and Tony Warren, "Wild Colonial Ploys: Currents of Thought in Australian Foreign Policy," *Australian Journal of Political Science* 35:1 (2000), 9-26.

Wendt, Alexander. *Social Theory of International Politics.* Cambridge, UK: Cambridge University Press, 1999.

Wendt, Alexander, "The State as a Person in International Theory." *Review of International Studies* 30:3 (2004), 289–316.

Wendt, Alexander. "Why a World State Is Inevitable: Teleology and the Logic of Anarchy." *European Journal of International Relations* 9:4 (2003), 491–542.

Whitaker, Reg, and Gary Marcuse. *Cold War Canada: The Making of a National Insecurity State, 1945–1957.* Toronto: University of Toronto Press, 1995.

Wierzbicka, Anna. *English: Meaning and Culture.* Oxford, UK: Oxford University Press, 2006.

Wight, Colin. *Agents, Structures and International Relations: Politics as Ontology.* Cambridge, UK: Cambridge University Press, 2006.

Williams, John. "ANZUS: A Blow to Britain's Self-Esteem." *Review of International Studies* 13 (1987): 243–263.

Williams, Michael C. "The Discipline of the Democratic Peace: Kant, Liberalism and the Social Construction of Security Communities." *European Journal of International Relations* 7:4 (2001), 525–553.

Williams, Paul. "Who's Making UK Foreign Policy?" *International Affairs* 80.5 (2004), 909–929.

Williams, William Appleman. *The Tragedy of American Diplomacy.* New York: W. W. Norton, 1972.

Wilson, Keith, ed. *The International Impact of the Boer War.* New York: Knopf, 2001.

Windschuttle, Keith. "Sphere of Influence?" *National Review* 44–46 (2005).

Wise, S. F., and Robert Craig Brown. *Canada Views the United States: Nineteenth-century Political Attitudes.* Seattle: University of Washington Press, 1967.

Woodard, Garry. *Asian Alternatives: Australia's Vietnam Decision and Lessons on Going to War.* Carlton, Victoria: Melbourne University Press, 2004.

Woodward, Bob. *Bush at War.* London: Pocket, 2003.

Woodward, Bob. *Plan of Attack.* New York: Simon & Schuster, 2004.

Wingfield, Adia Harvey, and Joe Feagin. *Yes We Can? White Racial Framing and the 2008 Presidential Campaign.* New York: Routledge, 2010.

Yaniszewski, Mark. "Reporting on Fratricide: Canadian Newspapers and the Incident at Tarnak Farm, Afghanistan," *International Journal* 62:2 (2007): 362–382.

Young, Thomas-Durell. "Cooperative Diffusion through Cultural Similarity: The Postwar Anglo-Saxon Experience." In Emily O. Goldman and Leslie C. Eliason, eds., *The Diffusion of Military Technology and Ideas*, 93–113. Palo Alto, CA: Stanford University Press, 2003.

INDEX

AASR. *See* Anglo-American special
    relationship
ABCANZ, 52
ABCA program, 52, 72, 101, 145
ABC program, 52, 95
Acheson, Dean, 93
Acton, John Dalberg, 29
Adams, Henry, 39
Adams, Henry Baxter, 31
Adams, John, 26
Afghanistan, 104, 110, 117, 119
Agency: broad conception of, 155; of elites,
    11; events and, 14; in International
    Relations, 154–55
Agrarian movement, 31
Alaska, 44
Alaska Panhandle Treaty (1903), 37
Alcoff, Linda Martín, 7
Allen, Ralph, 83
Alliances, 29, 47, 52
American guarantee, 59, 65–67, 69
Amery, Leo, 29
Amnesty International, 111
Anglo-American Committee, 35
Anglo-American League, 35
Anglo-American special relationship
    (AASR), 4, 51, 55, 107, 131, 150, 176*n*111
Anglobalization, 68
Anglo-Saxonism: and Anglo-American war,
    33–34; ANZUS and, 66; and arbitration
    movement, 34–35; Canada and, 45;
    and expansionism, 36–37; and foreign

policy, 46; and France, 134; German
influence on, 26; globalization of, 26;
and "great rapprochement," 24, 37, 40,
48–49, 131, 168*n*2; identity of, 38, 44; and
imperialism, 28–32; origins of, 25–26; as
racialized identity, 20, 24, 26–27, 29, 34,
169*n*13; realism and, 133–39; superiority
claims of, 3–4, 25, 27, 35–36, 47, 107;
in United States, 31; Venezuela I and,
39–40; Venezuela II and, 40–50
The Anglo-Saxon Review (magazine), 35
Anglosphere: accomplishments of, 52;
boundaries of, 53; in Cold War era, 74–100;
collective identity of, 141, 149, 154;
concept of, 8; cooperation in, 4, 144–46;
criticisms of, 4; ethnicity and, 100;
future of, 154–56; genealogy of, 15–20,
50–51, 153–55; Germany's relationship
to, 40, 46–48; growth of, 48; historical
development of, 3–4, 131, 154; identity
of, 5, 149–52; Iraq War and, 126; liberal
account of, 131; as object of study, 4–8;
origins of, 2, 22–23; path dependency
of, 153–54; persistence of, 127; politics
and, 6; race and, 3–4, 6–7, 71, 96, 99–100,
132, 141, 144; security cooperation in,
134–35; Self-Other relations and, 5, 129;
significance of, 3; terminology of, 165*n*1;
theories of, 8–10; values of, 2–3
Anglo-world, 48
Anti-Americanism, 44, 86, 94–95, 104, 111,
119, 121, 133